SYLVIA AND DAVID

Books by Richard Garnett

THE SILVER KINGDOM

THE WHITE DRAGON

JACK OF DOVER

CONSTANCE GARNETT: A HEROIC LIFE

SYLVIA AND DAVID

The Townsend Warner / Garnett Letters

Selected and edited by Richard Garnett

SINCLAIR-STEVENSON

First published in Great Britain in 1994
by Sinclair-Stevenson
an imprint of Reed Consumer Books Ltd
Michelin House, 81 Fulham Road, London SW3 6RB
and Auckland, Melbourne, Singapore and Toronto

A CIP catalogue record for this book
is available at the British Library

ISBN 1 85619 341 1

Typeset by Deltatype Ltd, Ellesmere Port, Cheshire
Printed and bound in Great Britain
by Mackays of Chatham PLC

Contents

Drawing   41
         No photos
Drawing   18

Introduction

'I am sure that the correspondence is worth preserving', Sylvia Townsend Warner wrote to David Garnett on 23 January 1965 when he was having doubts whether to publish his letters to and from T. H. White. 'It is a splendid record of how two superior mid-twentieth-century minds exchanged experiences and opinions, and were candid with each other, and contrived, by magnanimity, not to quarrel, and to evade expressing an exasperation mutually felt. It does you the utmost credit. Besides, you were obviously designed by natural selection to correspond with each other.'

Much of this is also true of the correspondence which follows. But David and Sylvia's love for one another was far more tranquil, untroubled by exasperation or any strains of physical passion, for, rather unusually for David, it never became a love affair. And their admiration for one another's work, which David later came to find embarrassingly enthusiastic, is in great contrast with the mis-givings expressed in *The White/Garnett Letters* about *The Witch in the Wood* or *Aspects of Love*.

The Townsend Warner/Garnett correspondence also lacks some of what Sylvia called the 'tit for tat, dock for nettle' quality of the White/Garnett, for, whereas 250 letters from Sylvia have survived, there are only 115 from David. This is not because Sylvia wrote more often than David, but because he was better at keeping letters than she was.

'Everyone tells me to write a fourth volume of my memoirs', David wrote to Sylvia on 8 June 1976, when he was eighty-four and she was eighty-three. 'But nothing is interesting except truth, and truth can be painful. At our time of life it is better to look forward to the pleasures of next week. So if I attempted a book a large part of it, all bitterness, hatred and unforgiveness would have to be left out and a very expurgated version of my heart produced.'

In the surviving letters there is very little bitterness, hatred or unforgiveness on either side. Though David was a more indiscreet correspondent than Sylvia, he says nothing, for instance, about the row which ended his association with Rupert Hart-Davis, and gives no more than a hint of his various extramarital affairs. The cuts that I have made have almost always been to remove repetitions or less interesting passages, such as the mass of letters about the obscurer details of T. H. White's life written when they were both working on books about him. In making my selection I have tried to put the main emphasis on their relations with one another, and also to redress some of the inequality in the amount surviving from the two correspondents. The present selection contains 162 letters from Sylvia and 103 from David, whole or in part, plus a few relevant extracts from diaries and other documents. There are only a few episodes that would be painful to the living. These I have not entirely removed, for it would have produced too expurgated a version of David's heart to omit all mention of such events as the deaths of his first wife, Ray, his daughter Amaryllis and his friend Michael Howard; and of the break-up of his marriage to Angelica. As to the last of these, the reader should not forget that this is necessarily a partial account – in both senses of the word – and that Angelica has already told her side of the story in *Deceived with Kindness*, where she provides a very frank explanation of why she felt she had to escape from David. It should be read as a corrective to his letters on the subject to Sylvia, just as they may offer one to her story.

Sylvia's letters likewise provide but a partial picture, for they say very little about Valentine Ackland. It was with Valentine that she lived in a lesbian 'marriage' from 1930 until Valentine died in 1969. This relationship has been fairly well aired already: Claire Harman's biography of Sylvia (1989) draws heavily on Valentine's diaries and features her largely; Wendy Mulford has written *This Narrow Place: Sylvia Townsend Warner and Valentine Ackland: Life, Letters and Politics, 1931–1951* (1986); no doubt Valentine will be equally conspicuous in Sylvia's diaries, edited by Harman and now in the press; and Sylvia's own account of their relationship will be available when in due course her correspondence with Valentine is published. The present selection may therefore redress an imbalance (Harman did not make use of any of the 333 letters from Sylvia and David that were then unpublished) and provide a useful reminder that the warmth of her affections was by no means confined to women.

David was working on an edition of this correspondence shortly before he died in 1981. At the same time William Maxwell, one of Sylvia's literary executors, was editing her letters, which were published in 1982. In his acknowledgements he thanks Janet Machen 'for the extraordinary lengths she went to in securing for me the complete correspondence with David Garnett'. Nevertheless it would seem that David kept some to himself, for Maxwell believed that there were no letters to David between 1932 and 1970, when in fact there were 115. His edition of Sylvia's *Letters*, now out of print, included substantial extracts from twenty-eight to David. Four letters from Sylvia and four from David were also published in the *PN Review*, 23, 1981. Otherwise, the correspondence is hitherto unpublished.

Both correspondents had fairly legible hands to the end of their lives. Apart from a very few idiosyncrasies in spelling Sylvia's letters provide an almost immaculate text. When her publishers wanted to make a book of her Elfin stories she wrote to David: 'I held out against it, saying I have longed to be published posthumously; but then began to think of what posthumously might entail: my punctuation being tampered with and a preface by God knows who – say, Malcolm Muggeridge.' I have spared her Muggeridge – or any prefatory puff – and have made only the smallest tamperings with her punctuation. David, on the other hand, was never a reliable speller, and his punctuation in his letters is very casual and hasty. None of the letters were written with any thought of publication, but to give one another pleasure: 'You enjoy my letters, I enjoy yours', as Sylvia wrote.

In preparing this text for the general reader I have hesitated between the pedantry of attempting to preserve the original exactly, adding punctuation only within square brackets, while amending proper names in footnotes, and the unscholarliness of making such emendations as they would have made had they been writing for publication. As the formality of print seems to make the idiosyncrasies of manuscript unduly obtrusive, I have settled on the latter. Contractions and initials have generally been expanded, but square brackets have been used for all other insertions. Some of the latter are frankly editorial and explanatory. Dates and addresses at the head of letters have been standardised, dates following the style they each generally preferred, and addresses being given in full the first time they occur and thereafter in brief. Postscripts have sometimes been silently omitted, and David's and Sylvia's own footnotes incorporated into the text within parentheses. In making the selections I have felt it only fair to indicate omissions with the customary '. . .', though with some reluctance, for I am aware that the reader who comes upon 'Fan . . .' will be only too likely to assume that David has said something wounding or scandalous about his daughter, when in fact he has merely repeated for the umpteenth time that she was one of the twins. I have not attempted to burden every passing allusion with an explanatory footnote – not that I would be able to do so.

David's note on *Lolly Willowes* (pp. 27–8) and 250 letters from Sylvia and 114 from David are in the Berg Collection in the New York Public Library. David's letter of 8 December 1969 on the occasion of

Valentine Ackland's death is in the Dorset County Museum. The two letters from Ray Garnett were returned by Sylvia to David on 19 August 1969 with the suggestion that my brother William and I might like to have them. I own the first of them and he the second. Prentice's report and the letters to Chatto and Windus are in the company's archives in Reading University Library. Sylvia's diaries are in Dorset County Museum, and David's pocket diaries at Hilton Hall.

I owe the warmest thanks to Susanna Pinney and William Maxwell, the Executors of Sylvia Townsend Warner's Literary Estate, who have not only welcomed the publication of this book but have also provided much practical help. I am very grateful too for the forbearance of members of my family in putting up with yet another public exposure of some part of their private lives. All writers on Sylvia Townsend Warner owe a great debt to Claire Harman, who has written her biography with an intelligence and sensibility matching her own. Claire Harman's generous appreciation of these letters has also been most encouraging, and I am grateful to her for allowing me to include some extracts from Sylvia's diaries.

I must thank Chatto and Windus for the use of material in their archives in Reading University Library.

For much other help of many kinds I have to thank: Michael Bott and Francesca Hardcastle of Reading University Library; Professor James T. Boulton; Professor François Gallix; Oliver Garnett; Jonathan Gathorne-Hardy; Gillian M. Goudge of the Royal Horticultural Society; Roger Lubbock; Francis O. Mattson of the Berg Collection, New York Public Library; Ernest and Joyce Mehew; Professor J. Lawrence Mitchell; Roger Peers and Richard de Peyer of the Dorset County Museum; Maggie Perham of the Royal Society of Literature; Angela Pitt; Hilary and Michael Rubinstein; Ruth Thackeray; and the staff of Cambridge University Library and the London Library.

1922

When Sylvia Townsend Warner and David Garnett first met in July 1922
she was twenty-nine and he was thirty. They were both the only children
of their parents. Sylvia was brought up in the atmosphere of Harrow
School, where her father, George Townsend Warner, was a housemaster
with a special interest in the writing of good English. He was, by all accounts,
a brilliant teacher, and she was devoted to him. She was exceptionally well
educated, largely by him rather than in any more formal schooling. Her
relations with her mother, who had never quite forgiven her for not being
a boy, were by no means so happy, and deteriorated after her father died in
1916. Her first ambitions were musical, and had it not been for the
outbreak of war she would have gone to Vienna to study composing with
Arnold Schoenberg. Instead she found herself working for a time in a
munitions factory. In 1922 she was enjoying living alone in London,
where she was coming to the end of a long and rather passionless affair
with Percy Buck, a distinguished musicologist who had been a music
master at Harrow. It was probably Buck who got her the job, ahead of
many other more obviously qualified candidates, as co-editor of an
ambitious series of volumes of Tudor church music, a task which she
performed extremely well.

David's background was literary. His grandfather, Dr Richard Garnett,
was Keeper of the Printed Books at the British Museum and a man of
letters. His parents both considered themselves outsiders in the society of
their time. Edward was an influential critic and champion of creative
writers; Constance translated Russian novels. Their friends were mainly
literary: Conrad, Galsworthy, Wells, D. H. Lawrence, and many others,
so that David took writers as a matter of course. Compared to Sylvia's his
schooling was poor, and his real education was in natural history, which
he learned for himself in the woods around his home. He trained as a
botanist, but his career was interrupted by the war in 1914. He became a
conscientious objector, spending much of 1915 with the Friends War
Victims Relief Mission in France. In 1916, and for the rest of the war, he
worked as a farm labourer, living with the painters Duncan Grant and
Vanessa Bell. He said afterwards that his writing was much influenced by
watching painters at work. In the spring of 1921 he married Rachel
Marshall, a shy but enterprising young woman who had travelled in
Russia before the war and worked on the land during it. She had trained as
an illustrator and wood-engraver and had already published an illustrated
children's book of her own. By the time David met her she was known to
all her friends as Ray. She called him Bunny, as did some of his relatives
and most of his friends. Sylvia, however, generally stuck to David. He had

I

not yet published anything over his own name, and was working in a bookshop at 19 Taviton Street which he had started with Francis Birrell, a friend who had been with him on the Quaker relief mission. He and Ray had as yet no home or children of their own and were living in Ray's mother's house in London.

David was to make his name with *Lady into Fox*, which came out later in 1922 and won two literary prizes, Sylvia hers in 1925 with *Lolly Willowes*, which was the first book to be chosen by the American Book of the Month Club.

In March 1922 Sylvia went to stay in a cottage at East Chaldon in Dorset with Stephen Tomlin, who had been a friend ever since her days at Harrow. Tomlin, or Tommy, as he was known, was a sculptor of great sensitivity, a man whose considerable charm concealed a complex streak of poetic melancholy. Sylvia was much attracted by him, but her feelings were never fully returned. The purpose of her visit was to meet a neighbour in Chaldon, Theodore Francis Powys, an original, but largely unpublished, writer, whom Tommy had made friends with. He was one of eleven children, and two of his brothers, John Cowper Powys and Llewelyn Powys, also became writers. David described Theo later as:

a grey-haired, elderly, heavily-built man with a big head and powerful rugged features. His very sharp eyes under bushy eyebrows summed one up; he was a moralist and a shrewd critic of men. The grey eyes were those of a relentless and severe judge. But the first impression was of a manner which contrasted with his rugged features and severe eyes, for he was exaggeratedly polite and spoke with excessive humility and gentleness, as though he were an unarmed man addressing gunmen ready to shoot on sight. That was indeed how he looked upon visitors from the outside world. (*The Familiar Faces*, 4)

When Powys produced a new story, 'Hester Dominy', Tommy and Sylvia read it and decided to try to find a publisher. Tommy had recently met David in the bookshop in Taviton Street, and they had taken to one another at once. Tommy knew that David had literary connections, so he left the story with Sylvia, asking her to deliver it to David. She has described how:

In the bookshop I found an extremely young-looking man whose hair was long and thick and untidy and whose suit was so blue that I felt he might blow up his horn at any moment. When I entered he retreated behind a desk, like some innocent wild animal that has never seen man before but who knows by the promptings of instinct that man is something to be mistrusted. . . . I asked if I could see Mr. David Garnett.

The young man came slowly and noiselessly padding out from his den. Staring at me very hard he said after a long pause:

'I am David Garnett.' (*Powys Review*, No. 5, 1979, 19)

David's recollection of the occasion will be found on page 35 below. He had recently completed *Lady into Fox*, and on 28 June had written to Chatto and Windus:

I am enclosing the typescript of a story for your consideration. It is designed to be illustrated with twelve wood-engravings by my wife, whose *Ride on a Rocking-Horse* you published. . . . I may say that it is not a book for children but for grown-up people – this in case you send it to the wrong reader.

The book was accepted by Charles Prentice, who soon became a good friend. Meanwhile David read 'Hester Dominy' and liked it. He made a note of his reactions:

It is very good. It is a work of art all right. It has form, the subjects are introduced in the right order: the effect is complete. The whole thing is most successful. . . . the story is an absolutely satisfactory work of art as it is, and the author seems to me one of the very small number who take writing seriously and have some idea about it. (*The Borzoi 1925*, 1925, 90)

Early in August he wrote to Powys about 'Hester Dominy', and also to Sylvia, who replied:

11: viii: 1922   *125 Queens Road, [London] w2*
Dear Mr Garnett, Very many thanks for your letter about 'Hester Dominy'.

I'm glad you think so well of it. It interests me that you should find in a critical reading of it that you find the rustics a little hard to accept, for I, reading as my first venture another of Powys's tales, made the same demur. Since then I have come to know something of the country people he writes about, and now I think his description of them is exceedingly just and clear-sighted.

He has written several stories besides 'Hester Dominy'. They all have the same pungent and earthy savour, but some of the earlier ones are so naif as to be almost unpublishable at a time when everyone is so accomplished.

One book of his has been published by Melrose. It is called *Soliloquies of a Hermit*. Not a novel, but a long meditative meandering essay. Personally I think he is much better within the framework of a story than spread abroad in soliloquy. The book fell flat in this country – it was published just after the war – but has had a considerable sale in America. He has tried various publishers for his other things, but so far has had no encouragement from them. I need not say that if you can do anything to help him find one, he would be most grateful.

Yours very sincerely   Sylvia Townsend Warner

David recommended 'Hester Dominy' to Prentice, and Powys's agent sent in two more stories, 'The Left Leg' and 'Abraham Men'. Chatto published them in the following year under the title of *The Left Leg*. The three stories were dedicated in turn to Sylvia, David and Tommy.

David and Sylvia had begun a friendship that was to last for the rest of their lives. Many years later he wrote:

Sylvia is dark, lean and eager with rather frizzy hair. She wears spectacles and her face is constantly lighting up with amusement and intelligence and the desire to interrupt what I am saying and to cap it with something much wittier of her own. I sometimes speak slowly, waiting for the right word to come to me, and when I am talking to Sylvia it very rarely does come, for she cannot restrain herself from snatching my uncompleted sentence out of my mouth and giving it a much better ending. She quivers with eagerness as though I were really going to say something good and then dashes in and transforms my sentence and my meaning into a brilliance that I should have been the last person to have thought of. In her company I soon come to think I am witty, though vicariously witty, it is true. (*The Familiar Faces*, 7)

Their friendship was forged in the Essex marshes. On August Bank Holiday 1922, Sylvia, having been attracted by such names as Old Shrill and Shellow Powells, set off alone to explore the marshes. She had left her map behind and got hopelessly lost. She was caught in a rainstorm and taken in, soaking wet, by kindly farmers. But she fell in love with that flat plain landscape. It was a curiously emotional experience and a turning point in her life. Thereafter she felt that she belonged to no one, and was her own woman. She was eager for David to share her experience.

8: xi: 1922   *125 Queens Road*

Dear Mr Garnett, This map – so threateningly named Southend and district – will show you something about the Blackwater marshes. At Mundon Hall is a large secret green pasture full of old oak-trees. If they would let you build a hut there I cannot conceive a lovelier place to live. It is the kind of place where one would have to have a flock of huge white Hans Andersen geese.

4

I am looking forward to some evening when you will bring yourself and the map here, when I shall be able to give you a confused but affectionately detailed account of the country.

Yours sincerely   Sylvia Townsend Warner

27: xi: 1922   *125 Queens Road*

Dear Mr Garnett, I was at *Figaro* on Saturday evening. And I overslept myself as a result and didn't ring you up early enough. I'm so sorry.

I couldn't have managed yesterday for a walk, anyhow. I had to revisit my childhood's home, which was extremely wet, and sad as only suburbs are on a wet day in November.

It was I, not you, that should have written. I said I would let you know when I came back from Dorset. But when I came back I was beset and bedraggled with things to do, and put off writing.

But do let us go and explore Essex. This Sunday I can't. But if the Sunday after would suit you, let me know, and I will keep it locked up in a neat box.

Yours sincerely   Sylvia Townsend Warner

Here is David's account of that Sunday:

It was a grey wintry morning and we spent most of it in the unwarmed carriage of a very slow train and later splashing through the mud while I listened, and Sylvia gave an extraordinary display of verbal fireworks. Ideas, epigrams and paradoxes raced through her mind and poured from her mouth as though she were delirious. Meanwhile we plodded under a grey sky across grey fields towards an invisible grey horizon. Finally we reached a bank of *zostera* and mud and the limits of the Thames estuary at high tide. Sylvia was right, the grey marshes had a melancholy eerie beauty that was all their own. But by late afternoon when we had climbed in the dark into another empty, badly lit railway carriage and were being trundled half-frozen from Nowhere back to London, Sylvia was silent and exhausted. Brilliance and shyness were alike forgotten, our hearts were warm to one another and have remained so ever since. That long day's tramp through the mud had been immensely worth while. (*The Familiar Faces*, 8)

1923

         125 Queens Road

Dear David, Please may I have the Essex Map back again for the week-end?

I shall be in on Friday evening if you would care to come round then. I want to ask you why I have never heard till today of Thomas Ellwood, whose prose seems to me even better than Defoe's. It is airier. I was sorry to hear from Tommy that you have not been well. However, we have found a nice godmother for you and arranged for a handsome christening.

Yours sincerely   Sylvia

David's wife, Ray, was expecting a child imminently, and I was duly born on 8 January 1923 without benefit of christening or godparents. Sylvia was later to write to another equally doting father:

Soon you will be like David Garnett, who looked at his eldest son sucking at the breast and said, It is rather difficult to make out whether he will prefer Keats or Shelley. (*Letters*, 93)

1924

David's second novel, *A Man in the Zoo*, was published in the spring, and he inscribed a copy to Sylvia.

1: v: 1924   *121 Inverness Terrace, [London] w2*

My dear David, I have just finished reading the *Man in the Zoo*. I like it very much, and admire you for having written it. It must have been difficult to write so unaffectedly about such a violent subject.

I'm sure that it is better than *Lady into Fox*. In any case I should prefer it, because I like your writing better than Defoe's – a macadam surface, I tell you. But apart from that it inspires me with more respect. This sounds either rude or ridiculous. What I mean is this: to tell his story the author has got to keep his reader at bay. From the moment the reader thinks: That's how I felt, or: I shouldn't have done that, the story isn't author's property any longer. It's nobody's property. It's the reader's booty.

You will find all these original thoughts much better expressed in Schopenhauer.

But I like your book so much, that, even to myself, these reasons for liking it seem rather quibbling. When next I see you I shall be able to express my pleasure less high-and-mightily.

Love   Sylvia

David and Ray had rented for the summer a cottage at West Itchenor on Chichester Harbour.

Tangley Hall is the name of a real house, some five miles north of Burford in Oxfordshire, which David gave to the ancestral home of the fictional Silvia Fox, the Mrs Tebrick of *Lady into Fox*.

22 July [1924]   *Itchenor, Near Chichester, Sussex*

Dearest Sylvia, So you have stumbled on Tangley, where your namesake spent her early life. Perhaps you will get to know the people who live there now – they have not been there long. There was once an attempt to rob the house, and the robbers very patiently bored a hole in the front door to slip an arm through in order to unlock it. But the owner of the house was waiting just inside with a billhook –

I was told all this when I was asking the way there a year ago. When I wrote about Silvia I hadn't actually been to Tangley but had only seen it on a signpost.

I was afraid it would be a disappointment, but far from it – it is just what I had hoped for. . . .

Here alas we have neither privacy nor electricity. We are semi-detached on each side, which means not detached at all. On one side is old George, a barnacle of eighty, very flea-ridden, but otherwise agreeable – on the other side are the junior family of Harker. The elder Harker paints the scenery for *Chu Chin Chow* or such things. The man talks in a lush voice about the murder trials: 'That fellow Ronald True, now – he ought to be vivisected to death.' The Jewess he has married is less theoretical and torments her small boy of three, but yesterday he bit her and then screamed for half an hour without drawing breath, so that people called in to ask if they could help or go for the doctor.

Such neighbours are disagreeable, but not so devastating as you would suppose. For the sun shines, we bathe and go sailing for most of the day, and I only suffer from them in the morning when I try to write my book.

Darling Bea!★ If you see her give her my love – tell her that Messalina and Melusina are nothing to her, fine women as they were.

With love   David

I'm sorry about the dog. You should have shaved him in this hot weather.

[September 1924]

Dearest Sylvia, I hope the weather at Tangley has not given you a cold – here I have got a touch of neuralgia in the head, like summer lightning a long way off.

Such excitements, my dear, have been happening to me. It's not a person, but a – no, not an animal – but a house that I have fallen in love with this time. And I feel as I did when I was twenty, that it was irretrievable, irrevocable – that if I cannot live in that house I shall

★ An elder sister of a boy Sylvia had known at Harrow, Bea Howe had, as Claire Harman wrote: 'Latin blood, English manners, the colourful background of being recently transported from Chile, and an affectionate heart'. She was to be the author of a novel, *A Fairy Leapt upon my Knee*, published by Chatto and Windus in 1927, and some biographies.

never live in any other – that if I am lucky I shall never be unfaithful even in thought to its bedrooms, though all the hotels in Europe shamelessly solicit me.

We were looking for a house to live in next spring – bought a copy of *Country Life*, and there it was – a smudged blurred photograph – but for the first time I became interested in Ray's idea of a house. I wrote, then went to see it, and here I am feeling sick with apprehension. Ray is viewing it today.

It is an early Jacobean farmhouse or small manor house – not too large. It is in very much the original state. There is a staircase of oak, carved beams, a wide hall, splendid dining-room and drawing-room, six bedrooms, a bath, hot and cold water, two w.c.s, a convenient kitchen with a good range. There is a pigeon house, a *columbary* as Bea would call it, in the garden, a tennis-court and two acres of orchard. The kitchen has been added recently, and the windows in front are sash and were altered some time in the eighteenth century. The house isn't a museum-piece, but it's convenient and beautiful. There are all sorts of drawbacks.

In the village there are four slate cottages newly put up and a dissenting chapel – otherwise excellent.

There is a horrid little cottage on one corner of the garden – in fact there are any number of drawbacks. But I'm in love all the same, and have been feeling slightly sick and had pains in my head since I went over it.

I don't know if you sympathise with these infirmities and aberrant passions. I hope you can, Sylvia, because if you cannot no one would.

I have been reading a book called *The Rector's Daughter* all day, Sylvia – I think it only just misses being a great novel – by an unknown elderly lady [Flora Macdonald Mayor]. I will lend it you. It's the first good new *novel* I've read for six months, and I read about one a week.

When will you be back in London?

With love   David

Ray has just telegraphed 'Lovely house, pretty village,' and has posted my offer to the agents.

Sylvia was also moving house, if only temporarily, and rented a cottage in Oxfordshire, where she completed *Lolly Willowes*.

10: ix: 1924   *Idbury Manor, Kingham, Oxfordshire*

My dear David, You must have thought me very ungrateful in not writing before to thank you for taking so much trouble about my

9

poems. My time has been taken up with visitors. I will certainly send them to Chatto and Windus – the poems: the visitors went this afternoon. Need I send them immediately? I should like to sleep a little longer on some that I brought down here. How shall I please you in return? I think I can do it rather prettily.

The visitors were my charwoman and her two little girls. When I had lit my wood fire these sat down on the rug and said: Now tell stories. It came into my head to put you to the test, so I told them the story of *Lady into Fox*. They sat listening like two owlets; and each evening they demanded that I should tell it again. On the last evening they had it almost by heart, and I suppose that, back in the Portobello Road, they will tell it to their friends. So it is quite probable that you will turn into folk lore. I hope you are as much pleased with this as I intend you to be. . . .

If you have begun bargaining for your house, you will certainly get it. Château qui parle, femme qui se tait. I assure you that the first half is equally true. I am so glad that it is in Huntingdonshire. (If you enquire, you may be pretty sure of finding that the Dissenting Chapel in your village was endowed by Selina, which will make it far easier to point out to visitors.* In any case you may say so.) That is one of my favourite counties. There is an extraordinary charm about that landscape of large fields and hedgerows dotted with clumsy elms, especially on some rather undistinguished evening when the sun has gone down without making a fuss about it. A cloudy sky goes best, one with a good deal of detail, as though it were a blurred reflection of the landscape. Large untilled skies and gallivanting cumulus should be kept for chalk downs. And I always like any place where there are quantities of hares, small soggy copses, Dutch barns looking like Cannon Street Station, and a number of useless ponds.

Some time you can tell me if it is really like this. I have always imagined it so.

Love from   Sylvia

David's offer of £1600 for Hilton Hall – against an asking price of £2000 – was accepted, and the success of *Lady into Fox* enabled him to give up working in the bookshop, but he remained a partner in the Nonesuch Press, which Francis and Vera Meynell had founded in 1923.

Charles Prentice reported to his partners on Sylvia's poems:

* Selina Hastings, Countess of Huntingdon (1707–1791) founded a Methodist 'connection' and several chapels, but not, of course, the nineteenth-century one at Hilton.

These poems were first offered to the Nonesuch Press. David Garnett told me of them. He said he thought they were very good, but that they would probably be rejected by his partners. Now Miss Warner sends them in, and in a covering letter says that Powys thinks well of them. One is glad to have such opinions, more than glad. But the quality of the poems themselves is their best introduction. They seem to me to be on the whole *excellent*. They have an eerie obscure force of emotion which comes thrusting up from some profound depth. There is no particular magic of language, just a curious compelling power and a rare appropriateness of expression. The style is harsh and sinewy Anglo-Saxon; in places perhaps reminiscent of Hardy. I think they are most peculiar things for a woman to have written, and a few are in a broader tone than that of most men. The author thinks deeply also. She is bitter at times and ironical and mocking. There is no facile pathos or ready-made beauty. The poems are distinctively individual. . . . I feel in a hurry to assert that I think we should publish them without delay.

11: xi: 1924   *121 Inverness Terrace*
Dear David, Chatto and Windus are taking the poems. I've just heard. My dear, I am so grateful to you. I am all of a tit-up with excitement.

It was ghastly when they were gone off to Mr Prentice. I nearly went the next day to ask for them back again. I felt like a cat whose kittens are taken away and she goes anxiously leaning about the house, and as her hope fails her mew grows harsher and more imperative.

My mews must almost have penetrated to Huntingdonshire. Are you there now, have you made a bonfire of the straw yet?

Love from   Sylvia

Friday [14 November 1924]   *Hilton Hall, Near St Ives, Hunts*
Dear Sylvia, I am very happy to hear that you have sent off those poems. I was afraid you would never bring yourself to, and I had heralded them with praises months ago. Well, my dear puffed and published poetess, you don't say who writes to you or anything about it. So instead I will say that I am here in my house, at home, already familiar with the uneven floors.

Did I tell you I had a Spanish table made of one walnut board an inch and a quarter thick to write at? If you are as virtuous as Mrs Browning you will have the same.

The ducks here have done something so pretty. You see, they

took a dislike to me. I was strange and perhaps domineering. They would not come to be fed or allow me to shut them up. And one night I went out and chased them, but they scattered in all directions, flapping their wings and screaming in despair. Perhaps I looked like a hawk.

So, having lost my ducks, I had to become acquainted with my neighbours, who turned out to be charming people. Last night two little girls brought back the last fugitives in a hamper under a seive. ?Sieve? Yes, sieve. There is a subject for a poem for you.

Today is bright and fine. We have everything to make the heart happy including an Aladdin lamp – but not a wheelbarrow, a daisy-spud, a dozen other necessities. We have no money until after Christmas. Tommy's aunt will have to wait for her three guineas. I have bought a kitten from her, but it hasn't come yet.

Love from   David
Siamese kitten.

[November 1924]   *121 Inverness Terrace*
Dear David, I hope you know about Siamese cats. They are half enchanted princess, descended, I believe, from the daughters of the Moon, which makes them very fickle and arbitrary. Will you teach her to play with the ducks? She should be just the right colour.

I can tell you more about the poems now. They will come out in the spring, and they are to be printed very plainly. Now I am having a ghastly time putting them in an order, they can't appear all higgledy-piggledy, and thinking of a title. Mr Prentice was rather firm about this. You will be naming the kitten, or I would ask you to think of a title. I think I must borrow Bea's Thesaurus of the English Language.

I went to see Mr Prentice. It was rather painful to begin with. I arrived feeling very sick and highly-strung because a bus had leapt at me sideways and only missed me by about four and a half inches. It was horrible and playful, like a drunk man. I was shown into a small room, and presently a stranger came in and looked at me without a word. I transferred a great many bus tickets from my right hand to my left, and we shook hands and sat down. After a very long pause I said: Are you Mr Prentice? And he said: Yes. And after another long pause we both began to speak at once. It was like a nightmare, or a religious ceremony. But he said such praising things about my poems that I soon felt quite at home with him. He said that they were a great surprise to him. Of course you had spoken very highly of them – my dear, you *have* done it handsomely – and that he had a great opinion of your judgement and all that, still – um – he himself didn't think it would be a real rabbit, or words to that effect. And he said that it was unusual to find a woman writing so objectively. And that I had such variety (this amazed me). And that my carriage chaste with slender waist would leave a swan repining. In fact he said so many pleasant things that I can't help repeating them.

Can't you get a wheelbarrow on credit, a squeaky one? You should always wear the same suit if you want the ducks to trust you. They can't bear black clothes or people in mackintoshes. My stepfather has quantities, and when they saw him in white flannels they fled into a thicket. You used to wear a snuff-coloured suit with checks and rather a tight waist. I should think they would take kindly to that. I love hearing about Hilton Hall. If you ever feel that you must boast about it to someone, remember me.

Please remember me to Ray.

Love from   Sylvia

[November 1924]   Hilton Hall

Dearest Sylvia, I was so glad to get your letter with further details. I had meantime seen Prentice – for I paid a fleeting visit to the Metropolis.

He said quite as many nice things about you to me as he can possibly have said to your face. In short he thinks you are very good indeed.

As to titles: I woke up at six this morning, and said to myself, 'Sylvia's poems are like the Essex marshes – more than that, they are like all land that has been reclaimed from the sea. They have the same calm solidity, a level fertile land, with no romantic mountain-tops. What is more, Sylvia is the sea, never able to rest herself, however much she wants to, but her poems have been reclaimed from her, and are land.'

Can you call them *Land Reclaimed from the Sea*? It is a little awkward, but very good. Are there any synonyms?

I try to think but can only think of ones which aren't serious, such as *The Townsend Levels*.

Perhaps *Reclaimed from the Sea* would do, but then all sorts of flotsam, drifting ships and drowned sailors are reclaimed from the sea.

Land Reclaimed from the Sea is better. Why *reclaimed*? Some land always was sea, and then is made land. Titles such as *Where Wild Waves Once Wandered,* though explaining my idea, will not do. *Blackwater Marshes* is too local. What is the opposite of erosion? Whatever it is, I feel sure it is no use. But there may be a word for

13

fields taken from the sea, a good English word, though a rare one, only used on large-scale parish maps, or in legal documents, or by farmers. I can only think of absurdities. Salt pans, mud flats, and so on. So all I can suggest is *Land Reclaimed from the Sea*. Not a poetical title, I admit.

I suggest you look up maps, Roget's *Thesaurus* and *The Misfortunes of Elphin*, also in accounts of Holland, for a word.

Well, my dear, I am in generally good spirits, I have no doubt you are, anyway you should be. Meanwhile, my dear, I have no news – except that the cesspool here is going to be emptied on the first moonlight night, and that I am going to have another well sunk, as it will be cheap.

Love from   David

28: xi: 1924   121 Inverness Terrace

My dear David, I have been reading aloud *Sir Charles Grandison* to Theo, but I don't think they write better letters than we do, or more constantly. I swim in melted butter with all this attention.

I went to Chaldon with a view to picking Theo's brains for a title, but he would do nothing but tell me to search the Scriptures while he read the standard Dictionary of Quotations. At last in despair I looked to the heavens for a sign, and pitched on *The Square of Pegasus*. You know that scant and dreadful constellation, with the black hole in it that is sheer space. Of course the name Pegasus has unfortunate associations, but the figure of stars is very much what I wish my poetry to be. The stars themselves look very rigid, and almost like tin-tacks, because of that black rent of nothingness, and that is how I should wish my few plain words to look.

But to be reclaimed from the sea is much the same as to be irreclaimable in the sky, perhaps better, for it has the advantage of being homely. I think your idea is better than mine, but I think my title might look better on the back of a book. The Dutch name for reclaimed fields is polder. I don't think that's possible; some people would confuse it with Balder (the god) and others with Babbitt. I suppose *The Sea Wall* wouldn't do? Another idea I had, connected with marsh country, is *The Decoy*. But I think your title is weightier than these. I shall probably use it, and keep the others for subsequent books. That sounds handsome, doesn't it?

Theo is much excited about Hilton Hall, and asked if it is in the fens. While I was there I read *Mockery Gap*, which may come out in 1927. I think it is the best thing he has done. There are an enormous number of characters including an ape and the Dorset Archaeological Society. The action is like the best twelve-part counterpoint, a counterpoint in which each part had a separate fugal subject which it develops quite independently of its share in the development of the whole. And the whole affair is as abstract as music. It has no relation to life except to the life of Theo's mind. The writing is very rapid, aloof and flippant, and entirely without transitions. It has nothing to do with any book since 1500. It is like a Gothic scene of the Last Judgement executed by a Chinese mind.

Chaldon was looking very beautiful and resigned. The undercliff was covered with lords-and-ladies, a devilish orange in the black slate. I scrambled down and wished I hadn't, for it frightened me.

Mr Jones the clergyman recently told his congregation that The Song of Songs was written by Solomon to his first wife. There is a new lych-gate at Winfrith which is promised to last for three hundred years and appears to be constructed of biscuit. Everyone was quite pleased with it until Mr Jones preached a sermon about it, and how it was to receive 'the corpse or body' on its way to wormy hole. He laid so much stress on corpse or body that hearers felt that any moment might be their next. It was opened by a Bishop while I was there, and we hoped he would give it a good send-off, but unfortunately he survived the ceremony.

Love from   Sylvia

Dig your well as deep as the well at Rothenburg.

10: xii: 1924   *121 Inverness Terrace*

Dear David . . . I hope your feelings won't be hurt. Mr Prentice doesn't like *Land Reclaimed from the Sea*. He says it sounds deprecatory, and that in this view he is supported by other opinion. Perhaps Tozer's, whom Violet★ believes to be a large Newfoundland dog sent tumbling downstairs to bark away bad writers. I have given in to him, partly because he writes me such kind letters, and partly because I agree with him. I can't admit the justice of any image which compares me to the sea. I'm sure you meant it pleasantly, and it is a beautiful thought; but I dislike the sea and fear it, unless it is at a safe distance. It is like Medusa's head, forever wakeful and writhing and dangerous.

On the other hand I am everlastingly grateful to you for obliging me to read about reclamation. I borrowed a great many books from my uncle on the Development Commission who is always brooding over mussel-beds. And I have learnt some charming facts about freshwater wells whose level rises and falls with the tide, and

---

★ Violet Powys, Theodore's wife. G. F. M. Tozer was a partner at Chatto and Windus who seems to have left little mark on the firm.

about warping salt-marshes and binding wandering dunes with marram-grass, and keeping waves out of a harbour by a reef of compressed air.

No doubt I should be less prejudiced against the sea if I could swim.

When will your new book be finished? I feel it is high time I read some more Garnett.

Love from   Sylvia

13 December 1924   *Hilton Hall*

Dear Sylvia . . . I am sorry you and Mr Prentice reject my title. But don't you see, my darling, that you describe yourself to a tittle when you explain what you dislike about the sea?

'Like a Medusa's head, forever wakeful and writhing and dangerous.'

Tozer? Do find out about Tozer. Ask Prentice point-blank. He only appears on notepaper. I have never dared actually ask. It seems indecent curiosity, and they have so many partners. Tozer may be a painful subject. Besides the people on the notepaper, there are also Whitworth and Swinnerton, and the last Chatto disappeared only recently.

My story [*Go She Must!*] is in an awful way. It's a *magnificent* story. And I am butchering it. In fact I cannot write a line properly. I plough wearily through my plot writing with labour what might as well be put into the fire. And it must be done by March.

Will you come here for Christmas? Come on the Tuesday before. My uncle [Arthur Garnett], an amusing fellow who stammers horribly, but who is charming, will be here. Please come, but we cannot have your dog. Must we have him? I love him, my dear, but Richard is terrified of animals, and there are two cats.

Let me know if you can come.

Love from   David

15: xii: 1924   *121 Inverness Terrace*

My dear David, It is very kind of you and Ray to ask me to Hilton for Christmas. I have never spent Christmas at anything so suitable as a Hall, and the idea that I might do so makes me feel like those enviable people who have town gloves and country gloves. But alas! I'm afraid I can't come because of bestowing the dog. I wouldn't bring him, it would be like a hair shirt in the midst of my delight, the anxiety that he might frighten Richard, or worry Ray. Would you be kind and ask me again at some less holy season (sorry as I am to miss your uncle) when either I could leave him with the Sturts in London, or despatch him to Little Zeal to my mother? But now the Sturts are themselves spending Christmas in the country, and I don't think guards are at their best. The prince of peace seems to rout them out of their natural good-temper just as he did Herod . . .

I expect you see the *Nation*, but in case you don't, here is a cutting from a review of your grandfather's heavenly book.* Did I ever tell you that it is one of the first books I can remember discovering for myself, and I had the fellow-explorer's pleasure of finding where so many of my father's quotations came from? Well, this seemed to me to express exactly what's wrong with modern fiction, and far better than I could, because the man who wrote it thinks it is what's right.

My dear, I *am* sorry you are having a bad time with your story. I suppose it's the inevitable result of a magnificent story. It is only the rather half-baked subjects that will lend themselves to an agreeable afternoon's writing. (And afterwards to an agreeable afternoon's reading.) I expect you will always write with an iron pen. First we build our houses of air and geometry. The stairs that no foot can tread go up undeviatingly, and underneath there is a convenient cupboard in which we can house darkness (or coats and hats: just as we please). Then we begin to write and build them of brick. The horror is, not that the bricks are square and solid, but that they are an insult to geometry, not a pure right angle among them, and no more solid than a crumpled mosquito net.

I can't imagine why we do it. I think we are both much to be pitied. And I am very sorry that because I am so tiresome with my dog we can't meet this Christmas and exchange our vows of woe and boast to each other about our works.

Please give my love to Ray, and ask me to Hilton Hall some other time, for indeed I should love to come. I saw a fine wheelbarrow the other day, green outside and inside painted a nice cheerful red, and I thought of you at once.

Love from   Sylvia

The bit about Medusa is beautiful. Did I write it?

---

* A disparaging review of a new edition of *The Twilight of the Gods*, 'not quite good enough of their kind', by Richard Aldington in the *Nation*, 13 December 1924. His remarks on modern fiction were: 'Much of our best fiction is a compound of acute analysis of individual characters set in a very personal world – aspects of modern life seen through a specialized temperament, often enough self-consciously original.'

1925

Sylvia's misgivings about visiting Hilton must have been overcome, for David wrote in *The Familiar Faces* that she came for Christmas, and 'this was the beginning of Sylvia's and Ray's friendship'. This is confirmed by subsequent references to the occasion. Ray wrote:

[ca February 1925]   *Hilton Hall*

Dear Sylvia, We are delighted with the wine glasses. I unpacked them while Bunny was in London and they looked lovely on the mantelpiece on either side of Henrietta★ – but still lovelier with wine in them when Bunny came home. Hilton Hall thanks you very much and is very proud. Bunny is roaming round now looking and imagining what this place will be like in twenty years' time. He has planted all the little apples in the orchard, the cherries and the peaches and the quince. We have planted a nut hedge between us and the ugly houses and apples on espaliers by the lawn. A walnut! And today a tiny mulberry not four feet high, but with a mulberry curve in its stalk. We considered carefully which way it should curve to look best in a hundred years' time from the drawing room window. But I think three months too long to look ahead.†

★ A bust of Henrietta Bingham, daughter of the American Ambassador, by Stephen Tomlin.
† She was expecting a second child in three months' time.

They should be a charming sight then, all these little trees among the old ones. I hope you will come again and see them.

Yours   Ray

The kitty has gone.

28: ii: 1925   121 *Inverness Terrace*

Dear David, I hear that your roof has blown off, and it will cost twenty-five pounds to put it on again. Please accept my sincere sympathy. Your roof was so kind to me that I feel it as a personal loss. However, I hope you will soon be so happy in the birth of a daughter that you will leave off regretting the roof.

That true-hearted Englishman Mr Prentice is now reading my novel. *The Espalier** is coming out in April. It is to be bound in mottle, like Garnett, only blue. It is a short square page, called I believe Pott. Did you see the prospectus? They put me next to Milton.

I hope you will review me for *Vogue*, and for any American papers you may have a hand in. You have done so much for me already (dear David) it would be a pity not to add a few substantial coping-stones. . . .

Please give my love to Ray. I hope your fruit trees have settled in nicely.

Love from   Sylvia

14: iv: 1925   121 *Inverness Terrace*

'near Whiteleys' if you like: personally I prefer 'far from Gamages'.
                                                                            More refined.

My dear David, Your letter was a great disappointment to me. I made sure it was to say that you had a daughter. I am growing quite tired of looking in *The Times*, I'm sure she should have come by now. It is all very well to tell me that your ducks lay eight eggs a day. I cannot take that as an extenuating circumstance.

I am not (now) going to be cremated. I am going to be buried with as much solemnity and as little privacy as possible in Kensal Green. I went there the other day, all the blackbirds and thrushes were singing, and there were the mausoleums like peers and peeresses opening parliament, or Indian elephants and potentates at the Durbar, or the gateposts along Eton Avenue. But nothing can convey how enormous, how ornate and how expensive they are. Angels, sphinxes, obelisks, soup-tureens, pylons, troglodytic

* The eventual title of her book of poems. Her novel was *Lolly Willowes*.

dwellings, gothic thingumjigs, Aberdeen granite poured out like water, animated busts, mosaic texts, tessellated sentiments, central heating, magnificent lounges, palms in abundance, three hundred and seventy-nine bathrooms, Church of England service – Hallelujah! And all for nothing. And all to oneself. Not a single mourner. Not a dry eye to be seen anywhere. Nothing except the neighbouring gas-works, looking like more mausoleums.

You see how eloquent it makes me.

I don't know what you might tell the American consumer about Theo. You might tell 'em that when he was a boy and lived at Montacute Rectory he used to catch snakes, and loose them down the stairs when his sisters were coming up. Snakes *and* ladders, that ought to fetch a refined progressive pure-souled people, I should think.

Darling Theo! I can't think of anything else that isn't libellous. I have been remembering him as I sit here, and it is as though he had come into the room with a cold face as though the moonlight were still shining on it, behaving with a rather guilty politeness, and propping up his stick with immense caution.

'Well, Theo, did you have a nice walk, with nothing frightening?'

'Well, my dear, I *did* hear a curious noise in the hedge. At first I said to myself it was nothing but a rat, but then I remembered *Who made that rat.*'

Theo is more afraid, more tunnelled and worked with fears, than anyone else I know, even than myself. That is why he is always considering death. He turns to death with relief, for it is so certain, so reliable, so safe. It is the judgement of a child to compare him with Donne and Webster, as all these intellectual idiots do, for *they* could not keep away from the thought of death, it was like pressing the sore tooth to them, but with Theo it is the only tooth that will not fail him. His despair of the universe is an intellectual thing, he knows there is nothing good, nothing true, nothing kind, that until he is dead he is at the mercy of life, and that at any moment from behind some impassive mask we choose to call blessed, a blue sky, a primrose, a child, a nicely-fried egg, life, not death, will look out with its face of idiot despair, idiot cruelty. So he is always afraid except when he is writing (thinking, I should say) about death. Then he is comparatively happy and secure, so he makes these charming jokes about it. But in his writing, because one has to use other people's language and other people's thoughts to be understood by them, and because for one Theo there are fifty Donnes and Websters – philosophically, I mean – his fear of life is translated into death-symbols. But these rabbits and girls writhing in the bloody

20

grass are horrible as reminders of what life is, when they are dead they have left off writhing. They are horrible no longer.

Still, this will hardly do for Knopf's Annual, will it? Perhaps you might tell them something chronological, and that he doesn't write two books a year in the order of publication. Not that I object to him writing two books a year, I wish you would too: but the general opinion seems to be that it is a little immodest.

Give Ray my love, I am glad to hear that she has once more got a roof over her head. I expect your orchard is beginning to look like green ghosts now.

Love from   Sylvia

Yes, I also look forward to seeing you. Bea said you looked very well when you were last in town. I hope you are.

David contributed an article, 'T. F. Powys' to *The Borzoi 1925: being a sort of record of ten years of publishing* (Knopf, 1925), in which he discussed Powys very much on the lines that Sylvia had proposed. It includes the extract from his note on 'Hester Dominy' already quoted on p. 3, and there is also an article on himself by A. E. Coppard.

David and Ray's second son, William, was born on 12 April 1925, and Ray wrote:

[ca 20 April 1925]   *Hilton Hall*

Dear Sylvia, It was very nice of you to write to me about our son who ought to have been a daughter, I know you think – but it can't be helped now. Theo told me it would be a boy, so he won't be surprised. He has dark hair which is growing instead of coming off, but I suppose it will come off, and long dark eyelashes, and the ordinary dark blue baby eyes. His eyes are wide apart, his nose is large, his mouth very firm looking, and he has a little pointed chin, but I see no resemblance to anyone.

This place is looking lovely, but so is every place now, and I almost envy you being at Chaldon. What a lovely valley it is beyond the Powyses'! Give my love to that little bridge and to Tommy's cottage.

We have cowslips here. I go out every day now. Before that I had my bed turned first this way then that so that I could see the plum blossom and afterwards the big chestnut in front of the house coming into leaf. It is aways full of birds and bees, the flowers will soon be out. We wake early and listen to the birds. No, baby doesn't cry very much. I think he will be a good baby. Richard was a good baby, but this one will be more placid. He is very strong and can hold up his head, he has very elegant hands with long fingers and tiny narrow nails. He seems to know how pretty they are, as he will never let them be hid but clasps them on the pillow or folds them on his chest or puts one finger to his forehead. Please give all of our loves to Violet and Theo.

Yours   Ray

They keep the bulls loose here too, tell Theo. I think I shall go away for August when they 'blair and holler' and escape from their fields.

29 May 1925   *Hilton Hall*

Dearest Sylvia, I have been meaning to write to you for many days now, only laziness and perhaps exhaustion have prevented me.

Your poems have been read and re-read a great deal here; you know what I think of them, and of you – all I can do is repeat tiresome praises, which I am afraid will bore you as much as the dirty billets-doux which were first passed you in the Harrow chapel, now that you are grown-up. But it is conceivable that seeing such a note a sentimental feeling might be awakened, and I hope now you have the admiration of the world, you will always regard mine with affectionate pity, with condescension and not contempt.

You are a true poet, Sylvia, you have your place in English literature. In the reading room of the British Museum you will never I think be one of the great names written round the dome (I seem to remember Carlyle and Emerson among them), but you will keep company with much the best-bred section of English writers – the late seventeenth-century poets. Lord Rochester will take you down to dinner, neglecting Mrs Barry, and Mr Congreve will find you much better company than the Bracegirdle woman. After your arrival Mrs Behn will be left to her own company; but she is a good-natured sort, and will forgive you. No – the poor ladies of the seventeenth century are utterly eclipsed – only one French lady is fit to be compared with you, Madame de Lafayette; and the Lord only knows how much of her is Rochefoucauld. I shall always feel a special pride in having inspired your 'Bride of Smithfield', but in the next edition I think you might thank me for the subject in a note.*

Very much love, Sylvia.

At the bookshop they rave over you.

Your country cousin   David Garnett

* Sylvia's 'Song from the Bride of Smithfield' tells of a girl's unrequited love for a butcher's slaughterman. There is an unfinished story by David in an exaggeratedly moralising Defoe manner called 'The Rose of Smithfield' about Angela Sharney who left her butcher husband for a slaughterman and ended up as a fallen woman. I do not know whether it is entirely fictitious or is based on a real character.

My dear David, I have been meaning for some time to write and
thank you for your pretty flatteries. Indeed I am not likely to feel
bored with your good opinions. So if you should happen to think of
any more, pray do not hesitate to send them – or better still to say
them. For I should love to see you again; and when I hear that you
have been in London I take it rather ill that you have not been to see
me.

I have been reading Eckermann's *Conversations with Goethe* with
much delight. Do you know what the Chinese novel can be that he
read and compared to Richardson? It has young ladies in it seated on
cane chairs, which (Goethe says) call up ideas of great elegance and
lightness. It must be very different to *Mrs Dalloway*.★ What do you
think of that? While I read it I felt like Joseph resisting Potiphar's
wife. But I did resist it, though I think she can move like a swan,
speak like a siren, twine like a convolvulus. What is the use of
describing feelings and thoughts, however vividly, if they are all to
remain the author's? This is *My* book, this is what *I* feel about it – It
made me feel almost ashamed as I read it to see such gifts made such
a schoolgirlish use of.

I met her the other day. She is so charming that I had the greatest
pleasure in stifling my scruples and telling her how much I admired
it.

I have not had any reviews to speak of yet, except a very
patronising insertion in one of the *Nation's noyades*. However, it is
only in their lousy little supplement, so I hope it won't be read.†

Give my love to Ray. She wrote me such a charming account of
the new baby that I felt perfectly converted to his sex.

Love from   Sylvia

My dear David, I have just spent the afternoon tightly reading *The
Sailor's Return*, and now I am trembling a little and feeling slightly
weak in the legs as I did on that winter's afternoon when we came
back from driving through the fens.

I think it is extremely good. I suppose objective is what I should
say if I wanted to please, but thank God there is no need to please
people who can do as well as you: so instead I will say more exactly

★ The Chinese work Goethe had been reading was *Chinese Courtship: in verse* by
P. P. Thoms, 1824. *Mrs Dalloway* by Virginia Woolf was published on 14 May
1925.
† 13 June 1925: '*The Espalier* is not startling but it is poetry.'

that it gives me the impression of something round, close-grained, and resilient with the kind of interior unapproachable life of a very good india-rubber ball.

You must have been pleased when you wrote the bit about the parrot saying 'Time'. I dare say you almost scratched it out again next day, though, for every miracle-worker has a moment of intimidation when he discovers that he has really brought it off.*

I have just come back from Oxfordshire. Tangley Hall was looking as charming as ever, they have a fine flock of white Aylesbury ducks there, and the garden was full of golden-rod and smoky-looking Michaelmas daisy. About a mile from Tangley there is a deserted farm called The Warren. I came on it quite by accident, for it lies in a little dell among woods, far from the road, and the field-path to it is vanishing from disuse. I found a way in and walked over the house as much as I dared, for the staircase is broken away, and all the timber eaten with dry rot. The parlour windows are grown over with nettles and gooseberry run wild, and growing up through the broken stone floor is a flourishing elder-bush, singularly bright green from its indoor life. The doors and chimney-pieces are carved with names and dates, mostly eighteenth-century.

I was very pleased with my find, and when I had done with the polite part of the house I turned to the back-kitchens and wash-houses. These were even more dilapidated and darkened, and I was just thinking that I had had enough of them when I saw an archway leading into a sort of cellar with a barrel roof. I went in looking at the roof and nearly fell into a well. It was so dark and smooth and plumb with the floor that it looked like a slate. It then seemed to me that this deserted house I had been pitying so was uncommonly disappointed that I hadn't gone a step further into its trap. It had been waiting so long for something to happen; and a drowned lady would have been a pleasant secret to hint of to the woods on a winter's night.

Afterwards I met a man who told me that the well was the finest and coldest spring in the district, and that three children had died of diphtheria at that farm in one week.

I wish you would come to see me. I am trying to write another story, the prologue is the best thing I have ever done, and the rest is

* William Targett, the landlord of the Sailor's Return, is dying after being injured in a prizefight:

> The boy sat silent for another five minutes till the door opened softly and Mrs Cleal put her head into the bar. 'Doctor says he cannot last through the night,' she said. The parrot scraped in its cage. 'Time, gentlemen, please. Time,' it said feebly.

like a dead codfish wrapped up in verbiage. I am blasted with discouragement, couldn't you come and flatter me a little?

Give my love to Ray. The woodcut of Tulip* is beautiful, I only wish there had been more.

I hope you are all well and happy.

Love from   Sylvia

[October 1925]   *Hilton Hall*

Dearest Sylvia, I have not seen you, nor written to you for many months, yet there is no one who has been more constantly in my thoughts; your name constantly on my lips, and on the lips of my friends.

We are always talking of you; but this isn't enough. I come to London almost every Thursday. Next Wednesday or Thursday (I don't know which yet) will you lunch with me?

Your letter delighted me, and it filled Ray with envy: she wants to go to Tangley, after which I suppose I shall lose her.

What you said about my Sailor was comforting. Strangely enough a reviewer, a little unsatisfied man with a red beard and the look of a genius – holds my parrot up to ridicule:

'The timely parrot dwells, with the last rays of the setting sun, in regions unexplored by literature.'†

But I even would approve *the last rays of the setting sun* if it hadn't been done before. In fact I think that art consists of such things. But the parrot is bad. I had thought of something much better for him to say – and forgot it – for many weeks tried to recapture it – alas, in vain, so I put 'Time, gentlemen, please' instead of scratching out the bird.

The same reviewer said: 'The theme is unsuitable for Mr Garnett's purpose', which shows he knows too much by half. I suppose I daren't confess I hadn't a purpose apart from the theme.

My father thinks well of you – has recommended your novel *Lolly*, and I gather that it has been accepted in U.S.A. as a gamble on your future, which is thought hopeful.

But you know that. What sort of knots are you tied in? Mine are desperate, and I am in the state of mind of a man setting out to sea in [a] sieve – a large specially made sieve which has been much admired by amateur yachtsmen on land.

Goodbye, dearest Sylvia. I send you all my love.   Bunny

* The frontispiece portrait of the heroine of *The Sailor's Return*, Princess Gundemey of Dahomey, known as Tulip when married to Targett.
† J. F. Holms in *The Calendar*, October 1925.

Dearest Sylvia, I have just read *Lolly Willowes* – and I like it so much
that I feel it almost indelicate to tell you how much – an
embarrassment which Adam may have felt in thanking God for
Eve.

No one told me how good *Lolly* was going to be. You said
nothing yourself. The American publishers asked my father if I
would write a note about it – you don't mind, do you? It will be
something quite meaningless and vulgar.

It came as a surprise to find *Lolly* such a beautiful and perfect
thing.

At first she's asleep like the Beauty in the wood. One bends over
asking does she breathe? And then she wakes up and goes about her
business, and at the end such a passion, a storm, fills her, I tremble
while she pants for breath. The end is the best thing in the book.

Yes, Sylvia, you have written a very wonderful story, with the
quality of some of your poems but with much greater force.

Lolly delights me, pleases me, much more than I can express and
fills me with hope.

If I can't write at least you can, and something solid will be left.
Don't be offended at my coupling myself with you like this – it is
not meant impertinently, but your performance makes me understand my ambitions.

Bless you, Sylvia, and vow as I vow

'And like a rat without a tail

I'll do, and I'll do, and I'll do.'

But, alas, I am feeling very much that I have no tale, and I must
tell one or the young rats will starve.

Much love   David

Dearest David, Your letter has given me a great deal of silent joy. It
has given me the assurance I wanted, and if it comes from you I can
believe it. Other people who have seen *Lolly* have told me that it
was charming, that it was distinguished, and my mother said it was
almost as good as Galsworthy. And my heart sank lower and
lower, I felt as though I had tried to make a sword only to be told
what a pretty pattern there was on the blade. But you have sent me a
drop of blood –

You would laugh if you could see the story I am writing now [*Mr
Fortune's Maggot*]. It is a lovely subject, there is nothing original
about it, for it takes place on a Pacific island (like Defoe and H. de
Vere Stacpoole), and the hero is a clergyman (like Mrs Humphry

Ward and Oliver Goldsmith), and it is written in alternate layers of Powys and Garnett, both imitated to the life. I roar with laughter at it and write on feverishly. The Rev. Crusoe is Theo, of course, and Man Friday is you. Oh, I forgot, there is the scenery out of a child's paint-box. *That* is Bernardin de St Pierre.

My dear, are you really having trouble with your tail? I am so sorry. I don't want the young rats to starve. How would it be to write the memoirs of someone picked at random out of a graveyard? Just the name, I mean; isn't that a tail that could be dipped into some pleasantly peaceful cream-bowls?

You could use *sortes virgilianae,* run your blind finger down a dictionary: Buttercups, my uncle's irrational dislike of. Cabinet, boule, at Parsley Manor.

No, I don't expect you to approve. You will grow your own. I hope we may never fail to admire each other's performance and reject each other's suggestions. What a heavenly state this calls up!

Love from   Sylvia

Thank you very much for writing to the Americans.

A note in David's hand among Sylvia's letters may be what he wrote for the Americans:

Lolly Willowes
On the authority of Mr Peregrine Pickle 'it is criminal by virtue of an act of parliament for any person to accuse another of sorcery and witchcraft, these idle notions being now justly exploded by all sensible men'. This eighteenth-century statute is probably still in force, and I shall not accuse Miss Sylvia Townsend Warner of being a witch. I do not want her to prosecute me for criminal libel, neither do I wish to rouse up some fundamentalist descendant of Cotton Mather to get *Lolly Willowes* burnt in Massachusetts. All the same even though 'the idle notion of sorcery has been justly exploded', sensible men have had time to reflect since the eighteenth century that it is as easy to be a witch without practising witchcraft as to be a member of the Salvation Army without being saved.

A careful study of the great witch trials of the sixteenth and seventeenth centuries has been made by Miss [Margaret] Murray, and her volume, *The Witch-Cult in Western Europe,* proves not only the existence of witches, but explains their practices and the organisation of their religion. It is interesting to learn that in poor parishes the local clergyman was sometimes also the devil's officer, that in this dual capacity he would repair to the witches' Sabbath after evening service. But, while Miss Murray has given us the facts, Miss Townsend Warner is the first woman to reveal the spiritual side of the witch-cult. In *Lolly Willowes* – the life story of a modern witch – she explains the psychological craving for witch-craft, and for the first time the reader can understand the great spiritual force which drove thousands of women during the middle ages out of the church and into the covens. But Miss Townsend Warner's story, *Lolly Willowes*, is much more than the story of a woman's deep religious experience. It is an extremely well written book, absorbingly interesting and the wittiest book I have read for a very long time.

No one who has read *Lolly Willowes* would willingly risk having his image made in wax and slowly roasted by Miss Townsend Warner. I predict that the book will get very good reviews.

1926

My dear David, I owe you such a pleasant afternoon that I must write and thank you for it. It was your good idea that a copy of *Lolly* should go to Miss Murray (*Witch-Cult in Western Europe*).

She liked my witch, though she was doubtful about my devil, and wrote to me a very pleasant letter to say so. Now I have just come back from lunching with her.

She is most fit and right; short and majestic, a Queen Victoria with the profile of Louis Quatorze and small fierce fat white hands. I wish I were in her coven, perhaps I shall be. Round her neck she wears a broad black velvet band, probably for a good reason. She said things that would make the hairs on your head stand bolt upright.

What charming things happen to me through your instrumentality.

How are they at Sparrow Hall?★ I think of gateposts set flush with a brick wall, stone knobs on top half covered with a shaggy mat of ivy. A white shuttlecock comes flying over – I am not sure what happens after.

But don't be nervous, I won't take and make a poem out of it.

Instead to show you how much I love you I send you my story about Hilton. I hope you will be pleased with your likeness, my dear Mr Slumber.

Love from

Sylvia

A young lady got into conversation with me in the Park. She pointed to the Serpentine and asked: 'Is that salt water?'

★ Hilton Hall. In Hilton there is a monument in memory of William Sparrow (1649–1729), who cut a turf maze on the Green to commemorate the Restoration in 1660. Sparrow did not, however, live at Hilton Hall, but at Park Farm. Sylvia was much taken with Sparrow's maze and wrote a story about it, 'The Maze', published in *The Salutation* in 1932. She has transferred the Hilton maze, much altered, with one of its inscriptions, 'AB HOC, PER HOC, AD HOC', into a land of Powys's countryfolk, in which the monument is destroyed by lightning when a visiting stranger stumbles upon the overgrown and forgotten maze. Mr Slumber remains aloof from the villagers, reading Herodotus and eating white currants.

My dear David, Perhaps I should have written at once to assure you
that I wasn't cross – but after all, I can't believe it was necessary. On
the contrary I am extremely grateful, and I shall show my gratitude
by instantly demanding something else.

Lolly is doing quite nicely, but we think she might do even
nicelier: so Mr Prentice is composing a little wreath out of her
reviews which is to be slipped inside the Chatto and Windus books.
Do you think Birrell and Garnett would accept a few leaves and
send them out in their parcels?

Some time before long I must see you, for my missionary has got
to dive into the sea somewhere about p. 115. The only time I have
been under the sea was quite involuntary, but I remember your
telling me that you loved diving, so perhaps your impressions are
more collected than mine. I have also to make some enquiries about
algebra, but the earthquake and the harmonium have had their
paws buttered and have settled in quite nicely.

Yet in spite of these gaieties it is not a gay story, and perhaps you
will not like it, for it is not like *Lolly*, it has none of her pretty ways.

It is more like Peeping Tom, I think.

Give my love to Ray, your fruit-trees have been in a year now, I
suppose.

Love from   Sylvia

Sylvia was asked by Chatto and Windus to compile an anthology on
winter. Nothing came of it in the end, but she was at first enthusiastic
about the idea and replied at once:

I should love to make a winter anthology, especially if it may
include a few illustrations. I must consult an astronomer: for a chart
of the winter sky seems to me most essential. Country dances
might go in too, tunes and recipes for the figures: skating-calls,
perhaps, a few: accounts of celebrated hard winters to make people
feel cosy: some words on fireworks – and, Oh joy! I've just
remembered it, that charming burlesque in the Chester miracle play
where the bad shepherd steals a lamb and hides it in the cradle. And
when the other shepherds come in to view the newborn, one says
suspiciously: What a long nose it hath!

4: viii: 1926   *Little Zeal, South Brent, [Devon]*

My dear David, Please will you write a disquisition or prolegomena
to the study of English cheeses for an anthology of winter that I am
going to do for Chatto? I know it is one of your special subjects. Of
course I would far rather you wrote an entire book on the subject:

but failing that I should like a few words from your pen. When I remember how happy I have sat drinking claret over your wood fire I feel that I am especially suited to collect 'wintry delights'.

I am also in need of your skill as a zoologist. In my earthquake I killed a parrot (the bough of a falling tree broke it: Victor [Butler] said this was improbable and should have a footnote to say that it was subsequently ascertained that the parrot died a natural death; however it happened to the raven in Selborne) and dislodged a hive of wild bees. But does one say hive for the wild bees, or is there a wilder word?

Indeed I will hold your hand, provided you will hold mine too. My missionary is an impossible length, fatally sodomitic, alternately monotonous and melodramatic, his only success is an aigredoux quality which will infuriate any reader after the third page. I love him with a dreadful uneasy passion which in itself denotes him a cripple. . . .

Give my love to Ray. I have got a cottage in Somerset till the 20th of September, at a village called Wayford which looks at Lewsdon and Pilsdon. Can't you come and pay me a visit? It belongs to a missionary (I took it for the sake of local colour) and has quantities of bedrooms. Do!

Love from   Sylvia

1: xii: 1926   *121 Inverness Terrace*

My dear David, You are a damned idle dog, why don't you send me that Latin tag on the Sparrow memorial that I want for my very good story? I tell you, you will regret it if you trifle with me. I have put you into it, a very agreeable character so far, reading the *Decline and Fall* and eating white currants. But it is well within my means to make you read the *Encyclopaedia Britannica* and drink Instant Postum. Now do you tremble?

I sent a set of Bristol glass marbles to Ray so that the young Garnetts could play an old English game during the winter, but I forgot to say it was from me. I hope it turned out all right.

Happy New Year,

Love from   Sylvia

1927

David's fourth novel, *Go She Must!*, is set very firmly in Hilton and the Huntingdonshire landscape. Hilton Hall has become the vicarage in which the Rev. Charles Dunnock has his doorstep ploughed up by the mummers on Plough Monday (a legendary Hilton event), and from which his daughter Anne makes her escape to France and elsewhere. The old gardener, Noah in the novel, is based on Reuben See, whom Sylvia would have seen working at Hilton Hall.

The copy of the book in its 'smooth Sunday coat', which Prentice sent to Powys, must have been one of the limited edition of 150 copies. Sylvia got one too.

2: ii: 1927   *Chaldon Herring, Dorchester*

Dear Bunny, You came today in your smooth Sunday coat sent by Charles to Theo. I have been reading you aloud. I read as far as page sixty-four, and though I have just enough self-control not to read on to myself yet, I am so excited that I must do something so I write and tell you what you have told me already that so far it is magnificent and the best thing you have done. What I most especially admire is the way it is timed. For all the time one feels the excitement of the world rolling irresistibly into an English spring, and yet it is lumbering and deliberate like days in the country.

Theo was delighted, of course Mr Dunnock would be congenial to him.

I hope it has already sold its first impression and that you are getting sensible reviews. Where they plough up the garden I was as moved as though I were seeing it done myself, perhaps more so.

It is a cold frosty night, and the foxes are howling and gnashing their teeth on the hill.

We all send our love to Ray and you.   Sylvia

9: ii: 1927   *121 Inverness Terrace*

Dearest David, We read *Go She Must!* with extreme parsimony because we were enjoying it so much: and we only walked back through those secretive large fields to their secret on Monday evening. My dear, there is no doubt that this is your best book, and the last chapter is the best of all. It is real virtuosity in the proper sense of the word: the slow unflurried grasp of the situation. I admire and love you more than ever, dear David, and I implore you to love and admire Oliver Cromwell with all your soul and with all your strength, and as soon as conveniently may be.

But stay in England: for when Anne bought her small hat and her lipstick she also bought a great many early novels by George Moore: and it was that that made her cry out: 'How extraordinarily different are the houses!' – a pseudo-Gallicism that she would never have learnt from her father or Reuben, I mean Noah. You are wrong about the Paris bit not being so good as the rest. It is quite as good, and the van scene is one of the best bits in the book. But here and there are little early Moore inflections, which muffle your outline just like the little films of cotton-wool which cling to peaches which have been too reconditely and cherishingly packed.

I find it extremely difficult to say this because I admire Moore almost as much as you do. And it is extremely courageous of me to criticise you because I am exposing myself to coals of fire when it's your turn to write about *Mr Fortune's Maggot*. Do not heap red-hot magnanimity on my head by refusing to tell me of its faults or I shall think I have offended you.

If I could meet you I would say such things that you would probably understand how fine I think your book is. Will you have dinner with me one day soon? I do not see you often enough; and what makes it worse is that it is often due to mismanagement and laziness in not taking steps to invite you.

I came back from Chaldon yesterday. The downs in their winter grass and flinty winter plough were like a tumbled basket of slack-baked loaves of bread. Lily —— has paid me a compliment, I think. For her illegitimate baby is called Sylvia. But perhaps the compliment is rather to my name than to me. At any rate she cannot suspect me of being the father.

Love from   Sylvia

Sylvia went to stay at Hilton when *Mr Fortune's Maggot* was in proof, and, as she later wrote to William Maxwell:

David took the proofs to read and shut himself up with them. When he came out, having read the book, he began to tell me that he thought it was good. His face swelled and reddened, and we both realised that he was in tears. *(Letters,* 11)

He wrote of the book in his review in the *Daily News*, 27 April 1927:

. . . And the only criticism one can make is that the author has been almost too restrained, that she has missed one or two opportunities, and that the end is so far above everything else that we feel for some reason slightly ashamed, both of ourselves and of Miss Townsend Warner. Here we have been laughing our way, unconcernedly, though not unkindly, through three-quarters of the book. Miss Townsend Warner has amused us, beguiled us, giving no hint of what is coming, and then, suddenly, our eyes are blurred with tears, and through them we see the truth, bitter and needing more courage than we can command. So we are rather childishly ashamed of having ever laughed at Mr. Fortune. Although he was always ridiculous, he was a brave man and good man, and though he lost his faith, and his last act on the island was to carve an idol for Lueli, he was a Christian also. . . .

30: iv: 1927   121 Inverness Terrace

Dearest David, I have just read your review in the *Daily News*. It is charming; you do really love Timothy, I see, and I am very glad, proud and grateful. There only remains one thing more: when you come to dinner (let it be as soon as you can) you must tell me which were the opportunities I missed, and where I should have let myself go more. It is not restraint always. Sometimes it is false shame.

Please give my love to Ray. Do your young fruit trees promise prettily?

Your loving   Sylvia

22: xi: 1927   121 Inverness Terrace

Dearest David, I think of you, I pull out your books; but I don't seem to do much else about you. This is a pity.

Now I have something to ask: two things, if the first doesn't put the second out of my head.

I am doing a book about Theo, a rather Shandean affair, which in the end I dare say will not go further than a limited edition.★

I am putting in as few facts as possible, they are dangerous things, but some I must put in. And I want to know when it was you first went to Chaldon, and what happened, and what happened next.

Isn't it triumphant about *Mr Weston's Good Wine*† being sold out?

Charles and I carried down the first copy to Theo last week-end.

He was extremely well and lively, and the first lambs-tail of 1928 was out in the Green Valley.

The other thing I have to say is that I think the Nonesuch should

★ It did not get beyond seventy-six pages of unpublished typescript.
† Powys's latest novel.

do a selection of the poems of Isaac Watts selected by me. He is extremely good. No one has any idea how good, because they have always read him castrated by hymnologists.

The Sailor's Return* has changed hands, and now Mrs Moxon has to walk over High Chaldon for a drink.

I hope Ray is all right again. I was very sorry to hear that she had been ill.

Love from   Sylvia

[ca 24 November 1927] The Nonesuch Press, 16 Great James Street,
London WC1

Dearest Sylvia, I was glad to see your hand, though the grey-bordered notepaper portended a sorrow – a death? An animal's death? Or stolen from *Vogue*?

About Theo: The order of events was this:

In the winter of 1921 – January or February or possibly December 1920 – Tommy came about five o'clock to 19 Taviton Street. We talked about Brancusi. He had come to see if we had some Maillol book. I began talking about sculpture – and Brancusi, whose work I had very much admired in 1913 at the Albert Hall exhibition – before I knew any artists or their work. We became interested in each other. He rushed off, and we met again and dined together at Gustave's that evening. Soon after I was invited to Chaldon. At Chaldon Tommy said there was a neighbour who would probably come in, who wrote, etc., etc. But Tommy was interested in it. He was a solitary, but not the bore one would have expected, I gathered. Theo came in and I was much struck by his politeness and his charm. It was obvious Tommy was very fond of him indeed, but had not wanted to alarm me by telling me too much.

We saw Theo after that on Sunday and walked to and fro several times in the dark, Theo rather scared of Mrs Ashburnham. Tommy annoyed me by forcing me to call on Mrs A. He walked with me over the hill to Wool. I was too much charmed and delighted with Tommy to consider Chaldon and its inhabitants as more than a setting fit for him.

A week or so later an alarming lady with a clear and minatory voice, dark, dripping with tassels – like a black and slender Barb caparisoned for war – with jingling earrings, swinging fox-tails, black silk acorn hanging to umbrella, black tasselled gloves, dog-chains, key-rings, tripped lightly in, and speaking to me in sentences like scissors told me –

* The inn at East Chaldon after which the one in the novel was named.

It was you, dearest Sylvia. You left 'Hester Dominy'. I read it and jotted down my impression of it at the time. That note I have got if you would like it. I sent 'Hester Dominy' to Charles afterwards.

Love from   Bunny

[Postcard] 25: xi: 1927   *121 Inverness Terrace*

Many thanks for your letter, which goes entirely against my own views of what happened. For Theo says you went to Chaldon in the summer of 1922, and I feel almost sure that you had not been there when I came to Taviton Street, which was after April, I know, as I only got 'Hester' then. But many thanks all the same. I shall print the two accounts in parallel columns, and then call for water to wash hands.   Sylvia

I have never had a single fox-tail. You are confusing me with another Silvia.

Sylvia's version is the more accurate. A letter from Tommy to David postmarked 11 August 1922 conclusively confirms her version. It is clear that they have only just met (he never again signs himself 'Stephen Tomlin'), that David had already written to Powys about 'Hester Dominy', and he invites David to stay at Chaldon.

1928

Sylvia visited Hilton with Prentice for the second week-end in March, and wrote in her diary:

10: iii: 1928: . . . Started for Hilton with Charles. In a very slow train . . . It snowed, and when we got to Huntingdon Bunny met us with the words: 'Sylvia's weather again.' We sat talking in Bunny's room till dinner time . . . Ray is doing illustrations for a book called *Pax the Adventurous Horse*, by a child of thirteen.★ Bunny read some aloud, and then we looked at each other in despair – each, however, thinking that even though we couldn't write like that it was much to our credit that we should wish to. . . .

11: iii: 1928: . . . During the night I had a fine dream of the Hilton ghost. We were sitting, the same party, in Bunny's room, but our chairs faced away from the empty grate, so that it must have been summer. The lamp dimmed for a minute, as it often does, and I said something jokingly to Ray about the ghost she kept in the cupboard. The lamp flared up again, and at that moment the cupboard door opened and a young man rushed out into the room. He was about seventeen, long and weedy with a feeble face, and was dressed like a cookboy in a long white pinafore and a tall cap. He ran like a rabbit that bolts out of a hole with a ferret in pursuit, making little darts this way and that. I cried out, Look, look! not frightened, but very anxious the others should not miss him. As I spoke I heard their chairs grate and they jumped up; and then I heard Bunny give a sort of groan of horror, and realised that whereas I saw only the boy they saw also what it was that he was trying to escape from, and which had followed him out of the cupboard.

David liked to think that Hilton Hall had a ghost, but I do not recall it ever showing itself except in Sylvia's dream.

Sylvia's second volume of poems, *Time Importuned*, was published by Chatto and Windus that spring.

★ By Muriel Hodder, published, with an introduction by Edward Garnett, by Faber and Gwyer in 1928.

Dearest Bunny, Bea has just been telling me that you like my poems, and are pleased with me. Please will you come and tell me all over again?

I am here in the [Harold and Vera] Raymonds' spare bed with a large confused dog-bite in my leg. Such sad scenes by the Round Pond. Sylvia being as brave as death in a pool of blood, surrounded by people saying they never did trust those Alsatians. It was a chow. He did it quite by accident, thinking my leg was William.*

I am perfectly well, but mayn't move. Next week I am going out in a bath chair. I have always longed to do that.

Will you ring up and suggest a time? . . .

Do come and see me, dear Bunny. I am so terribly pleased you like those poems. I was a little nervous that you might think them too noble and matronly, as they are, compared to the first set. Putting on flesh, I am.

My love to you on your Island. Has it blossomed well this spring? Have the fruits set?

Always   Sylvia

Tuesday [19 June 1928]   *Hilton Hall*

Dearest Sylvia, If you die of hydrophobia or tetanus, or gaseous gangrene, or worse, I will put on your headstone, and in your obituary notice in *The Times,* not one of your own moving epitaphs but the plain statement: 'She trusted the brute creation and was well paid out.' Sylvia – why do you get mixed up in such things – a dogfight – aren't you ashamed of yourself? Even a bitch would know better than that. Really, it is a disgrace. And actually you had so little feeling for the proprieties that you let it occur in Kensington Gardens, by the Round Pond. It's quite abominable.

Your poems want a great deal of reading, of re-reading, of learning by heart. I don't think I have anything to say about them. They have moved me more than any modern poems, except possibly one or two of Edward Thomas.

It seems to me Sylvia that you are a real poet: the only poet whose poems are any good at all. The art has fallen on very evil days, and it is not much praise to say you are the best poet today – with the desiccated dust of mummia in *The Waste Land* on the one hand and the humbug of Humberto Wolfe on the other – and the Sitwells crackling like broken wine-glasses or bladder seaweed on Scarborough front, underfoot. But I think you deserve to shine in a

* Her chow.

better world than this. In a world of stars you would shine brightly, now in the gloomy eclipse you suffer, not gain, by having no companions. Dear Sylvia – I don't want to pay compliments, and I can't criticise. But your poems will live in me as long as I love beauty, and they will live in hundreds of men's hearts, if men have hearts then, long after there's nothing left of us but our names, and long after anyone cares to try and clothe the name in flesh and blood, or cares to imagine what people were like who lived so long ago.

I will come and see you on Thursday or Friday: I will telephone.

Ray and my sons are in the South of France: they drive down to the beach in a donkey cart, from Duncan [Grant]'s cottage.

Well, well, it's the hour of ghosts.

Goodnight, and if I may, a serious (but not sympathetic) kiss, Oh – you dog-bitten slut: I promise you your books will be dog's-eared; not a nunnery of virgin, unopened sheets. Some copies will be torn in bits by puppies.

Love from   Bunny

12: x: 1928   *113 Inverness Terrace*

Dearest Bunny, Theo has requested me to find out for him what Chaste Honey / Harlot Honey / Virgin Honey is; he adds that I shall probably consult a clergyman. Instead, I ask you. I remember a picture of you, scowling beside a bee-skep. Perhaps you had just discovered that your bees were no better than they should be.

I cannot write about Aimée Semple McPherson.★ She is beyond my poor powers. I might perhaps snatch the hem of her garment in a very long, richly harmonised, mellifluously orchestrated Symphonic Poem, but she is quite out of reach of any words but her own.

I was perfectly carried away by her and wished with all my heart that I could be just such another thrilling the Albert Hall with the story of my life. Charles [Prentice] was not so much impressed.

He sat, a neat self-contained shape of suspicion, like a Lesser Cat who has been offered a dish of over-sweetened rhubarb.

I hear of you sometimes from him. It would be nice to hear of you from yourself.

Could you come to dinner one day next week, and see my new abode? And Ray? Couldn't she be in London buying roasting chestnuts and come too?

Love from   Sylvia

★ Much publicised religious revivalist, born in Canada and based in California.

Dearest David, Please write *soon* about Virgin, Harlot and Chaste Honey. Theo is hankering round a new book and only his doubts about the honeys is keeping him from starting it.★ He is like an oyster that waits for a little grit to start a pearl. So it is important, and you can easily find time to send grit by post. He is so uneasy and persistent about this, that I think he may be on the edge of another masterpiece. He is like a cat looking for the exact corner to kitten in, going round and round the house with conscientious restlessness.

Now that I have made him a cat and an oyster I may as well say that he is extremely well and lively. He sends his love to you and to Ray.

It is blowing and raining a tempest, and the sheep on High Chaldon stand quite still, unhappy enduring woollen clods.

Love from   Sylvia

★ According to John Mortimer's *Whole Art of Husbandry* (1721), 'The Honey which first flows of it self from the Combs is called Virgin Honey (as is also the Honey which comes from the first Years Swarm).' Powys was considering using *Virgin Honey* as the title for the novel which became *Kindness in a Corner* (1930). Chaste honey is perhaps a synonym for virgin honey. 'Harlot Honey' is the title Powys gave to a story, or perhaps a rejected chapter, from the same novel, which was published posthumously in the *Powys Review*, No. 3, Summer 1978. It tells of Mr Truggin, a widowed sexton in search of a tenant, who 'often used words that other people seldom used. As he saw the sooty piece of cobweb upon the bar of the grate, the word "Harlot" came into his mind.' When, in due course, his tenant arrives in the desirable shape of the young infant teacher, Chloe Huddy:

> Mr Truggin saw that her eyes were merry ones, and that she had no hat. . . .
> 'My hat is blown into a May bush,' she said.
> 'I will get it it,' said Mr Truggin gallantly.
> Mr Truggin walked beside Chloe. She had pointed out a tall May bush, the only green thing in that world.
> 'There be something in thee's hat,' said Mr Truggin as they drew near to the bush.
> ''Tis a swarm of bees,' exclaimed Miss Huddy.
> A word came into Mr Truggin's mind and met another. 'Harlot Honey,' he said.

1929

Dear Ray, I have had the title-page proof of *The True Heart* with the finished tea-set. I like it extremely, and I am so glad that when Charles asked me if I should like any ornament under the title I replied: a teapot. Thank you so much for taking so much trouble over it, and for pinning such a charming nosegay to my book.

In less than two months from now I shall be back from America. I put it in that way, because it is more bearable than to say that I go there next week.

I shall bring you a present from Woolworths.

Love from

                                                Sylvia

? drawing

Ray's engraving for the title-page of *The True Heart*.

Dearest Ray, I was so very grieved to hear from Charles of the scare you have had.★ I do hope it is only a scare, my dear. I expect it is. Anyhow, you have got to work on it so quickly that I feel comforted about you, for I know that that is the whole battle.

Would it amuse you to hear about New York? I got back in the small hours of Saturday morning, after a very rough voyage that ended with the *Aquitania* sticking on a mud-bank within a few yards of the docks, very tantalising. Then the train broke down, and we

★ The first intimations of cancer of the breast.

sat for an hour at Wimbledon. I felt exactly like a dreg trying to squirm down a blocked waste-pipe. When at last I let myself in at my own door William's feelings were so overwhelming that he could only express them by barking like a boiler factory at the taximan.

It is heavenly beyond words to be home, even though we have no hot water and plumbers at every meal. But I enjoyed New York more than I expected. It is impossible not to feel rather set-up when so many people are trying so hard to butter one's paws and be kind. And the climate was ravishing: clear cold with a strong sun and an air crackling with vitality. And I loved the city – the new parts of it, that is to say. Old New York is like the dullest reaches of the Edgware Road less solidly built, with iron staircases spidering up and down the house-fronts and the dust-carts on strike.

The skyscrapers crop up anywhere, as randomly as though someone had scattered a packet of skyscraper seed. The general effect of the skyline is much like a collection of medicine bottles of all heights and shapes rising from a solid floor of little pill-boxes. It is amusing to see the churches in the lower part of the town where tall buildings are general: they look absurd with their spires coming half-way up to the office-buildings that flank them: much as if God were really being put down among the lowly he talks so much about, to see if he really likes it. Judging from their expressions, he doesn't.

There is one large park with merry-go-rounds in it, and a small zoo, and quantities of chalets and artificial mountains and ornamental waters and notices saying: Keep off, and no grass. The trees glitter with ice as though they were mica trees in a ballet, and all the children wear leather jerkins and caps with earflaps. Gentlemen walk about in shaggy fur coats down to their heels, like grizzly bears. The grizzlies wear bowler hats at one end, and light spats at the other. The lifts were a disappointment to me, they are no faster than ours; though it is rather exciting to see them labelled: Express to 40th floor; Local to 48th; but the revolving doors to office-buildings are unnerving, they revolve so fast. Everyone going out or in gives them a terrific shove, they fly round like electric fans, and one has the greatest difficulty in not coming out in two halves.

I visited a Woolworth on Fifth Avenue for purposes of comparison. The glass is not so good as in ours, but they have superb kitchen ironmongery, incense, and beautiful jewellery. This is expensive, though. Earrings ten cents apiece.

Prices are rather awful, but as oysters are less than half the price of English oysters I had a false sense that I was living very economically. The food isn't so superlative as they make out, except the iced

42

puddings and some of the old-fashioned country things like apple butter, which is a sort of chestnut-coloured mush with a strong twang of wasp about it. The best bought food is at the speakeasies, where the competition is so violent that unless they can offer a decent cuisine people will go to the one next door. In ordinary private houses the prevailing drink is whisky, and if the taste is more than you can bear you drink it with ginger ale. In grand houses one has wine, but only the very grandest can afford to offer you beer. Tea is made by putting the leaves in muslin bags and steeping this in lukewarm water. You can then add preserved cherries or cloves to the brew if you dislike the flavour of warm muslin.

Quantities of people asked me if you were David's brother. This is not because of a masculine quality in your woodcuts but because your name is Ray, an American he-name. Any monosyllable will do for a male, apparently: Woy or Milk.

I spent one week-end in Connecticut, and walked about in snowy woods by the side of a river called the Saugatuck. The house I stayed in had one Polish orphan to run it. I came down to breakfast about 11.30 one morning and found her dusting the sitting-room wearing a pair of high-heeled gold dancing-slippers. This bit of country I saw was like the wooded parts of Surrey with a great many cardboard rocks from the last act of *Die Walküre* added to it. The houses were wood, painted white, with a great deal of fret-saw cornice, balcony, knops and gimp edgings. They look as if they had been cut out of paper with embroidery scissors to house a band of immigrant marionettes rather than stern New Englanders. All New England is going back to the wild. It is not worth anyone's while to farm those stony fields while land can be got in the West; so the woods are coming back, the snakes coming down from the mountains; a rattlesnake has been seen in Connecticut after seventy years' immunity. You can buy a perfectly good farm there, with land, for five hundred dollars.

Tell David that I found myself very famous. At one awful banquet a lady bounded up to me and said: I must thank you for your delightful, your charming book: *Mr Warner*. But after the first week I grew wily and avoided banquets and bores, and met people much like ourselves, except that they were friendlier and not so intelligent, and had some pleasant times mousing round with them.

Now that I am back, and relaxing into a reasonable climate, I am beginning to understand what a shatteringly active life I led there. I can sit back and feel the exhaustion just dripping off me. I think one reason why New Yorkers do so much all the time and do it so hard is that they haven't settled into their country. They are like visitors, not inhabitants.

43

My greatest boast is that having had five days' gale on the voyage out and the same measure on the voyage back I never felt sick for an instant. As this is nothing to do with me I feel justified in being proud of it.

Love from   Sylvia

21: iv: 1929   *113 Inverness Terrace*
Dearest David, I have just written my name in *No Love*. As I read it I remembered a cold March week-end at Hilton, when we sat in your room and you read aloud the beginning, and were very cross with me, dear Bunny, when I had the impertinence to suggest an umbrella-stand for the hall at the Jumblies.

I thought then the book would be a good one, and I augured especially well of your crossness at my daring to lay a finger on your property; but it is better than all my expectations of it, even though when I was in America I had a letter from Charles saying it was your best book; which made me hope very highly.

I do congratulate you with all my heart. I can't say I like this or I like that, I can't expatiate, my admiration is too comprehensive.

Charles is quite right. It is your best book, the roundest, the most living and growing. And more than any of the others it has that quality which I think of as especially yours: a decision and pride which keeps the reader in awe, that makes him know his place.

I want to see you. Can you come and have dinner with me one night this week?

Love   Sylvia

7 May [1929]   *Hilton Hall*
Dearest Sylvia, Will you forgive me for long silence – I wish I could flatter myself by saying cruel silence. I have been rather jumped out of myself by unwonted responsibility lately: looking after people for their own good, and someone has always been in the room. All very unusual.★

Thank you for saying *No Love* is my best book: it is. I am not going to repay the compliment by saying *The True Heart* was

---

★ Geoffrey Phibbs had become alarmed during an affair he was having with Robert Graves's mistress, the poet Laura Riding, who believed that if only they could get their love-making right they would actually 'stop time'. He fled to Hilton where he was pursued by telegrams and an imperious visit from Robert Graves demanding his return because Laura Riding was suicidal at losing him – and did indeed throw herself out of a window when Phibbs returned and tried to break off the affair.

yours, for, though it had extraordinarily lovely things in it, I liked
Mr Fortune better. The finest thing you have written ever I suppose
is the last sentence on p. 227 of *The True Heart*, but after her arrival
in London I don't like it at all. Indeed Sylvia, I'm going to make an
attack on you, and it's this: You do a very dangerous thing: you
invite the reader to feel superior to your heroine. You hand him a
stick and say: squail it at her – she's only an aunt sally and a half-wit.

And the author must never do that for fear of all the blains and
boils and murrains which break out on Mr Punch's face –   *why this?*
suppurations called A. A. Milne and A. P. Herbert and E. V. Lucas:
infectious micro-organisms.

No, my darling Sylvia – abuse from a stony prophet in the desert
won't do you any harm, and I see you playing with hellfire the
moment that dog arrives in Covent Garden. The end of the book is
lovely and serious and good, and is all part of the story; but the devil
tempted you, and you chewed the evil fruit, even if you spat it out
afterwards. This is a very harsh criticism, and Lord knows how
you'll take it after all your maple sugar. But if you are not cross with
me will you come to lunch on Thursday? I love you, and you'll see
that more in my face than in this letter. If you can lunch will you
ring up the Nonesuch?

Yours affectionately   David

She must have done so, for they had an amicable lunch together two days
later.

David had rather ambitiously installed white fantail pigeons in the
dovehouse at Hilton, but within two or three generations they had
become parti-coloured by interbreeding with the natives. I cannot recall
what more serious misfortune they suffered to inspire Sylvia's poem.

24: ix: 1929   *113 Inverness Terrace*

Lines on Four Fantail Pigeons
which were Kept Six Days in Captivity.

My brother died young;
My lovely sisters died
Young too, but I abide
These solid shades among.

He o'er this roof and they
O'er that now take their swing,
Or preen a supple wing
In voluntary stay:

45

But like a spectre I
Haunt my own dark, my own
Whiteness start at, and am grown
Afraid, now, to fly.

Dearest Bunny, this is all I can contrive in the way of being helpful about your pigeons. The young lady in Keats recommended white peas. But hers died, so perhaps she is not very reliable. In fact I can't remember a single pigeon in poetry who didn't come to a bad end, so I'm afraid there isn't much hope for you. You had better buy owls. Wordsworth stuffed one in his Later Poems, but otherwise they are hardy.

Today I talked to Ray on the telephone. She invited me to the Zoo, but I couldn't go, and was very sorry. I should have liked to have seen the Potto, a nocturnal animal with large ears.

Thursday week will suit me very well. I will call for you at the Nonesuch a little before one unless you ring me up with other arrangements.

My love   Sylvia

1930

Dearest David, . . . Not long ago Llewelyn and Alyse★ went home one night and found their door bolted against them, a window broken and a light in an upper room. They walked to Ringstead and telephoned for police. Seven policemen came, three from Wareham and four from Dorchester, in motor cars. One of them addressed Llewelyn as Mr Whitenose.

They then charged up the hill at a double, entered the cottage, drew their truncheons and crept up the stairs in single file. In the bedroom was a young lady wearing silk pyjamas, curled up asleep with the cat asleep beside her.

She explained that she was an artist, born in Kent, who had been overtaken by the darkness whilst walking out from Weymouth. So she broke in by the window, locked the door to be on the safe side, eat some supper, unpacked her pyjamas, made friends with the cat, and settled down for the night. Apparently she makes quite a practice of this sort of thing.

I suppose she always carries pyjamas in case she needs them. She inspected all the Coastguard cottages from the outside, and settled on Llewelyn's because it had a water-filter. She had eight pounds in her purse, and the police took her to Wareham. I fancy that Alyse saw to that. . . .

Bea and Mark have taken the house in Royal Hospital Road where the Todd used to live.† Her correspondence is still there, incriminating letters from all the old Bloomsbury Omnibus. So for some time they will live by selling autographs and blackmail. It was a lovely wedding: lots of champagne and no bridesmaids. So much champagne you could smell it in the air – like spring, but a good deal stronger. Wherever one looked there was a discarded swain in striped trousers. It must be gratifying to have a wedding like that.

Love from   Sylvia

★ Theodore Powys's brother and his wife, Alyse Gregory. They lived in a coastguard cottage at White Nothe (or White Nose) on the Dorset coast.
† Bea Howe married Mark Lubbock, composer and conductor, on 15 January 1930. Dorothy Todd was editor of *Vogue*, to which a surprising number of the 'Bloomsbury Omnibus' contributed reviews of various kinds.

1932

On 11 October 1930 Sylvia had entered into a lesbian relationship with Valentine Ackland, an unsuccessful poet twelve years younger than herself. They committed one another to a 'marriage' the following January, and Sylvia remained true to Valentine, despite her infidelities, for the rest of her life. At the time of Sylvia's next letter they were staying at the Hill House, Winterton, which had been the Acklands' holiday home, and to which Valentine was much attached.

David had obtained a Pilot's Licence on 24 September 1931, but he did not acquire his own aeroplane, shared with Hamish Hamilton, until May 1932.

23: ii: 1932   *The Hill, Winterton, Norfolk*

Dearest Bunny, All I know about Lawrence is this: that Secker is going to publish a 'drastically abridged and expurgated' *Lady Chatterley*, which is to be the 'authorised British edition'. Also that in the *Jolly Roger* tract★ Lawrence says that he was asked to produce a polite edition himself, and would not. That this, as far as we know, was his deliberate opinion; and that to castrate his book the moment his back's turned and he safe dead is a damned dirty act.

I'm afraid people who disapprove will do nothing, saying, 'Poor penniless Mrs Lawrence, she must live, so why not on her husband's carcase?' And I don't suppose there is anything to do but protest. But protest we should, if only we ourselves might ever be eminent enough to have conscienceless literary executors. I've written to the *New Statesman*, and to *Time and Tide* – a silly weekly, but I have a faint chance of getting into it, so I was practical. I wish you would write too.

Yes, I read about the scarlet-cloaked Montalk and thought it scandalous.† If one has boiled a cat alive or starved one's

---

★ *My Skirmish with Jolly Roger*, 1929.
† Geoffrey Wladislas Vaile Potocki de Montalk was a Polish count, born in New Zealand, who lectured on English literature and was a published poet. He had also written a small collection of poems, no more than six pages of manuscript, which were no doubt obscene by the standards of the day, and he wanted some copies to circulate to his friends. His publisher, who was also a printer, refused to print them, but told Montalk that if he could find someone else to set the type he could borrow the presses to do so. Montalk therefore

grandmother one has a chance of fair dealing in a police-court or court of law. None, if one is guilty of literature – as for poetry: if the fellow had written buttercups and daisies instead of cunt and bugger, he would still be writing something that wasn't a film scenario or an advertisement for bad legs, and criminal.

I should like to see you very much, dear Bunny. Why should you not fly here one day? There is a perfect landing-ground just by the house – a large expanse of sand-dunes. Do come. This place is just north of Yarmouth. Lunch or tea any day till March 20th or so, when I shall go to Chaldon with Valentine. . . .

Please give my best love to Ray.

Ever

Sylvia

[February 1932]   *The Nonesuch Press Ltd*

Dearest Sylvia, I have just read your letter in *Time and Tide*.

I agree with you that it is monstrous. The expurgation has been done by Lawrence's brother, aided by some other person (possibly Montie Weekley).★ The brother is an ex-revivalist, who has always been getting women into trouble – a sort of anaemic Rasputin trying to be respectable.

I am a very old friend of Frieda's and fond of her and for that reason not keen to rush into the fray.

But I think I should have done [if] your telegram had not reached me when I was being distracted by the most dreadful horrors: a little sculptor† I had made friends with and who had come down to live at Hilton, was stricken in agony, and I was sent for. While the doctor was being got hold of I cheered him and soothed him and told him it was often like that with the 'flu – and he believed me. It was lock-jaw. The doctor gave him morphia, I carried him downstairs, stowed him in the back of my car and took him to the hospital.

approached Leslie de Lozey, a professional typesetter. Lozey refused to set the poems and informed the police. Merely by showing the poems to Lozey Montalk was deemed to have published an obscene libel and was sentenced on 8 February 1932 to six months' imprisonment. An appeal, in which Montalk was represented by St John Hutchinson, an acquaintance of David's, was refused on 7 March.

★ It is not now thought that Lawrence's elder brother, George, and Charles Montague Weekley, the eldest of Frieda Lawrence's children by her first husband, Professor Ernest Weekley, had any hand in the bowdlerisation, which was authorised by Frieda, but not made by her.

† Frank Weitzel. He was only thirty.

He died the next day, and we buried him on Tuesday. Meanwhile Ray is in a nursing home. She'll be out in a few days, I think.

So you'll forgive me for not having done anything about *Lady Chatterley*.

I should love to come over, but are your sand-dunes level? and are they hard enough? I don't want to break my neck.

Love from   Bunny

[19 June 1932]   *Hilton Hall*

Dear Sylvia, At the oddly named village of Duxford (to provide which seems a work of supererogation to modern poultry keepers) they sing:

'The second, third and fourth of May
Are the chimney-sweepers' dancing day.'

On May Day they show garlands and say:

'Please to see my garland.'

I heard complaints of your unsociability from a young man who came to see me in order to talk so fast he couldn't hear me, until he was so exhausted that he shut his eyes so he couldn't see me. I had treated him with great politeness since his arrival was heralded by the announcement that 'Mr Rothschild wishes to see you.'

I am in a fizz. Tomorrow the fields behind and on the side of this house and the superincumbent cucumbers-cottages are up for auction and I shall be there to bid farewell to the last of Ray's investments.

Ten acres of good grass accommodation fields in the centre of Hilton named Scott's Close, two thatched cottages and a small slate-roofed one, surely is as good as moribund railway stock? Who knows? Not I, at all events but as the plain man says about art: 'I know what I like,' and I like Scott's Close very much indeed.

Yet that fizz is already flat and forgotten. My *Pocahontas* is nearly done. About four more chapters. (Can I write them in a fortnight? No.)

Now the young man Brewer thinks that I must visit America, or rather James and York rivers *so as to be sure* that I have seen the Virginia creeper growing before I describe it *so as to be sure* I have given it the right number of toes. (I am sure that is the style in which the whole of my book is written.) . . .

So I am going, and already you see the results. I woke up at four o'clock this morning wondering if my physique were good enough to stand America and became so worried that I had to get up on the spot and write a letter to H. M. Inspector of Taxes before I watered the lettuces and celery.

Am I riding into the jaws of death? I am. The heat will be appalling, and I shall wear canary-coloured socks and pants since they make Anemophiles bilious. (I mean by that the malarial mosquito.)

Oh, my dear Sylvia, what shall I do? I am in such low spirits that I can scarcely crawl. I can't bear Americans. I can't bear my book. I know nothing about it, and it will take a year to put any sense into the 100,000 words I've written already. Meanwhile I am absolutely broke. We can keep goats in Scott's Close or even cows. I won't have anything to do with them. I will buy myself a trousseau in the Burlington Arcade before I go.

I won't buy a dressing-gown. That would be wickedly extravagant. But shirts and socks and ties and shoes all in canary-coloured crêpe-de-chine.

Shan't I look sweet examining the morse hanging from the trees (a great feature of the Forest Primeval)? Oh, why do Americans insist on putting me on the spot?

I send you my love, and so does Ray. Please be sympathetic and send me a strengthening letter, because I am quite insufferable, and you don't have to be in the room with me the whole time as I do. I can't escape.

Love from
                                                          David

22: vi: 1932   *East Chaldon, Dorchester, Dorset*
Dearest David, I hope with all my heart you have got Scott's Close. In weather like this one wants to buy every field one sees; and I remember those as very nice fields, where I once took a walk with Richard, talking about echoes.

Next to that I am delighted that you are going to America, though personally I should be afraid of Virginia – it is, or seems to be, so cultured. I know all about the morse hanging on the trees. Did I not hear Gamel Brenan last summer telling old Arthur Machen – whom you met at my house once, and liked – all about the bilberries of her native clime?* They grow in bahgs, said she.

---

* Gamel Woolsey, American poet, was married to Gerald Brenan, writer on Spain and an old friend of David's. Arthur Machen, professional writer and connoisseur of the morbid, was married to Sylvia's aunt Purefoy. Sylvia had tried without success to persuade David to give him work with the Nonesuch Press.

Excuse me, said Arthur, who is a little deaf. Baaahgs, she repeated. Oh yes, yes, of course.

It was not all that they had hoped, that meeting, because at the onset Arthur said, I believe I have met you before. In Ealing. He meant no harm, to his mind Ealing is as remarkable a place as any other. But both Mr and Mrs Brenan looked a trifle nipped.

You will have a lovely time on the boat, eating caviare. If you explain to your waiter, you can have it at every meal. Try it for breakfast. And if you visit Richmond, Va., you will be introduced to Miss Ellen Glasgow, a dear old lady with an ear-trumpet and white crochet lapels like a first-class smoker. I was told, by someone else from Richmond, Va., that until I had met her I could have no idea of the graciousness and culture of the South. And indeed she was a charming old pussy.

I too am absolutely broke. My half-year's cheque from Chatto and Windus was Four Pounds Three Shillings and Fivepence. I have just dedicated a story to Charles, to show that there's no ill-feeling.★ It takes place in the Argentine. Thank God I do not know any young man called Brewer, or I should have had to go there. As it is, I have killed a rhea for local colouring, and put in some hens. They are invaluable animals, because they can be studied at home, and transplanted almost anywhere.

How far are you from East Dereham, where Cowper died? I am concerned about a man there, called Craske, whose pictures you may have seen at the Warren Galleries, where they were shown about two years ago. He is a fisherman, who was blown up in a mine-sweeper, and made an invalid of; and being slightly blown out of his mind, he began to paint. He is a sort of English Douanier Rousseau, but with an English seriousness, for I always feel with Rousseau, except when he's in the tropics, that if his tongue, just the tip of it, wasn't in his cheek, it ought to have been. Now I hear that Craske has fallen on very bad times, and is ill and miserable. I can't afford to go there myself, and I have been trying to think of someone intelligent in his neighbourhood, who would go, and look at his work, and revive him. It is attention he needs, more than L.S.D.

His address, just in case you or Ray should feel inclined to go there, is 42 Norwich Road, East Dereham. He has a very nice wife called Laura. His tariff, I may mention, is moderate. One guinea for water-colours, thirty shillings for the larger needlework pictures. They are both so respectable and speechless that it is worth knowing this. The pictures really are magnificent, Defoe-like

★ 'The Salutation', published as the first story in Sylvia's book of that name in 1932.

pictures, stuggy, exact, and passionate. What I should really like would be for Ray to go and choose one she like[d] and let me give it to Hilton as a present for your return from America. I would really like this.

Talking of Defoe, dear Bunny, have you ever read a story called *The Island of Pines*? It is about a shipwrecked Englishman, who was cast up with three white women and a Negress, and by the time he was eighty he had in children, grandchildren and great-grand-children one thousand, seven hundred and eighty-nine. It is a sort of animated Malthus, I haven't enjoyed anything so much for months. It was written by Henry Neville, an early seventeenth-century writer. He only lay with the blackamoor in the dark.

This place is exquisite. The fields, hay-cutting has only just begun, are so full of flowers that in the evenings they smell exactly like the breath of cows. On Tuesday old Mrs Moxon brought us a young owl, which she had caught, with the recommendation that we should kill it and have it stuffed for an ornament. We kept it caged in the woodshed till dusk to save it from being mobbed. When we let it out it gave one shove with its claw, like a fenland skater, leaving a deep scar on Valentine's wrist, and was gone in one swoop, with nothing to tell where it went but a shrill scolding from small birds abed.

My love to you both, and my best wishes for America. I shall think of you in your canary-coloured spats.

Sylvia

19 October 1932   *Hilton Hall*

Dear Sylvia, Ray has just read me the first story in your book, 'Some World Far From Ours',★ and it is, I think, the most beautiful thing you have written, and it moved me very much. It is the best thing I have read of yours in prose – and it is poetry – for it is the most direct, simple and economical, with no safeguards of wit.

Don't think I am depreciating your bigger works – I'm not – and they are bigger, and the end of *Mr Fortune* is far far more impressive, I know. But this story is perfect and ranks with the works of the great artists, the conscious artists, so rare and so few in literature.

In a book of stories there are bound to be some one cares little about, that is why, feeling so moved by the first, I thought I would write while the words were still in my ears. I'll write again saying I don't know what, later on. But this is simply to tell you Sylvia that

---

★ Published with another story, 'Stay Corydon, Thou Swain', as a small book in 1929.

you're a great artist and a true artist, and I love you, and that I don't undervalue you because you are an old friend.

Yours affectionately, Bunny

On this note the correspondence lapsed for twenty-three years. William Maxwell, in his edition of Sylvia's *Letters*, suggested that this lapse was imposed by Valentine Ackland, who may well have been jealous of David and discouraged or even forbidden the relationship. There is no direct confirmation of this in the surviving letters, but the circumstantial evidence is strong. Although Valentine did not prevent Sylvia from resuming the friendship and the correspondence as warmly as ever in 1955, it was a long while before Sylvia mentioned her as freely in letters as she had done before the hiatus; and when Sylvia and David met they did so out of Valentine's way, at Hilton or on neutral territory in London.

1933-1954

Sylvia was now living entirely with and for Valentine. In 1933 they published a collection of poems, *Whether a Dove or a Seagull*, bearing both their names, but not saying who had written which. The experiment was not a success. Sylvia on her own, however, began to acquire a substantial reputation. In May 1935 the *New Yorker* first published one of her stories and so began a most profitable relationship which was to last until her death 144 stories later. William Maxwell, the novelist, who was on the editorial staff of the *New Yorker* from 1936 to 1976, became a close friend and, in due course, one of her literary executors. She continued to write poetry, several novels, a brief study of Jane Austen and a mass of letters, many of them to friends in America, made as a result of her stories in the *New Yorker*. Under Valentine's influence she joined the Communist Party, as the only bulwark against Fascism; and they were both active in support of republican Spain, which they visited twice during the civil war. On their return they settled permanently at Maiden Newton, near Dorchester and not far from Chaldon, where they had previously had a cottage.

David completed *Pocahontas*, which was published in 1933 as a Book Society Choice, and in 1935 a further novel, *Beany-Eye*, which was likewise founded on fact. After that he lapsed from creative writing. He edited the letters of T. E. Lawrence. He was literary editor of the *New Statesman* from 1933 to 1935, and thereafter wrote its leading review until the outbreak of war. He joined the R.A.F. and worked in the Air Ministry until shortly before Ray's death from cancer on 24 March 1940. Hilton Hall was let for the duration, and he went to live with Angelica Bell, daughter of Duncan Grant and Vanessa Bell, in Sussex and London. He served in the latter part of the war in the Political Warfare Executive, where he was concerned with propaganda to France and clandestine relations with the Resistance. He married Angelica in May 1942, and in July 1945 they returned to Hilton, where a pig club and digging for victory soon grew into active farming with a Jersey herd as well as poultry, pigs and bees. He and Angelica had four daughters, Amaryllis, Henrietta and the twins, Frances and Nerissa.

All this while, by his account, he had no contact with Sylvia, though I am puzzled to recall reading his copy of Sylvia's *Cats' Cradle-Book*, published in America in 1940. It is hard to see how he could have got hold of it in wartime except from her; but it has no inscription to settle the matter.

1955

David had published the first volume of his autobiography, *The Golden Echo*, in 1954. Then in 1955 he brought out the second, *The Flowers of the Forest*, and his first novel for twenty years, *Aspects of Love*. He sent Sylvia an inscribed copy, and she replied with her new volume of stories, *Winter in the Air*.

[November 1955]   *Frome Vauchurch, [Maiden Newton],*
                                      Dorchester, Dorset

Dearest David, If I had not been so deeply delighted by *Aspects of Love* I would have written to praise it much sooner. But whenever I sat down and wrote *Dearest David* I went back to the book to make quite certain of some passage or some development, and then instead of writing I went on reading. (The house is littered with sheets of paper beginning *Dearest David*, you are as berhymed as an Irish rat.)

Even now, when I know it so well that I don't have to make certain of any shade of approval, I can only say that it is as hard to praise as a cloud or an apple. So my instinct was right, one must just read it and be thankful. But after all these years of verbiage and solemnity and shit, O God, David, what a pleasure it is to see real writing again, and real construction and pleasure in life. It was like coming to a perfectly cooked fresh chicken again after sitting at endless tables of Birds Eye and bad cocktails, or looking at a Matisse, or being in a boat and feeling the water alive beneath it.

I hope you enjoyed it some part as much as I did. You must have enjoyed carrying your great scene where Alexis has it out with Rose to its finish with never a pause and never a flop. And are you *consciously* grateful that the haunt of George Moore that was, I remember, such a nuisance to you in *No Love*, has been made to repent to a diadem in becoming the exactly right, the delineating idiom of George Dillingham? (I hope you were aware of this – anyhow, you are now).

With my love   Sylvia

Dearest Sylvia, I wrote half a letter of thanks in reply to yours, but am glad I left it as now I can tell you how enchanted I am with your stories. I have waited impatiently to say so until I have read every one.

I suppose I am the only person alive to catch some of your allusions and enjoy some of your jokes.

'The Bride of Smithfield' – she figures in *The Espalier*, of course – but I suppose even you don't remember that her name was Rose Sharney?★

Your book came just as I had written half a dozen pages about meeting Tommy and being taken by him to visit Chaldon. From that has followed my meeting with you and a friendship founded on a mud-splashed exhausting walk across Dengie Flats.

Oh, my dear Sylvia, not having seen you (and not having thought about you much of the time) for nearly twenty years, I had forgotten your *wit*.

Perhaps I always rather despised it, ranking your capacity of a calm simple restraint in hitting the nail on the head in your poems far higher.

But how enchanting your wit is in these stories. Not that I like the purely witty ones best. I think 'Idenborough', 'Winter in the Air', 'Absalom, My Son' are the ones that mean most to me.

Really the subject you treat best and know about is love. The superficial emotions are amusing, great fun, dated perhaps, a private joke between sexagenarians. (I suppose you must be getting on that way – or are you only a girlish fifty?) But when there is a deep agonising wound you are able to write simply and like a master.

I am altogether stirred up and am determined to throw aside all other occupations in order to write. Yesterday and today I wrote six typewritten pages about my mother. On the whole I was satisfied with them and shall put them in volume three. I hit off a phrase about my father – 'he always saw the exception before he knew the rule' which pleased me because it was so exactly true.

My dear, I can't come to Dorset, but if ever you come to London, do let us meet.

Really I'm getting old and should be indulged, and it would give me enormous pleasure to see you. I wish I could exhibit my daughters to you. Four of the most lovely, noisy, tearing, romping,

★ See above, note on p. 22. In 'Absalom, My Son' Matthew Bateson, an author, is musing: 'He must find a title for his old story made new, for *The Bride of Smithfield* smacked of the twenties and wouldn't do.'

roaring bookworms you can imagine. The twins got stilts as a birthday present, and now look down on one from six foot six, and yap like hyaenas. All four are beautiful and intelligent, and Amaryllis paints, writes and is learning the violin. Could I decoy you here? It would be lovely.

Yours affectionately   Bunny

17: xii: 1955   *Maiden Newton*

Dearest David, You will have to christen this bird. I hope it won't take you too long. But I think you have a natural vein for christenings. One of the things I remember about that walk over the Essex marshes was that you said Dengie would be a good name for [a] spoiled bad son who would ruin his respectable family. Another thing I remember is how you pulled an acorn out of your pocket and planted it in a field. And when we were passing a pump on the edge of Southminster, and I said 'The Parish War Memorial', after a moment of looking startled you put on a suitable expression without a hitch or a hesitation. But the thing I remember best, and I dare say you don't remember it at all, was that when we were back in London, having dinner in some Soho restaurant, you told me I should read Stendhal. That is something I have particularly to thank you for, my dear. I have been reading him ever since; and continually changing my mind about his characters, and never about him.

I have only just read *The Flowers of the Forest*, as I asked for it as a Christmas present, and the anniversary-minded giver didn't send it till last week. I like it a great deal better than I did the other, you are in the midst of it instead of on the edge (though this distinction really implies a merit in *The Golden Echo*, because children do live in the suburbs of their parents' lives), and it has a terrific sense of drive, as though you were compelled to relate it. As for the mauvais amour – p. 170 – it is passion recollected with no damned tranquillity, and magnificently plain.*

It disturbs me that you have had such inadequate and peevish reviews; not only because this must be disagreeable for you, but because it shows such a stingy state of mind in the reviewers, as though they resented every experience of freedom or enjoyment. I'm afraid we are living in an age of faith. I've always known in my bones that such ages must be rather depressing. We should have realised earlier what Bishop Eliot was up to, and taken him to

* An unhappy love-affair with Thea Fordham, disguised in the book by the initials T.T. She later committed suicide.

Canterbury Cathedral. But it is not too late to meet. Let us meet in London. The next time I'm likely to be going there I will let you know, and perhaps we could coincide and have a cosy sexagenarian chat. I'd love to.

Affectionately   Sylvia

1958

No letters have survived for the next couple of years, though no doubt some were written. Then David sent Sylvia *Morals from the Beastly World*, a collection of animal fables by his son William. Its title was derived from a phrase, 'love of the beastly life', a chapter-heading in an Italian girl's thesis on David Garnett, describing one of his salient characteristics.

1: x: 1958   *Maiden Newton*

Darling David, I think myself very fortunate. *The Twilight of the Gods* had been my delight for years before David Garnett wrote his first book, *Lady into Fox*; and now here's William. William shall be the comfort of my old age, I shall peer out of my bath chair looking forward to another William.

It seems to me, David, that he is a fine addition to the Garnetts. This is a judgement at first glance, but first glances are usually keen. The moment some impending bores are out of the house, I shall settle to a proper reading; but I have already seen enough to know that I must write at once to congratulate you and thank you.

With love   Sylvia

18: x: 1958   *Maiden Newton*

Dearest David, I am very much impressed by William Garnett. He has an admirable manner of narrative, don't you think? – a narrative that appears leisurely and rolling, yet moves forward at a lope. And how well he makes himself clear! I was particularly struck, I was entranced, by the skill with which all the elaborate short cuts and routes in the Rat story were managed. It was masterly – an extremely difficult thing to do, and he did it like Stendhal.

With William and Nerissa you will have good grounds for serene doting.*

---

* Perhaps it was at this time that David sent Nerissa's poem:

> Puss
> A sleeping shape lies on the bed
> A cat morose, at peace, well-fed.
> Oh Puss, you sleeping mass of fur
> Give me your voice and let me purr.

I should love to have lunch with you at the Café Royal. I should love to have lunch with you anywhere, but the Café Royal grill-room will make a beautiful golden frame. I will let you know when next I go to London.

With love   Sylvia

1959

Darling David, How delightful – that I shall be meeting you at one
o'clock at Rules on the 11th, and that Henrietta has become a
Buddhist. Merely speaking as a Voice from the Sink, I welcome the
thought of so many greasy plates the less; and beyond these
practical womanly considerations, how agreeable to see people
manifesting Spiritual Pride. I don't wonder you brag about it,
though veiling your brag behind tomatoes and hard-boiled
eggs. . . .

With my love   Sylvia

From Sylvia's diary, 11: iii: 1959:

Walked to Rules to meet David, and as the table had miscarried, we
went on to Boulestin. He has grown a little deaf, and at first it was
uneasy, dimmed; then he began to talk about the wall-paintings
discovered in Sparrow's Farm, and the pheasants made by the
Women's Institute falling dead to the Victorian sportsmen, and
about his daughters; alas! he is very hurt and smouldering about
Chatto and Windus's rejection of his book. Finally we talked of
Charles.

David's conversation was of:
    Paintings of the Royal Arms and Prince of Wales's Feathers discovered
on the eve of war in Park Farm, a derelict house in Hilton in which William
Sparrow, maker of the Hilton maze, had lived. In 1945 David and William
found in the farm, by now a ruin, a further set of paintings of 'Jacobean
pin-up girls', two of which were thought to represent a notorious
highwaywoman and 'Roaring Girl', Mary Frith, known as Moll
Cutpurse.
    A historical pageant David had written for the Queen's Coronation
which was performed at Hinchingbrooke, and in which, for lack of any
real history, late Victorian times were represented by a shoot, where
pheasants, made of stuffed socks with tail-feathers, came hurtling over a
high wall to land at the feet of the guns.
    His new novel, *A Shot in the Dark*, turned down by Chatto.
    Charles Prentice, who had committed suicide in 1949 as a result of an
unhappy love affair.

Darling David, Thank you for giving me *A Shot in the Dark*, thank you for writing it. It is an enamoured book, Stendhal could not have written of Italy more loverly. But Stendhal could not have done Mr Bannerman. Mr Bannerman is a native glory, and he *is* a glory. You have done him superbly. He watches the whole book, just as his wife overhears every word of it.

'A large white greyhound of a kind seldom seen today in Italy.' Its appearance is enchanting, it fixes the scene, yet you seem to have thrown it in for love, as if you were Tiepolo throwing in several more blue satin cloaks from the sheer excitement of the brush between his fingers. I adore *brio*, and the book is full of it, *brio*, and splashes of paint flying, and juice squirting out of bitter fruit.

I think Chatto and Windus were fools to turn it down. Prudent virgins; and we all know what the Bridegroom thought of *them*. Even if there had been a prosecution over that bed, how infinitely better to fight the battle over your book than over that dreary *Lolita* – which I devoutly hope will be made into a successful popular film like *Gigi*, and that will be the end of that.

I laughed aloud over the two gentlemen from the F.B.I. in their suits from Brooks Bros – but after that I was in exile till you got back to Italy. It seems impossible to avoid these chapters ten. They have to be written and got in somewhere, but I wish one could hire them for the evening. It is the glory of music that it absolutely refuses to admit a chapter ten. . . .

Love from   *"these Chapter Tens"*   Sylvia

1962

Once again there is a gap of several years in the surviving letters, and once again they resume with the gift of a book.

19 January 1962   *Hilton Hall*

Dearest Sylvia, Thank you very much for *A Spirit Rises*. I have now read all the stories and have been continuously delighted. If your name had not been attached I should have known them at once – for the intense flavour of your precise humour is always striking out. No one else living or dead, or to be born in the future, would have described St Jerome's 'small lion for ever waiting for a word of recognition'. Oh dear – oh dear. How delightful it is to hear the voices of those people one has loved. And *you* are there in these stories. I won't pander to your vanity by describing my delight in each of them in turn. But instead I will tell you a story from real life which came into my mind after reading 'A Dressmaker'. It concerns people whom, or some of whom, you may well have known. I've forgotten the heroine's Christian name, but her married name was Mrs Jones.* She was a lively cockney girl, whose parents made a packet in the fruit trade, and she insisted on going to Art School, where she met Ray, who liked her. Then the 1914–18 war came to an end, and Tom Marshall [Ray's brother] came home from Ruhleben with his friend Jones. Ray, knowing a young man ex-Ruhleben prison camp needed a girl, and not caring for Jones herself, introduced her friend – who became Mrs Jones. Both had money. But Jones didn't like the great world and settled down to a craft in Essex, bookplates or something. Mrs Jones was rich, happy, lively, bored.

By chance Mr Queer met them. He was a charmer, a painter with a certain following, and Mrs Jones fell headlong in love. So she gave him the cottage by the estuary on their little estate. She bought his pictures of waterfowl. She knew Mr Queer was queer. No hope. And the price she extracted was that he should dine once a week

---

* The heroine of this story, which probably owes as much to art as to real life, was Vivien Gribble; her husband was Douglas Doyle Jones and their friend Sir Cedric Morris.

with the Joneses. For the whole week she dreamed of that evening and prepared for it. And so she bought for these dinners dresses by Molyneux, Schiaparelli, Worth, Hartnell. (She died before Dior came on the scene.) And the three would dine – truffles, caviare, lobsters, oysters, vintage champagne, boeuf en daube or coq au vin with Chambertin (1923) or Mouton Rothschild (1924). And every other week a new dress. Mr Q. loved it; he was charming to her, and their conversation tinkled away piano with Mr Jones sometimes playing a slow loud note at the other end of the keyboard – but usually silent. Suddenly Mrs Jones died.

What happened? The dresses hang in polythene bags untouched. Old Jones every week has Mr Q. to dinner. But Mr Q. has been independent for years. Mrs J. left him the cottage and enough to live on comfortably. And though Jones in old age is even more of a bore than he was as a young man, Mr Q. has taken on the job of keeping him going. What do you do with real life, my dear, when it apes art?

Well, perhaps I should give some account of myself and family. Richard, big and solid, has two sons, five and two. I gave him the cottage next door. They come down for weekends, and Richard builds and hammers, and is slow and smiling and always genial and interested. He has a sweet wife who adores him – she's a granddaughter of old Sir Herbert Grierson. He is a director of Rupert Hart-Davis, now bought by Harcourt Brace.

William continues to play the oboe in local orchestras and makes cider we drink all the year round for lunch and dinner (when there's no wine). He's madly interested in the theory of sails – aerodynamics of them.

Angelica, my wife, is at this moment in Mentone, as she had to drive a car for Clive [Bell]'s use there. He is old and has had two operations, from which he has recovered and sounds fairly cheerful. She comes back next week. I love her.

Amaryllis, eighteen, is the apple of my eye. The most sensitive, intelligent, lovely, understanding creature – a phoenix – a paragon of her sex and already complete, definite and important to others (not herself). She's at the Central School for Drama and has a room in London.

Henrietta, sixteen-and-a-half, wants to be a film actress or a T.V. announcer and is perfectly equipped to be one. She is stunningly good-looking. A whizzer. . . . She is at Dartington College – went there on Tuesday.

Then the twins (fifteen) Fan and Nerissa. At the moment they are on the mat in St Ives being taught judo by our fishmonger. They are young Persians. They shoot, and tell the truth and despise their sex and their sisters. Nerissa is a genius – she paints masterpieces.

Nobody quite realises it. She is very gentle, liable to be embarrassingly unselfish.

Then Fan – defiant, greedy, clumsy, honest as it is possible to be – and with a head on her shoulders. Both look very like me at moments and like Virginia Woolf* at others.

At the moment I'm cooking breakfast and dinner and doing a fair bit of housework, and then I've started making marmalade. I've made twenty-two pounds. But I've another eighty to make, which will keep me busy. You see, with this vast family we eat a lot.

Forgive all this egotism, but I thought it might amuse you and is all I can give in return for your enchanting witty perfect stories. I've finished my third volume – a rather painful work – of memoirs, called *The Familiar Faces*, and when it is typed shall send it to Chatto.

Let's meet again. Have dinner with me when you come to London, will you, and perhaps see Amaryllis?

Very much love   Bunny

P.S. Do you want to see what I've said about you before it is printed?

24: i: 1962   *Maiden Newton*

Dearest David, You can't have read my stories with greater pleasure than I read your praises of them. For I think you would not praise unless you meant it, and your approval means a great deal to me, and has for – how many years? 1924, certainly, for *The Espalier* was published in 1925, and it was you who took some of my poems to Chatto and Windus.

No, I don't want to see what you have said about me in *The Familiar Faces*. The thing I really want you to say you probably have not said: that it was you, dear Bunny, who made a serious writer of me. You were my godfather, you held me at the font, you saw to it that I knew *Moll Flanders* and *Roxana* in the common tongue, you called on me to hear sermons – your own, in due course you sent me to the Bishop – l'évêque Stendhal –

I am much, much more grateful to you than I can possibly say; and the people who have enjoyed my books should be grateful to you too, and should know where their gratitude should be directed.

If you could put this in, how pleased I would be. But I won't write your book for you.

You can't keep art out, you know. The story about the Joneses and Mr Queer is magnificent. But what pins it is your 'their conversation tinkled away with Mr Jones sometimes playing a slow

* Their great-aunt.

66

loud note at the other end of the keyboard'. You ought to write to me oftener.

I saw Amaryllis at the Bryanston play this last summer. In some of her movements she reminded me of you. She has an excellent stage presence. I hope she will go on and be a glory to the name of Garnett as well as the apple of your eye. I had half a mind to ask if I could meet her after the performance, as that boring thing, an old friend of her father's – she must have them in dozens – but she was spared, as complications of hospitality took me away before the play ended. When we met last Henrietta was being a Buddhist, a vegetable devotee, and you were eating underdone beef at her. Which won? I hope you didn't set her down too soon. For all we know, she may have been right.

I sincerely grovel to the young. I wish they didn't grow up so shockingly fast. They flash by like meteors.

My fond true love, dear Bunny. Do you make your marmalade in seven-pound jars? I don't see how you could store it unless you do.   Sylvia

If you see the *New Yorker* February 10th it has a spirited piece by me in it, (vide) marmalade. *

re?

13: ii: 1962   *Maiden Newton*

Dearest David, I am very sorry that I can't come to your [seventieth] birthday party, and see you standing like a Turk with your lovely daughters round you; but I have a weekend visitor arriving on the 9th. I must be a hostess when I would infinitely rather be a guest.

My love   Sylvia

David sent an inscribed copy of the third volume of his autobiography, *The Familiar Faces*, to Sylvia on 8 October 1962.

17: x: 1962   *Maiden Newton*

Darling David, Yes – that's how it was. Thus did we dance, thus did we sing.

I suppose we were like the spray blown off the crest of a wave. For underneath the wave rolled on, a post-tempest wave, turbid with weed and shingle, travelling from one war to the next. As you say, they were years of faith – faith that enabled us to disregard the general condition of the majority; and a certain amount of

* 'One Thing Leading to Another', in which the housekeeper to a couple of Catholic priests gets rheumatism in her shoulders through making marmalade too vigorously – with quite unexpected consequences.

superstition, Do you believe in Freud, do you believe in Jung; but not a shred of piety, horrible, deforming, stupefying piety. We have lived in a society where no piety was, *that* was the vital principle, everything flowed from that.

You have called back so many ghosts, evoked so many others of my own, that I had to be hostess to them before I could turn round and write to you. Ray coming silently down the stairs into the empty hall furnished with a naked Christmas tree; Tommy arrested in the Queen's Road by a placard on a barrel-organ: *needs must when the devil drives* (a weed in a travelling wave) and trying to establish the grammar of needs must; reading all Marvell's poems when they came out in the Nonesuch, the 'Glo'worm' and the whole length of 'Appleton House'; and you, dear David, sitting on a muddy baulk in the Essex marshes, and driving a few acorns into it.

I love you more than ever since this book, and esteem you more highly. Do you realise that there is not a grudge or a whine in it? And that that is something extremely rare? I like it even better than the other two. Not merely because I am no stranger to it, as I was with them; but absolutely because of its warmth and judiciousness and fortitude. And I am glad and proud to be in it.

With my love   Sylvia

22 October 1962   *Hilton Hall*

Dearest Sylvia, Thank you for your letter. If there is ever a question of getting past St Peter, I shall show it as one of my best testimonials.

I have just written a new story [*Two by Two*] with which I am delighted: I hope you will like it. It is about my youngest daughters – twins they are – Fanny and Nerissa – and their adventures in a much earlier age.

I wonder if you could bear to come to this place again? Angelica has urged me to ask you. I think you would like my daughters. Amaryllis has started her second year at the Central School for Drama and works very hard. She is living on a houseboat permanently moored close to Battersea Bridge – opposite Cheyne Walk.

She is the pride and joy of my life: beautiful, sensitive, intelligent. She has great literary judgement – and she likes my new story, so I feel happy about it. Then Henrietta, about whom I was a bit worried a year ago, is now a source of happiness. She wants to be a writer, by the way, and has no idea that she might not have the instant success of a Mlle Sagan.

The twins, who are just going to be sixteen, regard female arts with aversion and contempt. . . . Fan goes ratting on Sunday with an ex-Scotland Yard detective, they sleep out in hard weather. Nerissa is probably the most gifted of all of us. She is a painter and very talented. Fan aims at science. They are all beautiful in different ways, and really I'm lucky to have such adorable different creatures. William is a quietist. His chief interest now is sailing and [he] is designing and building a catamaran on revolutionary principles.

Come and have a look at them. If you don't want to perhaps you would have lunch or dinner on the houseboat when you are in London. But it would be much better to come for a weekend.

Much love   David

30: x: 1962   *Maiden Newton*

Dearest David, I should love to visit Hilton again, and meet your daughters, and see how the trees have grown. I seem to remember a walnut and a mulberry. It is very kind of Angelica to suggest it. Do you realise that I shall be meeting her too?

I may have to go to Cambridge before long, and this would fit in with Hilton. May I wait till I know about this, and then consult you?

May I read your new story when I come? Will you read a short one of mine in the first November *New Yorker*? It is about a detestable old businessman who dies of an attack of poetry.★

With my love   Sylvia

2 November 1962   *Hilton Hall*

Dear Sylvia, Your letter came this afternoon and rejoiced me. Please let us know when your visit to Cambridge takes place, and we will come and fetch you from there, and you must spend a couple of days or so here. The mulberry was four feet high when I planted it and must be twenty now.

The autumn-winter has a curious fascination: the last pink poking up unexpectedly among the scattered seed pods of its predecessors, the rotting pears in the grass. Even the vegetables have an unexpected charm. We ate a dish of french beans last night, picked from the frostbitten row. Then the rain comes slashing everything: then the lemon tree has to be put under shelter for the winter.

It will be lovely to see you. Try and make your visit include a

★ 'Swans on an Autumn River' in the *New Yorker* of 17 November 1962.

weekend, as then I shall be able to decoy Amaryllis down – and possibly Henrietta, who is setting up at seventeen as a professional author. We are all longing to see you.

Love from   Bunny

I shall read your story in the *New Yorker* when next I go to London in the Reform Club. And I'll give you my tale when you come here.

I think it would be a delightful end to die of poetry. At least it might be, or it might be long and exhausting: I would not care to be killed off by Southey.

There are two Bishops of Cork. When the R.C. Bishop was on his deathbed, news was brought him that the Protestant Bishop had died in the night.

'Ah! He'll have learned by now who is the Bishop of Cork,' said the R.C. Bishop and expired.

1963

On 10 October 1963 David sent Sylvia *Two by Two*, his apocalyptic account of the adventures of the twins at the time of the Flood and what happens to them when they disguise themselves as monkeys and stow away on the Ark.

20: x: 1963   *Maiden Newton*

Dearest David, I came back from Italy two days ago, and found your new book waiting for me. I must have seemed ungrateful not to have written sooner, but in fact I am both grateful and prompt. There were a great many things to be done; and I put them all by till I had finished *Two by Two*.

No one could enjoy your inventions – the use of snakes, the dolphins, the phoenix – as intensely as you yourself; enjoying one's inventions is like eating out of the saucepan; but I swear I can't be far behind in enjoyment. All through the book I was conscious of your making mind, and this entranced and delighted me. Your Defoe-like comprehension and practicality and minuteness made me feel that now I know exactly what it was like in the Ark. Defoe was a little late for the Plague, you are a little late for the Deluge. In both cases, this was fortunate. The dust had settled, the subject was clear before you.

I am praising. I shall continue to praise your invention. But in the last part of the book your imagination takes over, and the last part of the book is best of all.

With my love   Sylvia

1964

Dearest David, I thought of you when I read of the death of T. H.
White. I send you my sympathy. Your portrait of him in *The Familiar
Faces* is so living, so engaging, that I can realise your sense of loss.

When we are old (how strange it seems; but indeed, my dear, we *are*
old) there is a sense of being bankrupt by the death of a friend younger
than ourselves. We have reposed a part of our future in them. Losing
them, we are that much disabled of ourselves, see less clearly, become
less interesting, are forced another step down into being fogeys.

And he must have been such a cordial, various, animating creature.
My poor David.

With my love   Sylvia

Less than two months later, on 16 March 1964, Michael Howard of
Jonathan Cape wrote to Sylvia suggesting that she should write a life of
T. H. White, the author of *The Sword in the Stone*, etc. Sylvia replied on the
following day:

I very much incline to the project. I would not hesitate at all if it
were not for the thought that David Garnett would be a better
choice. (*Letters*, 211)

But David did not want the job. He did, however, plan to edit his
correspondence with Tim White for publication. So Sylvia was signed up,
and Howard, in his capacity as literary executor, gave her access to the
material in White's house in Alderney.

Their correspondence about White soon became very heavy: 85
surviving letters from Sylvia and 59 from David up to the publication of
The White / Garnett Letters in 1968, with letters sometimes crossing in the
post. Only a small selection has been included here.

Darling David, I am just back from a trip to Alderney with the
Howards. In between meeting everybody on the island Michael
and I went through a quantity of his books. We discovered that he
used them as notebooks and post-offices. Here is a letter posted to
you in one of them. O David, that house is so strange and haunted,

with his suitcases back at the foot of the stairs. I worked there late one night, determined to finish a set of bookshelves and when at last I went downstairs and out of the house and locked the door behind me it was like going out of a wood at night – you know, as one leaves it and it turns into a bulk of darkness, one feels all the creatures resuming their lives.

Yes, *what* an undertaking! So far, I only know what I want to do. I won't cheat; and have a beginning idea of what I can't do, which is a bottomless pit. It is a sad reflection, darling David, that after all the years intelligent people like ourselves have been illuminating English society it is still totally impossible to be honest. . . .

About meeting. May I come to Hilton some time in October before you go off to America? I shall be better fixed then for knowing what I want to ask and discuss. . . .

Love from   Sylvia

22 July 1964   *French address: L'Ancienne Auberge,*
                        St Martin-de-Vers, par Lauzès, Lot

Dearest Sylvia, We haven't met, and now I'm off to France – or rather to Belgium, where I have secreted a Morris Mini Traveller which I drive to France and meet three of my family – William, Angelica and Fan. Perhaps it's just as well we should meet a bit later. I may possibly do a rough mock-up of the Tim–Bunny and Bunny–Tim letters while I am in France. But on the other hand I may spend the time asleep, or climbing the vertical mountainside to buy eggs from an old girl who lives in the deserted village where the vineyards were never replanted after phylloxera, and the church is cracking, and elder bushes push bunches of berries out of the windows of the new school built about 1899. I can't tell you what a lovely place Fage is: scarcely any people except my henwife, but the largest most glorious gravid female adder I have ever seen. She was asleep in the sun on a wall bordering a vineyard which still insists on producing grapes – nobody prunes the vines or picks the grapes. I woke her, and she poured herself slowly down a hole between the stones. I've never seen any movement more beautiful. The Javanese dancers couldn't compare with her. . . .

I hadn't met Michael Howard before – but what a delightful man he is. I like him very much. I hope you do. What I really want with you is a long gossip about Tim. No doubt everyone else does. But mine will be different.

Very much love   Bunny

73

Dearest David, There is such masses of White material to read, and such gaps to bridge, that I put off coming to see you in your boat, and persevered. Also, never having written a biography, I had to think how to write biographies. And decide what to call him. I have decided to call him White. This strangely simplifies everything, including how to write biographies. Wherever possible, I shall let him speak for himself, and for the rest, I shall write like myself. . . .

I love you and hope you will have a fine holiday.   Sylvia

3 August 1964   *St Martin-de-Vers*

Dearest Sylvia, Your letter arrived shortly after we did. I wish you had come yourself. . . .

Certainly call him White. The chief thing in a biography – not that I know anything about writing them – is to exhibit your subject, or let him exhibit himself, from all angles, which is what a tailor does when making one a suit.

Luckily for you, White exhibited himself in the most contradictory ones. In fact his metier was to do so. He was inspired by his own multiform image, which is not how you and I work.

We live in a narrow little valley with flat green pastures and a trout stream, the Vers, shut in between walls of grey rock half covered with bushes. Above, on the Causses, there are scrub oaks, abandoned vineyards, derelict villages, motorcars pouring along the N.20.

Angelica bought a half-derelict inn here. It is all huge beams, floors made of immense oak boards which tremble as one walks about – a little garden with a spring in it.

We have electricity, hot and cold water, a shower, a W.C. and a refrigerator, and we cook on butane gas.

We drink wine and live on vegetable soup. William and Fan . . . are here and play duets, he on the oboe and she on the flute.

She has also brought her new love, a French horn, and makes startling noises on it. She is persistent rather than good. William is good on the oboe (and in every other way).

Very much love   David

12 August [1964]   *St Martin-de-Vers*

Dearest Sylvia, . . . I am in a horrible quandary. I don't think this book of letters will be worth anything unless I put in almost everything . . . Even so I foresee it would run to several volumes. So I may be driven to abandon it. The thing is I think my letters are interesting also, so these would be fearfully long if they are put in. Without them the interplay of love and irritation is not shown. . . .

One of the things which always astonished me about Tim was that although he prided himself on being a master of all arts: fishing, shooting, riding, hawking, carpentering, sailing boats, etc., etc., he was very bad at those I watched him at. He was a worse fisherman than I am, and I'm terrible. He wasn't a good shot, he trained gun dogs so badly that they were wild, the bookshelves he put up at Butt's Intake* might have been made by a lunatic. Don't take my word for this. Ask Richard about the bookshelves. He imposed himself on others as a master of various skills, and many accepted him. And sometimes he may have gone on until he learned. Also he handicapped himself by accepting a theory and explaining how to do something before he had learned himself. . . .

Love from   Bunny

14 August 1964   *St Martin-de-Vers*

Dearest Sylvia, I think you will have the field clear: I have finished reading Tim's letters and piecing them together with my own, and I don't think I can make a selection. I want to publish them in several volumes in extenso, omitting only the boring salmon fishing and the Cape–Collins trouble.

But no publisher will face doing this, and it will take me a long time to write notes and so on. I shall have to break this to Michael Howard personally when I come back, so don't tell him this at present.

One or two things occur to me that I might forget to tell you. . . .

Charles Chapman-Mortimer invited me to his flat in Sloane Street and introduced me to Ylla, the woman who took excellent photographs of animals. I realised they had hatched a plot: I was to write the letterpress of a book of her photographs. She was a fine personable Belgian blonde, but I had other fish to fry, and hate writing to order and found myself in fierce revolt against the idea. I therefore said Tim was the man and sent him a telegram saying:

Priority. Will you consider writing five thousand words for most wonderful photograph animal ever known stop If yes

---

* David's cottage in Swaledale, properly known as Duke Mary's, where White spent the winter of 1945–6.

sending Ylla by Saturday plane reply immediately David
Garnett.*

Tim had no notion what an Ylla was and afterwards wrote and
called me a bastard to play such a trick. But I think he liked her and
wrote what was required. I think he had wired back, 'What is an
Ylla?' But I did not reply.†

In or about 1962 the telephone rang about 6 p.m. at Hilton. It was
Tim, who said he was in St Thomas's, had just come to from an
anaesthetic after an operation. He told me his room number and
asked me to come to see him. Then his voice faded into mumbles.

The next afternoon about 4 p.m. I went into his room un-
announced. He stared at me in astonishment and exclaimed: 'How
on earth did you know I was here?' He had completely forgotten –
and could not remember – having rung me up, or even that he had
come to and had a lucid interval after the operation.

Of course, all the letters are yours for reading whenever you
want them.

William went back today after identifying forty-one species of
birds, the most striking of which was the hoopoe.

We are happy to be in France and love this place and district. But
there are rather too many visitors this summer and too many cars.
Gay voices resound and a young woman strolls up and down with
her marmalade cat on a leather leash.

William found a ruined farm on the tops from which one could
see to the Pyrenees and to the Puy-de-Dôme – a view all round.
There was only one farm within a mile, and the hoopoe. We rather
fancy ourselves as hoopoes.

Huppe-pupet is the French for that curious butterfly bird.

We expect you on the 9th October.

.   Yours affectionately   David

25: viii: 1964   *Maiden Newton*

Dearest David, You appal me. If, as you say, the Tim–Bunny letters
complete would fill two volumes, how on earth am I to fit them,
even with the severest bill-hook, into my book? I nauseate
summaries. I abhor snippets. . . . I have got the shape of the book
more or less planned, and I have begun to write some of it. And

* The actual text of David's telegram has been substituted for the version in his
letter.
† White wrote the introduction to Ylla's book, but the project fell through,
ostensibly because he had paid too much attention to her and not enough to the
animals.

however much I now replan, throw away, cut myself out, in order to put in letters when obviously [they] must be put in, the come-and-go quality of the Tim–Bunny volume will be lost. And that was too good and too rare not to be preserved. I shall be stuffing and setting up half a goose, instead of the whole animal being displayed as in life.

I shall send this to Hilton Hall to reproach you on your return. I don't know when you return. I don't know whether I love you or not.   Sylvia

5 September 1964   *St Martin-de-Vers*

Dearest Sylvia, I feel terribly guilty for upsetting you. Actually there is nothing to be worried about. I think it is probably laziness and the dog's revulsion from his vomit (but they haven't one, have they?) which made me decide I couldn't do a selection. I shall have to one day.

But meanwhile I will hand all the photostats over to you when you come to Hilton, and you will read the whole thing in forty-eight [hours] and pick the pearls out of [the] pile of wheat with the swift unerring eye of an osprey, or whatever bird lives on pearls. . . .

We will have a roaring fire and sit up late, while you explain about Tim, and I try to explain why I didn't know him better, which is something I don't really understand myself.

Very affectionately   David

Sylvia went to Hilton on Saturday 9 October for the week-end.

12: x: 1964   *Maiden Newton*

Darling David, . . . I may neither write nor type, because the young cat is so busy making addresses of welcome, having processions, and performing loyal masques and cantatas that he gets in the way of whatever I try to do.

But I do hope you know, dear David, how grateful I am for all you have told me, for your encouragement, for the way you have helped me make up my mind – and for the letters; and that I don't need to be eloquent about it.

It was a marvellous visit, and I have come back feeling like the Queen of Sheba.

My love   Sylvia

1965

Dearest Sylvia, I have just got back from a very interesting tour of the U.S. and a holiday in Mexico. . . . Mexico is fascinating. I went and looked at all the pyramids and palaces of the —— nobody knows what most of them were called, built by the predecessors of the Toltecs and Aztecs and Zapotecs.

It was nice dodging the winter too. I want to write a 200,000-word novel about the U.S.

Please let me know if you think the Tim White–D.G. correspondence is worth publishing.

All my love   David

Dearest David, . . . I am sure that the correspondence is worth preserving: it is something that posterity (I dislike that damned posterity, I shan't be there; but still, I feel my duty towards it) would be the wiser for, and the happier for. It is a splendid record of how two superior mid-twentieth-century minds exchanged experiences and opinions, and were candid with each other, and contrived, by magnanimity, not to quarrel, and to evade expressing an exasperation mutually felt. It does you both the utmost credit. Besides, you were obviously designed by natural selection to correspond with each other.

There are two ways to preserve it. One is the Box in the British Museum with directions that seven Regius professors must be present at its opening. The other is to publish it. There is something to be said for either.

But we must make up our minds; at least, we should make up our minds.

So far, I am doing my book on the assumption that you will do the letters; that is to say, I am quoting the minimum, and not quoting it if I can get it from anywhere else. . . . If you decide not to do the letters, then I shall quote a great deal more; but even so, I shan't be able (because of balance) to quote an equal amount of you. And this would be a pity, because the tit-for-tat quality of the correspondence is part of its excellence.

For my part, I seem to be getting on fairly well. My great difficulty is making the eels lie down in the pie. . . .

With love   Sylvia

25 January 1965   *Hilton Hall*

Dearest Sylvia, I much enjoyed your letter. I have decided to publish the letters and have invented the following reasons for doing so.

a. They will be published anyway, and I shall not make so many errors as the Professor from Alabama would in 1990. Also I shall be able to make myself appear less unpleasant, without actually rewriting my own letters (though I suppose I have a right to do that?).

b. Tim and I will be completely forgotten in a few years' time. If published now some of the readers of your book will go on to read the correspondence.

c. If I don't do them now I shall have to do something far more difficult and shall be running my head into a stone wall.

Will you therefore send me the facsimiles that you don't need?

I don't want to hurry you. Actually I am making marmalade and shall go on contentedly doing that until the pots run out. . . .

I need not tell you that I was a stupendous success in the United States.

The trouble is that I can't take any interest in England now: I care nothing about Mr Gordon Walker's defeat, or Churchill's death, or the Pakistanis in Smethwick. Instead I dream of the students' strike at Berkeley, of Mario Savio, their leader, and of whether the children in Mississippi will escape being educated at all now the Federal Government is cutting off school funds.

New York was detestable, but I enjoyed good weather everywhere else. Mexico is delightful, except for Mexico City. But I don't care for some of their food.

My daughters grow in beauty. Amaryllis leaves for the U.S. on Wednesday, touring with an agreeably gay amateurish performance of *The Beggar's Opera*. She is Mrs Peachum and a bit miscast.

Much love   David

[Postcard] 27: i: 1965   *[Maiden Newton]*

I am convinced by all your reasons, and bowled over by the force of reason 3. And I am very glad they have convinced you, too. *Please* don't change your mind. . . .

Love   Sylvia

Dearest David, This letter was stuck in the T.H.W. diary and hadn't been noticed. I have copied it – exactly, I believe . . .

Has it ever struck you that in many ways he was remarkably like Turgenev? Not just the hellcat mothers, but the mixture of brag and diffidence, and all that shooting and fishing.

Love from   Sylvia

Sylvia's copy of David's letter to White of 2 February 1940 is appended. It is not included in *The White/Garnett Letters*, where David, having presumably forgotten that Sylvia had sent it to him, says he must have written such a letter:

2 February 1940   *Air Ministry*

Dear Tim, I was delighted to get your absolutely lovely account of going to Inishkea. I will read it to Ray tomorrow when I go down to Hilton.

Your account of the night, of the geese, of the God, could not be better and made me feel as though I had been there alone. I have had such experiences as a young man, when I went to strange places alone.

I spent two days quite alone in Germany in the Black Forest, for example.

Well, I wish I were on Inishkea now. Or I wish I were at Belmullet with you. Or catching salmon. Shall I ever be at peace again?

Well, a friend of yours rang me up at Hilton and asked your address. I told him Mrs McDonagh, Doolistown, Trim. He said that you had been too long in Ireland, that you would never shoot a goose there and must come to the East Coast soon, as he was soon going into the Army and wanted a few days of your company first.

Well, I can't write about the War. I know everything and so can never remember what is a deadly secret and what I read in the newspaper (except that the newspapers usually lie).

So the only thing is not to say anything whatsoever – which accords with my inclinations. I don't want to think about the War. It is not really a fit subject. I work here long hours and do very little – practically nothing in my own opinion – but I have won the hearts of my superiors.

Ray is very ill indeed. She is in bed all the time now, and has a nurse, one of her sisters, and a friend down there. I get down two days a week. If you write, you must not let out that you know she will die soon.

When it comes to the point the dying cannot face that, at close range.

She said once: 'Bunny, you must lie to me and lie well.'

That freezes the lies on one's lips, but I do my best, and she is always calm and happy after I have been there a few hours.

There has been more fear than pain, but there is a good deal of pain now, or would be except for drugs.

She was wonderful at Christmas, insisting on the Richards family (with whom they had been staying at Ventry) coming. The house was full of little girls. Ray could get about then, even out into the orchard, and she enjoyed it immensely.

There have been weeks of ice and skating for the boys in the holidays. William can dance on skates now.

I have been out twice: once far out over the Atlantic with a convoy – once almost to Norway looking for German battleships in very bad weather. It was very exciting and an odd feeling looking about the clouds for enemy aircraft.

Well, goodbye, dear Tim. I long for the time when we shall meet again. If you write to Ray be very careful what you say. Don't talk about her illness, I beg.

Love from   Bunny

3 February 1965   *Hilton Hall*

Dearest Sylvia, Sorry not to have written sooner, but I had a near go of pneumonia – sore throat and temperature at night – but have now been cured by huge pink pessaries (alliteration running away with me) that one swallows – something ending in -mycine. . . .

I don't think Tim was at all like Turgenev. He was (to begin with) far less intelligent.

Tim was very easily satisfied with superficial explanations and accepted conventional standards easily. Also he had very little understanding of women – no knowledge of their potentialities. Not even interested in psychology, science, foreign literature. Turgenev's relations with Pauline Viardot were of a complexity quite outside Tim's range.

Tim, though brilliantly gifted at expressing himself, *wasn't an artist.* (I mean he had very little sense of form and his books though full of brilliant patches are all imperfect.) Turgenev was one of the greatest literary artists. Also Turgenev was lethargic, mild and gentle. Tim was a swashbuckler. *He was very like Falstaff.* Turgenev was a masochist; Tim a sadist. In the obituary I wrote in *The Times* I said that at the end of his life he looked like a cross between Sir John Falstaff and Nubar Gulbenkian. But the obituary editor, Colin Watson, cut that out. He played at being himself, just as Falstaff did. . . .

Very much love   David

Dearest David, Here are four more years of White/Garnett . . .

If you think he was 'very like Falstaff' the diaries would disconcert you. Of course, diaries are not infallibly representative; for one thing, they are safety valves: if Falstaff had kept a diary, the record of his feelings after the affair of Gadshill might have been nearer to White than the exterior Falstaff would wish one to suppose. But I can't imagine Falstaff being anything but a man. White the diarist is often womanish – clever-womanish, i.e. self-deluding, giddy, lonely, [bewailing *crossed out*] and shrewish. I cross out 'bewailing' – common 'tis to either sex.

I didn't mean a total comparison with Turgenev – only with the young Turgenev.

No, he wasn't an artist. He was too much of a devotee for that. He was devoted to writing, to what he was writing, and then cared no longer about it, just as religious people turn their backs on their dead stepping-stones. I think he was a scholar, at heart. The prowess he admired most was learning. It was for your erudition he admired you, not for your books.

I suppose the true reason for all his fickle devotions was that he fastened his mind on any plank that could carry him across the snake-pit.

Do you think William could be persuaded to put down what he remembers? I particularly want views of White as seen by the young . . .

I liked William very much. He reminded me so strongly of Ray that it stopped my heart to feel that I knew him while knowing that I never would.

Keep those pessaries handy. Pneumonia makes second tries.

With my love   Sylvia

12 February 1965   *Hilton Hall*

Dearest Sylvia, I hope you aren't angry with me for my disagreeing that Tim was like Turgenev. Turgenev is one of the people I am most interested in . . .

Also when I say he was like Falstaff it is because I am very fond of Falstaff. Tim was always putting on an act and was well aware of it – in fact on one of the last occasions that I saw him he drew my attention to his hand-made silk shirt, his cape and his big blackthorn stick and said most engagingly: 'It's all part of the act.' . . .

I feel so much affection for you that I will willingly agree that Tim was like Goethe or Leonardo or Michaelangelo – so long as you continue to feel some affection for your loving   David

Dearest David, . . . David! I shall have another book of short stories coming out this autumn perhaps. May I dedicate it to you? You once said that I wrote well about love. There is a good story about a brother and sister falling in love (and living happily ever after, I am glad to say). At least, I am pretty sure it is good.*

I don't forebode any severing of our loves before then – or after – however briskly we may disagree over Tim. . . .

Your loving   Sylvia

26 February 1965   *Hilton Hall*

Dearest Sylvia, . . . Did I tell you that your American rival, Mr Eric Molin, came to call on me . . . He was small, dark, bearded, with that infinite blind patience that is frequent in American scholars and which reminds me forcibly of beagles – which as you probably know are small slow splay-footed hounds which hunt hares. But they never *see* a hare – unlike a greyhound which sees the hare and rivals it and catches it by speed. However close a beagle may be to a hare, it never lifts its head to look at the living hare. It goes by smell alone – by the printed page left by the hare's pads. So it never knows what a hare is like. So with these scholars. Incidentally beagles are popular in the United States.

Forgive the digression. Mr Molin was a very pleasant beagle and has sent me an extremely good photograph of Tim and two of his Irish poems. . . . I feel so inadequate and woolly about these letters and about Tim. The photograph shows how unhappy he was. And I always avoided seeing it as much as I could, and I still do.

Very much love   David

3: vi: 1965   *Maiden Newton*

Dearest David, . . . White is killing me. I don't see how I can give the book any air of proportion. Do you realise that all his creative work was over by 1945? From then on, he splutters and gutters. If I could use his lust and rage and frenzy and defeat over the —— boy I could make a real dragon's tail ending. But everybody's bloody feelings are in the way, and if I observe them I shall be reduced to the portrait of a frustrated Scout-Master.

---

* The story was 'A Love Match', and the book, which was dedicated to David, was published in America as *Swans on an Autumn River* and in Britain as *A Stranger with a Bag* for reasons explained on p. 97 below.

And I feel so much affection for him (maddening and caddening though he was; and really he was a considerable cad), and so much compassion. . . .

With my love   Sylvia

9 June 1965   *Moby Dick, Chelsea Yacht and Boat Co.*
                                      Opposite 103 Cheyne Walk, London SW10

Dearest Sylvia, . . . Indeed, yes – I do realise that his creative period was extremely short. I also discovered his caddishness, which is hard to reconcile with his compassion. There is a great deal I know little about because he concealed a good deal from me. I know very little except by hearsay of his homosexuality. . . .

He told me that he was a sadist and that his sadism had wrecked his love life, because he never felt sure he was loved until he had been cruel to the object of his love. And he certainly liked to *think* of beating women's and boys' bottoms. But was he actually a sadist, physically? He certainly wasn't with Brownie [his red setter bitch].
―― was such a horrible girl that any sensible man would have flung her out of the house if on land or overboard if at sea. Cruelty to her doesn't count.

Well, what I *really* want to say is that you *must write your book without thinking about anyone's feelings.* Then when you have completed your masterpiece, you can bowdlerise the 1966 edition, knowing that the whole thing will appear in 1996 and that there will be long reviews saying that you were not only a poet, not only a master of the short story, but the most brilliant and perceptive biographer of the era after the Second War and before the final one. Please do this. It is really the only sensible and practical way of dealing with him.

Very much love   David

10 July 65   *Hilton Hall*

Dearest Sylvia, . . . I have just recovered from a go of laryngitis–bronchitis and a course of antibiotics. It is wonderful to have the energy to write this letter and sign myself

Your devoted and affectionate   David

13: vii: 1965   *Maiden Newton*

Dearest David, . . . Fond love always – I wish you wouldn't catch bronchitis and antibiotics. Neither will do you any good. You should catch your bronchitis in the bud, and drive it away with onion soup last thing at night, or garlic chopped fine and eaten in sandwiches. Add chopped parsley if you feel elegant.

Sylvia

Sylvia sent 'parts of my book for wholesome hours of idleness' to David on 28 July.

Saturday 30 July 1965   *Hilton Hall*

Dearest Sylvia, Your book is wonderful, it could not be better. It has the effect of making me feel that I never knew him. As a matter of fact I have been realising this, though it isn't really true. . . .

It is a lovely day here, and the house is full of beauty – all four daughters, my granddaughter Sophie, her grandmother Frances Partridge (Ray's sister) and Duncan Grant. The first golden french beans are ready. I send you all my love and admiration. . . .

PS. May I keep the pieces you sent me for another week or so? I want to reread them slowly. If the whole book is like this it will be a masterpiece.

2: viii: 1965   *Maiden Newton*

Dearest David, Your approval is life to me – I feel as excited as a girl.

Please keep the bits as long as you like. You cannot keep them too long, indeed, for it is a comfort to think that something isn't under this roof. When I have nothing else to clutch my heart about I remember that I am housing about half a ton of White manuscripts – irreplaceable. . . .

Do you grow coco beans? They are the colour of aubergines, and dangle among very dark green leaves.

Dearest David, you have filled me with pride and joy.

My love   Sylvia

If Duncan is still with you, please give him my affectionate remembrances. . . .

3 August [1965]   *Hilton Hall*

Dearest Sylvia, . . . I have sent off my collection of letters to Michael Howard, though it is still much too long. But I have cut out too much already and am getting sick of the whole thing. I have no idea now why the book should be published. It seems more unnecessary than most, and I am just nerving myself to start another, which being all my own, will be even more unnecessary. . . .

Love from   David

Dearest Sylvia, . . . The weather has suddenly changed, and we have had four days without a storm of rain. I am beginning to fuss about my departure to France at the end of the month. I must unite weak lots of bees, and feed them up – a month too early. And there are lots of complications. Nerissa is going to stay here, either alone or with Fan, while we are away.

At this moment we have Quentin [Bell]'s three children and Sophie here – but Quentin and his wife return and carry them off today. In the meantime I shall have to play stump cricket unless I hastily put on my bee-veil.

I don't suppose you ever employed an agent. I did, and he has just died. Peter Watt. He was the cousin of some early friends of mine – one of whom, T.T., I have written about in *Flowers of the Forest*.★ He had a lot of their gaiety and gentleness and sensibility and hidden deep down that wild streak that makes one love and feel akin – that the Fordhams had.

Very much love   David

In October 1945 David and Tim White had a memorable row at Ridley Stokoe. The details are not relevant here, but Ridley Stokoe is. It is a hill farm with three hundred and forty acres, reaching from the North Tyne through fields and woods up to open moorland, which David bought for £2200 in April 1942. The farmhouse and farm land were let, but an old army hut provided a haven for holidays.

Dearest Sylvia, I got back here today to find your letter after a week at Ridley Stokoe, which left me physically much the worse for wear, exhausted, but madly in love with the place and wishing I could live there from the spring to the autumn equinox.

The border country has a fascination and mystery about it. The Yorkshire dales are grander, but somehow the emptiness of Northumberland, the hill beyond hill, stretching out for so far brings back the past. Hesleyside, five miles from us down the Tyne, was where the women served up the men's spurs on a dish as a hint there would be no roast beef until they had driven it back from Scotland. The abominations and ferocity of these border people [were] extraordinary. And why? Because there was a frontier. Once the frontier was abolished they became one kindly gentle people. Or perhaps that is putting it too high. But the English stopped living by raiding the richer Scots, and the Scots stopped

★ See above, p. 58.

burning English farms and pitchforking the babies back into the flames by way of reprisal.

I went up with William and Fan and Nerissa and we stayed in William's hut (built since Tim's visit). Perhaps I haven't told you that I gave him Ridley Stokoe some years ago.

However, all this, if you have read so far, is not to go without meat in the sandwich. For I found what I had forgotten, a 'game book', which is in effect a diary, and in it a full description from my point of view of Tim's visit with the dogs.

William is typing it out and I will send it along presently – before I go to France. . . .

Meanwhile I have chucked my material at Michael Howard, who complains that I have left out too much of my own letters – but how else to squash 200,000 words into 120,000?

One of the things which stands out plainest in my relations with Tim is my solid stupidity. I never asked myself the most obvious questions about Tim. I suppose that kind of stupidity is a measure of affection to some extent. The unquestioning belief that wives have in the capacities of imbecile husbands and vice versa are examples.

Very much love   David

24: viii: 1965   *Maiden Newton*

Dearest David, I love you very much, but I want to box your inattentive ears. When you were havering about the White/Garnett letters, did I not tell you they were inestimable because they were that extreme rarity, a give and take correspondence between two interesting people? And now it seems you have gone and upset the balance by leaving out too much of yourself. Michael Howard is quite right. Please put more of yourself back, and if need be cut Tim. The letter about going back to Hilton, the air-raid pastorals about growing vegetables: these letters are already historic documents. Do please treat yourself with more respect. For that matter, treat me with more respect. I haven't been sitting idle and just being witty since we first met.

The letters didn't give me any impression of your 'solid stupidity' about Tim. I think your heart was constantly interposing between the questions you might have asked and him. You didn't want your head to plumb the depths of his dislikeability; and during the war we all tried to save what we could of our endangered vital private lives; so you were practically kind but evaded rape. Not to mention murder: you must sometimes have been near wringing his neck.

But you went on being yourself with him. That is the essential. You did better by him than Wordsworth did by Coleridge.

Can you make out Wordsworth? I can't. The last time I was in the north I went to the Museum and gazed at the Hat. But it told me nothing of what went on inside it. . . .

It is a marvellous good chance that you found the Ridley Stokoe game book. Happy William to have Ridley Stokoe as his portion. Nowhere else in the country smells so delicious. I know the other side of the border very well indeed: twelve summers in the Ettrick Valley and there-around. My father fished, my mother painted, and I went as I pleased. Your theory about the frontier would have pleased Tim. But there are frontiers on frontiers' backs. I remember the Yarrow and Ettrick Agricultural Show, the Yarrow shepherds fighting the Ettrick shepherds, their dogs fighting around them, their wives with steely lips being polite about each other's rowan jelly.

Part of the fascination and mystery of these empty leagues is the dense population of names: every hill, every smallest stream, every pool in the river with a name. Happy William with so much to listen to that isn't conversation. Does Grass of Parnassus grow on his wetter acres? . . . I hope you will be happy, well, and not too active at St Martin. There will be some White for you to read when you come back.

With my love   Sylvia

27 *August 1965*   *Hilton Hall*

Dearest Sylvia, . . . Thank you for what you say about my letters. I will try and keep the better ones. Everything depends on what Michael's reader, whoever he or she is, says about the book.

Can't you post me some more to St Martin? There is a fine morning. Last night William and Fan and Nerissa returned from Ridley Stokoe.

On this visit no game was shot except for three hares (which have replaced the rabbits after myxomatosis). All three were shot dead by Nerissa, two of them with a rifle, one with a bullet through the heart at fifty yards. She is a hawk-eye.

I expect all this attempt at slaughter disgusts you a great deal. But you must try to restrain the propagandist in writing Tim's life. However, I am sure you will.

Love from   David

Dearest Sylvia, Your letter has just come and I cannot resist replying, though I have nothing to say. I am alone: Angelica and William set off for home and Hilton yesterday . . .

I am a long way from Tim in spirit at the moment, thank God.

The weather has turned bad again: the woods, which grow on the sides of ravines, are full of toadstools, mostly 'immangeable' but sometimes venimeux. William brought in two which we ate without dire results, and I also bought some *Lactarius deliciosa* in the market, which wasn't fearfully good hot, but provided a wonderful salad cold with lemon juice and oil. I continue to collect them, but am a poor hand at identification. If I die of mushrooms, and you write my biography, please say: 'He was never a systematic botanist.' Which, alas, is true.

I have started writing in French and send you my first effort. I wish I knew the language better. I often think in it, but it is depressing to know that one is thinking incorrectly.

The people here have two languages: French, which they pronounce badly, and Patois, which is not a dialect but a totally different language and more like Spanish than French.

The difficulty about keeping house for oneself if one is alone is that one can't eat enough. Last night I stuffed a large green pepper with chicken liver, minced chicken, tomato, mushroom, egg and cheese. It was marvellous – but I could only eat half and shall have the other half tonight. The same was true of the soup. So meals become monotonous. There is a marvellous market at Cahors with ducks, geese, fowls, guinea-fowls, rabbits, all dead and alive, every known vegetable and fruit with wood mushrooms of every size and shape, cheese, cow, goat and sheep, butter, eggs, fish – tunny, fresh sardines, loup, baby cuttlefish. I got three last week, and Angelica cooked them supremely well in their *ink*, but after I had taken out eyes and the bone you pick up on the seashore. She made a sauce with relics of aubergines.

I shall go in to Cahors on Saturday – but how many cuttlefish can I eat? (I have a refrigerator.) Not more than 150 grammes at the outside. And it is no good my buying a fowl – the cheapest meat in France except horse – as I shall never get through it. It would have to appear at five meals. Well, you see I've turned into an old bachelor in twenty-four hours. In another month I shall spend all my time airing my socks before I put them on. Perhaps I shall become like Tim. Certainly my writing so far isn't encouraging.

And great works loom in the offing: a path, half the length of which Angelica has laid in stone to be completed, and a bay tree and some rose bushes to be put in and a tree trunk to be sawn up and split. Will you write my biography, even if I do turn out like Tim?

By the way I am invited to lecture in California at Davis, Irvine, Los Angeles and Santa Cruz. Also at Oregon . . .

The trouble is I don't like lecturing – what I like is to sit in a room and give advice to students who are writing theses on Sylvia Townsend Warner.

Well, I must stop and do some work before it is time to break off for a sip of wine or Vichy water.

Very much love   David

Mort de la vieille France

C'était un hameau de la vieille France,
Trois familles de paysans y vivaient dans la misère
Sans argent, sans espoir.
Les maisons vides tombaient en ruines.
Les vignobles, envahis de ronces,
Le bétail vendu; quelques chèvres suffisaient.
La vie devenait dure.
Quand même on trouvait un lapin au pot le dimanche;
Autres jours on mangeait quelques escargots,
Un lièvre pris au hasard, soupe à l'oseille, cèpes de bois, haricots.
On faisait du pinard et fabriquait une liqueur de noix.
Oh oui! On vivait dans la misère.
Les saletés partout, la merde dehors aux coins de toutes les
    maisons
Les ordures dans les basses-cours.
Quand j'arrivai les puces dansaient en gavotte sous la table
Et s'abritaient sous les jupons des vieilles femmes.
Tous les jeunes étaient partis dans la banlieue de Paris.
L'école était fermée depuis longtemps,
La tour de l'église fendue par un coup de foudre.
Aucune messe.
J'aimais Fage.
Je grimpais par le sentier du vallon,
Je passais entre les vignes ensevelies de mauvaises herbes,
Je regardais avec adoration une vipère grosse d'une dizaine de petits
Elle glissa sous les grappes dans une muraille,
Me laissant le souvenir de rubis vivants,
Et je passais acheter une douzaine d'oeufs à la vieille
Que je nommais 'La Vecchia' – elle ressemblait à la vieille de
    Giorgione.

Toujours difficultés d'estimer le prix;
Et le bonhomme de quatre-ving-dix ans me demandait:
'Vous prenez un verre, Monsieur?' 'Merci, pas à cette heure-ci.'
Il ne me pressait pas – parce que, à vrai dire – il n'y avait à quoi
    boire dans la maison.
Je parlais un peu de l'Angleterre, saluais, emportais les oeufs
Et me mettais sur la route.
Mais, cette année-ci
On a arraché les vignes, on a tué mon beau serpent;
Partout la commune est divisée avec fils de fer barbelés comme à
    la guerre.
Paysans et paysannes mortes.
Une écervelée envoyée a l'hôpital
La vieille France abolie.
Massey-Ferguson a remplacé les bons boeufs à la charrue.
Le main d'oeuvre est mobile: les deux-chevaux
Arrivent de Cras à sept heures.
Hommes sans habitudes, mécaniciens sans loisir, robots sans
    visages
Ils ont arraché les vignes, ils ont tué mon beau serpent.
Les escargots sont empoisonnés, les cèpes ne poussent pas.
On se demande: 'Vaudrait mieux laisser les dernières maisons
    tomber en ruines
Ou y installer les frigos pour les louer aux vacanciers?'
Fage et la vieille France sont mortes.

D.G., St Martin-de-Vers 24 September 1965

4: x: 1965   *Maiden Newton*

Dearest David, You make me feel proud – sending me your poem.
It is a beautiful poem. I would know it was yours whatever
language you disguised it in. It is pace. Writers have a pace which is
recognisable as a gait. The poem brought back to me, exactly as you
told me, the old horse dying in the hard spring of 1917. It's in your
book, I know, but I remember the spoken version much better.

So that has gone too: the fleas and the oxen and the slow cooking
on a little heat. The grief one feels is raw, yet familiar. Here, they
cut down all the trees. It is wretched to survive a tree with so much
more life in it than one's self. . . .

I think you are sinning your mercies. You ought to buy a chicken
at Cahors, some gammon, a small rabbit, some boudin. On your
way back you should pick half a dozen juniper berries and some bay
leaves. You should anatomise the chicken – if you can désosser a
cuttlefish, boning a chicken will be nothing to you – and stew its

91

bones down to a broth that will set into jelly. When you have hacked, whacked and pummelled the rest and made it lie down in a pâté, and added the chicken broth (garlic, of course), all you need do is to write some poetry while it cooks; and when it is almost cooked, make an incision and pour in a good dose of brandy.

There will be no more cooking for a week, and with a coarse-cut pâté one slice is never like another, so you won't weary of it.

That's what I should do, if I had Cahors market: except that I might have a duck instead of a chicken: but the jelly isn't so good.

I refuse to contemplate your biography. I have other views. You are to rise and speak the Epilogue. Will you please write my obituary for *The Times*?

Meanwhile, and to ensure this, don't pick any bolets de Satan. It's bad enough to think of you going to America all over again. I missed you dreadfully last time. Make them pay you a rich advance fee and then cable that you have a nervous breakdown, due to financial worry. Surely they would be too sorry and humane to want the advance back?

With my love   Sylvia

It is a lovely poem. Please write several more.

To encourage him, she enclosed a poem of her own about Hilton Hall and L'Ancienne Auberge:

> Nobly grammatical in a puritan landscape
> The house stands waiting at the end of the journey.
> The house of the journey's outset, the former inn,
> Submitting to its fate of being departed from,
> Blinks after him once or twice, grows cold, grumbles
> Itself into a winter sleep. He travels between them,
> Alone, in a farewelling time of year.

7: xi: 1965   *Maiden Newton*

Darling David, I believe you are home. Here is the remainder of the Ireland section of White. It is the centre arch of the story, so I have let myself go over it. . . .

Did you write any more poems in French? May I see them?*
Love from   Sylvia

11 November 1965   *Hilton Hall*

Dearest Sylvia, I think you have done it brilliantly; that's to be expected – and much more than that, you really understand Tim

---

* For other poems in French, see below, pp. 131–2 and 186.

(much better than I ever did – but of course you are not hampered by having him there in front of you). And you reveal him completely to the reader. I think the whole thing magnificent. But I am not sure whether (speaking from memory) I agree about *The Book of Merlyn*. Of course, I haven't actually read it, which puts me in as weak a position as many reviewers. . . .

Many many congratulations and all my love   David

14: xi: 1965   *Maiden Newton*

Dearest David, . . . I wish you would read *The Book of Merlyn*. . . . I don't like being the only person to pronounce on it. I am not a fair judge, because I often dislike his writing to the point of embarrassment. (I am never embarrassed by him.) Someone said that Fielding reading *Pamela* was like a dog reading a book by a cat. I am a cat reading a book by a dog show, for much of the time. . . .

I love you very much. And please remember me to Angelica.

Sylvia

17 November 1965   *Hilton Hall*

Dear Dorsetshire Pussy Cat, I am a cat too, and it is exhausting living with this overpowering smell of dog. Curiously I feel it more with Tim himself and less in his books. . . .

At present I am preoccupied by writing a paper on Cybernetics, which I am reading to the Huntingdonshire intellectuals – a club called the Bigots, which meets about six times a year and consists of two local doctors, the headmaster of the Grammar School, a man who rebuilds old Rolls-Royces, Lord Hemingford, the schools inspector, the director of education, a dentist, two clergymen and an amateur archaeologist and two scientists.

Cybernetics is the technique of running factories by automated machinery directed by computers, and I am interested in its long-term results on the human race.

At our last meeting Lord Hemingford asked how he was to vote in the Lords on homosexuality. Only two out of sixteen wanted it to continue to be a punishable offence – which surprised me.

My novel [*Ulterior Motives*] . . . is like a bag in which a child puts everything it may want in the holidays: a map of Peru, a tin of dried milk, a cutlass, etc. It is in fact a ragbag, and I keep thinking of bits I want to add. It was stupid of me to take it up again and finish it because it will never be coherent. I dare not show it to a living soul either. I feel like the parent of a deformed child of which I am secretly proud. . . .

Love from   David

93

Dearest David, I am very sorry to disappoint myself; but I can't come this weekend. I've got pleurodynia – an insignificant plague if I throttle it in time. But then if I throttle it by the eleventh, jouncing in a train will encourage it to come back and spend a happy Christmas with me.

I am so sorry; and I feel so shamefully valetudinarian. Please forgive me. I find it hard to forgive myself.

With love from   Sylvia

12 December 1965   *Hilton Hall*

Dearest Sylvia, Please take the greatest care of yourself. When I had a bad throat George Moore wrote me a letter asking me to promise to tie a woollen stocking round it. I wish I could think of an equivalent demand. But really I can't think of anything except sleep and warmth and possibly a hot double whisky, brown sugar and lemon juice before retiring.

I feel rather ashamed of myself because I am in the rudest health myself. It is a great disappointment you are not here. Angelica and Fan and William are playing in the dining-room – fiddle, french horn and oboe. I fancy the french horn (Fan) is playing something written for another instrument – possibly cello. But the result from my room is agreeable.

I wish you here, because I wanted to tell you, to confess to you, by word of mouth what I hesitate to say on paper. The fact is I am horribly bored, not by Tim himself, but my friendship with him exemplified in all those idiotic solemn letters written from false premises. And I simply am *not* going to look at them *now* any *more*. This may involve my telling all sorts of lies to you and Michael. You are warned.

The thing is that I have regained confidence in the very dubious novel I have written, and I realise that the end was cut much too short. Also the diagram of the story is this:

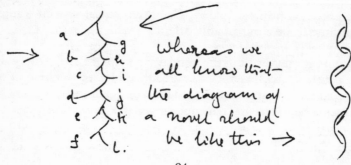

I have therefore got to get hold of a, b, c, d, e, f, g, h, i, j, k, and tuck them in as one did when weaving cane mats in kindergarten. Even if I don't and defy the rules I have got to make one of my chief characters come alive. At present only two characters really wriggle their toes of their own free will.

So you see how things are.

Also one of the characters disappears after the third chapter. I forgot him. Now I realise he is important. But what he thinks, feels or does I have no notion. So I have to wait till he arrives and knocks things sideways.

Love   David

Take care of yourself.

16: xii: 1965   *Maiden Newton*

Dearest Bunny, Your letter has done me more good than half a dozen hot double whiskeys with brown sugar and lemon juice, because of its kindness, because of its *news*.

I am totally delighted that your novel has asserted itself, and won't be cut short, and that a, b, c, d, e, f, g, h, i, j, k, etc., will lie harmoniously down in it, and the characters you forgot about come back and bang on the door. My dear, I wish you the liveliest of torments – one can't say higher than that. As for all that plaiting in or whiskering out, I can only give my own opinion: that novels should be approximately globular or perhaps the shape of the best baking potatoes.

Oh, I am so pleased. But let it be very long, and very substantial and full of eddies and opinions – a novel for winter nights.

As for the D.G./T.H.W. letters, why shouldn't they wait? If you leave them long enough, they will come back to life, and you will be able to accept the false premises as part of the set-up: which they are. True, I don't at the moment see how you can editorially remark: At this moment I hated his guts. But you will find a way, if you leave them to simmer at the back of the stove.

The hatred in the game book is as blue as a thunder-cloud. And if the letter he wrote to Lanie Wheeler on his first day at Hilton is typical of what he was like when he arrived, I don't wonder at the hatred. His Dublin friends, McGraths etc., cherish it as his epitome. It is about the crossing: it is the broth of a letter. It is painful.

Some time – *not* to interrupt the novel – you must tell me what impression he then made on you, what changes you saw. He was havocked with jealousy, do you know, because of your war importance (were you decorated, or knighted or anything? I ought to know this for the book). And though he knew Ray was dead, it wasn't till he saw Hilton that he realised she was gone. There is a passage in the Duke Mary's diary, when he was sucking his wounds, where he speaks of missing her as a mediatrix. I find it only half-touching, because it is mixed with his self-pitying. There are times when the diaries remind me of a crack of mine: 'Scratch an Englishman and you find a martyr.'

Let us turn to giraffes. What a ravishing picture! I have never seen it. I have been looking at it during all the interstices of today, they grow taller every time I look at them. As a rule I hasten to give my Christmas cards to organisations who make albums for legless orphans; but they won't get this.

I enjoy the poor gnu too – if it is a gnu – waiting for the lady to recognise him as also a work of providence.

There is nothing I can send as a match. As a matter of fact, this little book was marked for your Christmas some time ago. For God's sake don't read it all at once, for you would then dislike me.

With my love   Sylvia

I am better, thank you.

Sylvia sent David a copy of her privately printed *Sketches from Nature* inscribed 'Merry Christmas, dear David, and love from Sylvia'.

1966

Sylvia sent David a copy of her latest collection of stories, dedicated to him, in the American edition, entitled *Swans on an Autumn River*. The British edition was called *A Stranger with a Bag*.

4: i: 1966   *Maiden Newton*

Dearest David, I send this U.S.A. copy of your book (see dedication) because it is out now and because it has the title I intended. T'other had to be altered because a spiritualist came out with a book called *Swan on a Dark Sea*, and I did not wish our locks to intertwine.

I hope this will get to you before you go away to Mexico – I think you planned to go there? I send it with a great deal of love and gratitude for your direction. If it had not been for you, by now I would probably have given up writing poems and keeping them in a drawer. And if I had written any prose it would have appeared in the *Musical Times*.

Fortunately for me you have inherited your father's gift for fostering – as I have said in the White biography.

With very much love   Sylvia

8 January 1966   *Hilton Hall*

Dearest Sylvia, You should not write such letters. You make me insufferably proud, and it will require the united efforts of Angelica and my three daughters batting me over the head with a spoon and exclaiming 'Down, wanton, down!' – as though I were an eel in the pan – to reduce me to my proper place. Nobody has ever had such a wonderful letter. And if it is true, what you say, seldom has an ancient barnyard fowl hatched out such a Swan as you.

I like all the stories, but best of all, I think, 'A Love Match'. I am surprised that you got away with it in the *New Yorker*. My book *A Shot in the Dark* was rejected by Harcourt Brace because of references to sapphism, which Mr McCallum informed me had scarcely been heard of in the United States.

Love which has to be kept secret has a greater intensity than love which is accepted by society. But I think passionate physical love never is accepted, and society does everything possible to destroy it. My *Man in the Zoo* was about the private nature of love and the hostility with which it is regarded.

I have never known a happily incestuous couple, and I dare say you have not either. I have known a couple who called themselves brother and sister at first, and then had a baby and got married; and I have known a family in which Papa 'interfered' with his offspring – but that is not love; and also a Jewish mother who seduced her son aged eleven – but that was a mix-up. Usually it is Papa who seduces his children – which I can well understand, as I have four wildly attractive daughters. But unfortunately I think falling in love between the generations is impossible, unless perhaps one came back after eighteen years' absence to meet one's daughter aged seventeen-and-a-half. It is not the difference in age, but the familiarity, which inhibits.

I like 'Johnny Brewer', 'Reparation', 'Total Loss', 'Fenella', 'Their Quiet Lives'. I like them all very much. And I shall go about for some time like Johnny Head-in-Air. When will you come and visit us? Any week-end in February. I should like you to see something of Nerissa, and no doubt Fan (who plans to be a horn-player and musician) would like to see you and get you to listen to her noises.

Henrietta is here this week-end with her daughter. She is going to a ball in a wonderful 1898 dress in which she looks marvellous.

All my love   David

The 'separate sheet' which follows was filed with David's letter of 30 July, but seems to belong earlier, perhaps here.

I don't think I have written to you about *Sketches from Nature*, which demands a separate sheet. Reading them is extraordinary for me, as I can hear your voice and visualise you (I visualise you as you were in 1923).

Really there is no more to be said. You set out to record your girlhood, but the printed page reveals you in the act of recollection – or of improvisation – as well as the memory.

And your wit! Much as I should like to insinuate that it is not quite fair to be so clever and so witty, I cannot do so, because the witty things are like needles of light focussed on the past and revealing them as the doctor's little flashlamp in a sort of electroplated fountain pen reveals a monstrous tonsil. Not that your childhood was a morbid growth. It seems to have been singularly happy. Like me, you were lucky in your parents, who must have been delightful company. I envy Philip staying in the Devonshire cottage, though I should never have had the savoir vivre to fall on my knees.* I was an impossible hobbledehoy. But I wish I had had the luck to go to Harrow and get to know the Warners in that way.

Very much love and gratitude   .   David

31: i: 1966   *Maiden Newton*

Dearest David, I have been respecting your novel and gazing on you with holy dread and keeping out of your way, but I do want to know how Tim struck you when he came back from Eire: I am uncertain how to be struck by him myself. The diary and the first letters to [Sydney] Cockerell give me an impression of uneasiness, déracinement and clean pinafore, but this may be my creative mind. And how far was that pub from Duke Mary's?

Thank you for writing as you did about the short stories. By the way, the *New Yorker* never turned a hair at incest, but set up a considerable hackle over 'Johnny Brewer'.

With my love   Sylvia

PS. *pp. sotto voce.* I hope it goes on well.

3 February 1966   *Hilton Hall*

Dearest Sylvia, I am deeply grateful to you for your sympathetic treatment.

I sent my novel called *Ulterior Motives* on the 31st January and immediately remembered that the wife of one of the characters – a widower – is called Marie-Thérèse in one place and Marcelle in another. Actually she is Marie-Thérèse, but I shall probably forget. A certain emptiness is left, and for several reasons I am starting immediately on another.

The thought of Tim nauseates me with its unreality, and general idiocy (on my part). When he arrived from Ireland the noise and physical presence of Quince, who stood four foot six on his pads and knocked everything off any table when he turned his back to it with his amiable tail, and Killie, bouncing, ingratiating and all too female, were a scintillating halo around Tim, who was, I think, rather full of self-pity after a hellish journey, which I think he blamed on me (i) for inviting him, (ii) for being an Englishman. But he was very anxious to like Angelica and make the best of things.

---

* Because the postman happened to look in as Sylvia's mother was reading aloud the Fifty-first Psalm as a means of timing boiled eggs – see 'Fried Eggs are Mediterranean' reprinted in *Scenes of Childhood* (1981).

The Punchbowl at Low Row is visible from Duke Mary's. But it is about six hundred feet less in altitude and about a mile, or three-quarters of a mile, away as the crow flies.

It is easy to get there, but if one walks much more difficult to return from, as one has to walk up the Stripe, a narrow field with a gradient of about one in three in some places. And even in a car the road by Whita Bridge is a severe test for a drunk driver. I think it essential that you visit Duke Mary's. It is now Richard's property, and it is a most marvellously beautiful place and habitable from May till November. Why not borrow it for a week or a week-end?

When can you come here? I heard you had taken refuge in Cornwall, but it is now mild, and I saw a bee in the aconites. Why not the first week-end in March 4th? Unless we are deep in snow.

Amaryllis has returned from a disastrous visit to U.S., as the company hadn't got the right visa owing to the inefficiency of their lawyer and was refused a work permit. They lay about starving for three weeks and then returned, and she is now going to auditions.

Very much love   David

2 March 1966   *Hilton Hall*

Dearest Sylvia, . . . Will you come here on April Fools' Day week-end, Friday 1st (or Saturday 2nd) or 8th/9th? You won't find Angelica here, but I shall hope to have some of my daughters, William, and Richard next door. I must explain that Angelica has bought herself a house in Islington and has left me. I am old enough to see her point of view. She is forty-seven, and it is a last chance to lead another life. I am seventy-four (next week) and like all old people am irritating. Unfortunately in the twenty-four years of our marriage I have become dependent on her. I have always tried to train her to stand on her own feet – manage her own life – and it seems I have been too successful. I have determined not to feel bitter and only to do so when I lie awake in the early hours when one sees things with perfect clarity but in a distorted atmosphere, so that what one thinks then is stark reality is really a mirage.

Actually I have been very lucky all my life, have enjoyed success, love of exceptional women, intelligent and loving children, enough money to get along without hardship. Angelica has unfortunately not got another man. I should, of course, be jealous if she had, but it would be better for her. Physical love is the most important thing in life.

I may go for a fortnight to France at the end of April – shall spend the summer here, September and October in France. Jean Renoir is said to be going to shoot *Aspects of Love* during the vintage – but you know how film people always let one down.

Then if I can concoct some lectures I may get to the United States from November till January and return by way of Mexico and Guatemala. Please come if you are fit. We will have the central heating on; everything will be comfortable, and I am becoming a competent cook.

Very much love   David

3: iii: 1966   *Maiden Newton*

Dearest David, Your letter has just come.

I feel deeply distressed for you. I'm afraid, since both you and Angelica are rational beings, it must have been a protracted wrench with discussions and arrangements and seeing each other's point of view; and so with none of the anaesthesia of shock. One pays rather heavily for being civilised – and suffers as much post-shock, or more, for a negotiated calamity, as one would if it had fallen on the back of one's neck like the axe.

You say you have been lucky all your life; but you forget to list the greatest blessing of all: that you have an exceptionally wide and sensitive intelligence. You still have that. It won't go and live in Islington. And you won't have to go outside yourself for succour.

But these wise reflections don't make me any the less sad. Even at my age I am still childish enough to want people to be happy. And to that I have added a maturer concern: I don't like people to be wounded, especially if they are, like you, proud and fostering.

I will come and irritate you – 'all old people are irritating' you say, not that I wholly agree – on Friday 1st April. I would come coughing on one leg, but as it happens I am now through with winter ailments and very well. I hope I shall see some of your daughters, and that they have a penchant for crones. I had, at that age.

I am sure you cook admirably. But one tires of cooking. My impulse was to write to Mr Nolan in Dublin telling him to send you a side of his extremely good smoked salmon, to prey on when you didn't want to cook. But now I think it will be exasperating if it came just when you were going to be away and there was no one to put it in the refrigerator. So please send me a card, quick, quick! And I will act accordingly.

I love you very much   Sylvia

Dearest Sylvia, Forgive me for not writing to thank you by return, but I have rather had my head in the sand. The salmon arrived very apropos on Saturday, an hour or two ahead of Amaryllis and Fan, and it added great distinction to our menus.

William and I have had two good slices each tonight, on my return from thirty hours in London. *Moby Dick*, on which I live when in London, is a fascinating hide-out. For about six hours out of the twenty-four she is afloat, joggling about at the turn of the tide, the rest of the time resting on the mud. Swans come and take one's stale bread. Seagulls swoop down to pilfer. Last night I heard a curious conversation going on, very gently, close to my pillow. Not quite human. I knelt on the bed to look out through a window on to the foredeck, and there, a foot or two from my pillow but the other side of the wall, was a couple gently conversing in the semi-darkness: mallard drake and duck – not quacking.

The most human voice is that of the eider. In Scotland my cousin and I searched the loch with field-glasses to find the boat from which voices came over the water. Finally we realised it was a party of eider ducks close in to the shore.

Longmans are publishing my book in the autumn. I have got to write a blurb. *Lady into Fox* is out of print in U.S.A., and the rights have reverted to me. Now a strange firm have offered to reprint it with the original illustrations as one of their children's books!

This strikes me as odd. However, I am accepting. . . .

Very much love   David

From Sylvia's diary:

30: iv: 22: David was on the platform, looking in the wrong direction. As I approached I saw him and the look was frantic and foiled: as much as to say: *This* is going wrong. We drove soberly along almost empty roads under green trees, and he correctly made me tea. . . .

All this while David was cooking. He is still riddled with shock, and talks slower than ever, and though we were all gay at dinner there was a sensation of how well we were all keeping it up – except William with his tranquillity like Ray's: a deer about the house. . . .

2: v: 66: Inevitably, I suppose, I left feeling I should not go there and find him again. But he is working on another book, so perhaps that will rebuild his interior.

Darling David, My mind is full of space and trees and happy young creatures – and friendship. It was a lovely week-end; you are the most comfortable of hosts, I could even say 'Down, wanton, down!' to my restless conscience, which felt it should be expressing itself in the sink. It couldn't urge me to cookery since you cook so extremely well – and so unobtrusively, the mark of the master. . . .

Goodnight, dear David, and thank you.

My love   Sylvia

Dearest Sylvia, . . . I am suffering from a hangover, partly emotional and partly due to drinking a lot of champagne, whisky, burgundy and Grand Marnier – but principally the former (emotional) reason. Angelica has come to the conclusion, unaided, that she has made a mistake. She came and spent a day and a night on the boat on Tuesday–Wednesday. This was followed by a warm reconciliation with my closest female friend, who also thought she had made a mistake, and by my going out to a dinner with charming young creatures at which I consumed the whisky, burgundy and Grand Marnier. I enjoyed myself and didn't get at all drunk, but have felt a bit deflated today.

Angelica returns here for the week-end tomorrow.

Obviously there may be more surprises in store – probably painful ones. But I am feeling very happy, and what is equally important, I think Angelica is much happier and also everyone else, all round. She wrote me such a comic letter in which she said: '*Not having a lover cannot be a reason for leaving you.*' I have forborne to ask why not. It seems to me that it is a reason, and perhaps a good one. Anyhow there – or rather *here* – we are.

Very much love   David

Five months of solitude and heart-searching have made her more beautiful. Shattering.

Dearest David, Your letter came this morning. I am very glad that Angelica has rearranged her mind and that Hilton Hall will have its proper pattern again. Thank you for writing to tell me. It is a grief off my mind – off my heart rather, for my mind was engaged in thinking how admirably you were behaving. I would rather reflect on your happiness than on your merit. Happiness is *much* the rarer achievement, so I hope to admire you more and more.

With my love   Sylvia

Dearest David, . . . Please congratulate your old cat from me. Hilton has need of them. If you haven't got the mole plague already, you soon will. My younger cat has brought me four engaging corpses in the last four days. Besides, Hilton is inconceivable without its cats. How else would Nerissa have found that sublime 'morose'?*

With my love   Sylvia

14 June 1966   *Hilton Hall*

Dearest Sylvia, . . . I went last week-end to a very beautiful spot in South Wales, on the banks of the Tywi. There used to be a great house with a park full of ornamental trees and rhododendrons on a bluff just above the river, and a view of the open valley stretching away with the winding silver river. The house was burned, and now the garden is so wild that only white foxgloves mixed with the red and syringa and the rhododendrons show that it once existed. There was an adder asleep on what was once a terrace, buzzards nest among the yew trees.

The owner is a fishing companion of my cousin Dicky. He caught two glorious salmon and a big sea-trout. I caught a sea-trout, or sewin as the Welsh call them, and Dicky caught two. They have caravans, but I slept in a tent. That and wading about in the black river at midnight made me feel young again.

May I read what I wrote about the visit to Alderney? I am alone in the house with *six* cats. One contented tabby would be better company than three querulous orientals and their illegitimate offspring.

Very much love   David

Yes, *Morose* is good – almost genius. But it is I who am morose just now.

15: vi: 1966   *Maiden Newton*

Dearest David, . . . I wish I had been in your wilderness, especially at night when I needn't have disliked the rhododendrons as rigidly as I do by day. If I could have my wish, I would send them back to their Himalayas. Isn't it astounding how wild Wales still is when one gets away from its poor debauched coast; and how wild it smells. Natural wild, not incensed.

Very much love   Sylvia

* See above, note on p. 60.

Dearest Sylvia, . . . I don't think rhododendrons come from the Himalayas exclusively, do they? The honey they produce is poisonous, and I always imagined that the honey which poisoned Xenophon's men in the Caucasus was rhododendron. And the Alpenrosen of the Tyrol are alpine rhododendrons also.

Did I tell you that two nightjars swooped down on me in the darkness to investigate my salmon fly and that I had to scare them away for fear they would catch it?

My daughters arrive today: the garden is full of peas, globe artichokes, spinach, strawberries and raspberries starting. Angelica busy bottling fruit. Hives bursting with honey.

Love from   David

Dearest David, . . . I have been reading the second volume of the Moorman *Wordsworth*. I am appalled by the resemblance between White and the decaying Coleridge: the same petulance, the same scrabbling over the past – of all useless and merciless occupations! – the same love, and incompetence to implement it. But, not being a genius, White wasn't to the same extent impeded from walking by his wings.

I am glad your garden is so thriving. Ours is pretty good. We have no artichokes, as the plants had to be divided and replanted. But we have quantities of wild strawberries – not that sour Baron S. but wood strawberries – and hope to have quantities of figs.

We also have ten young great tits, bred in our letter-box: the second year it has been taken over as a nesting-place. It made the postmen extremely paternal. They stood listening on the doorstep with mild grins.

With my love   Sylvia

Dearest David, . . . ten baby great tits . . . are now eating the green peas. Faulty ecology. It is not ecological to foster tits in letter-boxes.

Have you used Scaraweb? It is *terrifying*. I suppose it is made of the left-overs of bad dreams.

With my love   ? ?   Sylvia

Dearest Sylvia, Thank you for your letter. I do indeed know Scaraweb, as it alone preserves buds from bulfinches. But what inconvenienced them six months ago is, as you say, a nightmare as one picks the hair lines from the white and red currants. Gooseberries are relatively easy. . . .

Time seems to run short in the summer. I suppose it is the effect of age, but I simply cannot bear to do any work. I don't include in that term cooking the meals, looking after the bees, preparing and gathering fruit and vegetables, bottling gooseberries and raspberries, entertaining visitors and playing Oh Hell! with my daughters after dinner.

But I can't think, tidy my table, write urgent letters, or read anything but *The Times* – and that isn't the same any longer. And so many things loom ahead. I forget them by day, but the sleepless conscience at night reveals them, like radar – enormous across my path – dark and solid, and collisions are inevitable. So I hurry out to pick peas, and even the strands of nylon on the currants are welcome as a distraction from duty.

Very much love   David

3: viii: 1966   *Maiden Newton*

Dearest David, I was just going to send you a telegram when your letter came.

FORSTER TWO CHEERS FOR DEMOCRACY PENGUIN PAGE 91 THIS IS A MUST.

It is. Pray turn to p. 91 if you haven't been there already. . . .

I am in a state of contained delirium with the last years of the biography. Something that isn't me appears to be doing it irrefutably. Michael Howard has entrusted the final diaries, in a massive yellow tin trunk, to the Dorchester Museum under vows and padlocks. I sit reading them in a large calm library with an old gentleman or two turning over the day's *Times* and saying, Tk. Là, tout n'est qu'ordre et beauté – and Tim raving in my ear.

I long to tell you all. But when? Finishing and titivating and compressing will keep me here till the end of September. Then I want to go to Cape Wrath; and you, I suppose, will be going to America. Or are you too happy at home to go? I would like to think that.

Wish me well.

Love   Sylvia

Dearest Sylvia, Demon woman. How can I turn to p. 91 of *Two Cheers for Democracy* (Penguin edition) when the Cambridge booksellers declare it is not in Penguin?★

Don't flatter yourself that I drove off to Cambridge on receipt of your letter. But William was going, and I asked him to get the book as well as two Porter bee-escapes and vast quantities of honey tins.

For honey and bees occupy my thoughts more than literature. Today I took twenty-three sections from one hive, and then, becoming impatient because the bees would not go downstairs (or the bee-escape didn't work), I took two racks of shallow frames stuck together with a lot of bees inside – about fifty pounds altogether, I suppose.

As a result the kitchen table was running with pools of thick golden honey. The kitchen was full of bees trying to get out and outside hundreds of bees trying to get in. All most friendly. No stings. . . .

I am overjoyed that you are in up to your neck [in] the last diaries and horrors. My engagements are at present only with my bees. I take a hive to Butts (Duke Mary's) for the heather. Before then I clear out the attics at the Cearne (my parents' cottage) of five thousand books and pictures and junk and dispose of them.

Then I write four lectures. Go to France on 1st September. Return about the 10th of October. Feed bees for a fortnight and fly to New York about Guy Fawkes' Day, Angelica has the idea of coming to New York about 8th January and meeting me in Texas or New Mexico about the 14th, and then we shall take a bus – several buses – and visit all the pyramids in Mexico and the buried cities in Yucatan.

★ The Cambridge booksellers were mistaken, and David eventually acquired a copy. The passage Sylvia has in mind seems to be:

> Just as words have two functions – information and creation – so each human mind has two personalities, one on the surface, one deeper down. The upper personality has a name. It is called S. T. Coleridge, or William Shakespeare, or Mrs Humphry Ward. It is conscious and alert, it does things like dining out, answering letters, etc., and it differs amusingly from other personalities. The lower personality is a very queer affair. In many ways it is a perfect fool, but without it there is no literature, because unless a man dips a bucket down into it occasionally he cannot produce first-class work. There is something general about it. Although it is inside S. T. Coleridge, it cannot be labelled with his name. It has something in common with all other deeper personalities, and the mystic will assert that the common quality is God, and that here, in the obscure recesses of our being, we near the gates of the Divine. It is in any case the force that makes for anonymity.

collective unconscious? [handwritten annotation]

After that we propose to return via the West Indies. It is cheaper by boat, but James Strachey tells me that there is piped music in every saloon and that every passenger has a transistor in his pocket. So that a boat is hell. So is Hilton. Fan plays scales on the horn or the same unending tune with the same fumble. William plays the cor anglais – the oboe – but well. Angelica scrapes away at the violin. Nerissa listens to the B.B.C. – Test Match – Archers – whatever is on. Often all are audible at the same time. In the garden the American Phantoms – jet fighters – deafen one.

Why can't we meet in London either last days of August or mid-October?

Very much love   David

18 *August 1966*   *Hilton Hall*

Dearest Sylvia, We all feel so much sympathy with you and with Pericles. It is rare for a cat to be mauled by a dog. I suppose he was taken unawares. I do hope he recovers. Let me know. I have just got back from Duke Mary's after taking a hive to the heather. Whether we get any honey depends on the weather. It was lovely while I was there, but not hot as it is here. Richard has done many repairs and improvements, and the children enjoy it almost as much as I do. . . .

My bees travelled well, being given ventilation – perforated zinc both below and above the hive. Only two died on the journey.

A colony of Richard's friends are being attracted to the North Riding. Tim Bagenal at Gunnerside. Stephen Keynes (a nephew of Maynard's) on the hill above Gunnerside, and a lecturer of Anglo-Saxon called Raymond Page beyond Hawes at High Houses between Dodd Fell and Whiddale Fell. It is a house of some pretensions – four main rooms fifteen feet by fifteen. Eighteenth-century staircase with good balusters. Altogether very attractive in a marvellous Wuthering Heights position and at the end of a road which stops. As though that was not enough defence against the world since *Beowulf*, there was a great Charollais bull roaming loose. . . . They have been there a week and have nothing but a cooking stove, two beds and four chairs and a tiny round bedside table.

Very much love and hopes for Pericles.   David

22: viii: 1966   *Maiden Newton*

Dearest David, Pericles is better: thin as Rozinante and limp as spaghetti, but back in his senses and functioning. He had convulsions, one after another, all the first night, hurling himself about and mewing *like a kitten*: an agonising conjunction of these feeble cries and the muscular strength of a wild cat. . . .

I am going to outrage Tim's more respectable friends by *not* deploring his Naples wallow. Those appalling photographs of him like Silenus among the pimps and parasites shocked me, I admit, when I first saw them. But it is better to fatten rascals than solicitors. Besides, the photographs are flashlight photographs, and flashlit mothers' unions would look as villainous.

The elder Lane boy, writing his view of Tim for me, began with a magnificent phrase: 'I think the first thing that struck anybody was his stature and sloppily dignified appearance' – *sloppily dignified*. Unfortunately he can't keep it up.

With my love   Sylvia

David: This is going to be a very rum biography.

30 August 66   *Hilton Hall*

Dearest Sylvia, . . . We – Angelica, Duncan and I – fly from Southend to Calais, complete with my Mini and then drive, stopping for one night with a French painter. I shall have to refurbish my lectures for Americans and am getting nervous – ready to scream, like the White Queen, well in advance. But I dare say I shall settle down to drinking my litre of wine a day contentedly and looking for wood mushrooms and Roman snails.

I regret having fixed up the American visit, as I want to write – or rather finish – another book, and the winter months are the only ones when one has no excuses of bees and garden for not working.

I got seventy-three pounds of honey from one hive and could take at least another thirty pounds from it. But I am leaving it for them to winter on, as I shall not be here at the right time to feed them with sugar.

I hope Pericles is making a good recovery. Write to me in France.

Much love   David

18: ix: 1966   *Maiden Newton*

Darling David, Today I killed and buried White. Not that the book is killed yet. . . . But having begun at the beginning I have now reached the end. It is a disagreeable insubstantial feeling – a form of convalescence with nothing to get well for. . . .

I have a very old-fashioned mind. Valentine came into the garden where I was giving Pericles a refresher course in tree-climbing – his illness left him rather uncertain of deftnesses, though he has reassembled them all now – and told me about Verwoerd's assassination. I said, after a reverent pause, 'And done with a plain old-fashioned dagger.' Assassinations were more gratifying when we were young, and could rejoice in the death of tyrants without second thoughts. Now one thinks of all the other deaths that will be consequent.

How are you getting on at St Martin? Is it a good year for mushrooms, have you made that pâté yet? Here it begins to be chilly at night, which is agreeable; the mornings feel excited and new, and when I look out of the window I see pigeons in the yew tree. . . .

With my love   Sylvia

27 December 1966   *D. H. Lawrence Ranch, San Cristobal,*
                                                                      Taos, New Mexico

Dearest Sylvia, Here I am, snowed up in the cabin where Lawrence and Frieda lived, and writing you a long letter about my experiences seems the best occupation. No doubt they will soon get a snow-plough at work, and cars will arrive. But at the moment all is peace.

I spent a month visiting five universities, including Toronto in Canada, lecturing at each and talking impromptu to classes and seeing students. So it was a relief to get to this place, which I borrowed from the University of New Mexico, and be alone. It is now fully equipped with electricity, oil heating, W.C., bath, constant hot water – very different from Lawrence's day. All I have to do is to buy food and cook it. Sometimes I split logs with an axe. On Christmas Day I was in Taos, and Brett* took me to see the Deer Dance at an Indian Pueblo. Brett is eighty-three, drives her station wagon, full of vitality, dresses in moccasins, wadded coats, trousers and a cap of deerskin which Monty would envy. It has an eagle's feather, an enamelled scorpion, and silver tassels. She came up here to lunch one day and was in fine form – bursting with scandals which would have rocked England to the core and brought down the government in 1910. I can just remember a few of the names.

To get back to the Deer Dance – or mystery play. The Pueblo consists of two halves about two hundred yards apart, with a stream in the middle with occasional bridges. The buildings are up to five storeys in height in two main blocks, rectangular, flat-roofed, the upper storeys reached by ladders and each storey set

* The Hon. Dorothy Brett, painter and disciple of Lawrence in New Mexico.

back. The Pueblo has not cha[nged]* much since the Spaniards came, but they now have doors and wind[ows], which were too dangerous when attacked by the Plains Indians. There is [a] small R.C. church at the lower end of the plaza.

Two lines of Indian women with bare arms and shoulders, with lo[ng] hair loose down their backs, wearing high white buckskin moccasins [and] gay tunics began dancing with a drum. A dozen men – the clowns – jo[ined] in – rhythmic cries rather than songs. When the dance was over the[y] went to the other end of the plaza and repeated it. There was a long wait. My feet grew cold. I was standing with Brett's great-nephew Simon and other acquaintances on the roof of an Indian house. Presently I noticed four or five Indians lighting a fire. They were sending a signal smoke to the deer. And then in the distance I saw a line of antlered figures crossing the most distant bridge. The party of perhaps fifty or sixty was led by the two Deer Chiefs – old men dressed entirely in white deerskin with white antlers on their heads and leaning on white sticks. Behind them two men – the guard – with bows and arrows, and two superb women, tall, massive, immensely dignified – the Deer Mothers. On their heads two tall eagle plumes rose from a gay patch of parrots' feathers, shoulders and arms bare except for necklaces, and high white moccasins, coloured dresses, a rattle in one hand, a bunch of feathers in the other. They marched into the courtyard of the church followed by the animals – men in deerskins, with deers' heads and antlers over their own, two buffalo with horns and humps, a wolf, some children as fawns and wildcats, a puma. Each leaning on two sticks – the forelegs. They formed two lines.

Drums, rattles, grunts and rhythmic cries as they dance. The two Deer Mothers pass up and down between and round the lines with magnificent dignity, with a shuffling dance, hardly lifting their feet, commanding all the animals, which shrink from them. Then the clowns join in, and one suddenly seizes a deer, flings it on his shoulders and tries to escape. But the guards seize him, the deer is released to dance again. This happens again and again – one of the evil 'Black-eye' clowns succeeds and escapes with his deer. This happens again and again. Then the dance is over. The Deer Mothers lead off the troupe of animals. The captured deer pull off their skins and masks and walk off with them over their arms. Later the dance is repeated at the other end of the plaza. It is a symbolic fight between the Goddesses of Nature and the destructiveness of man, and it is done every year – nowadays with two hundred American

* The edge of the letter has been torn away.

cars parked about and getting in the way, and the enemies of the Indians watching in crowds. Only they may not bring in cameras. Any camera seen is smashed. In three days' time I am going back to California. Then on the 12th January I meet Angelica at Austin in Texas, we fly to Mexico and drive down to Yucatan in a hired Hillman car. Heaven knows when we shall get back. I expect early March. The sun has come out, and a light wind is blowing snow off the benches.

Very much love and a Happy New Year   David

1967

Dearest Sylvia, My chief feeling, as Henry James would have noted in his story of the Ithaca ladies in Florence, is that we have really got here. We have done things the H. J. ladies would have done. We spent the day before yesterday at the ruins of Palenque, a city discovered in the jungle . . . [by] an Indian in 1773, which flourished between 600 and 900 A.D., and where in 1959 a pyramid proved hollow with the tomb of the 'pure man', buried with all his jade necklaces and huge pearls – Well, that is not the impression the place gives. To begin with, the 'jungle' is more like the parkland of [a] great English country house than anything else. Then except for the colossal scale and solidity the ruins might have been built by Beckford (in solid masonry) if he had read *Kubla Khan* and determined to create Coleridge's vision. There is the sacred river, running through a vast conduit, a waterfall, orange groves, the various pyramids which might have been built to hold an eighteenth-century hermit.

But, to leave this first impression, the Maya were artists of exquisite sensibility, and the half-dozen heads – naturalistic – and hundreds of little clay caricatures, are among the works of really great sculpture. We spent two nights in the village of Palenque – primitive – potholed. But the second night we moved to a lively primitive hotel – two clean beds of tin to discourage the insects, a cold shower and W.C., dirty floor, no troubles except the loudspeaker blaring away U.S. Negro music for hours – for twenty-five pesetas = fifteen shillings. The previous night had been hell, with church music, a marimba serenade, a chorus of dogs and cocks crowing so loud you could see down their throats – all night and double the price. I have the usual Mexican tourist complaint of diarrhoea, but Enterovioform holds it in check. Angelica has been well apart from thirty-six hours' headache at Tehuantepec. Tomorrow we set off for Merida in Yucatan.

PS.   *Hotel Colonial, Campeche*

You would like the women of Tehuantepec, on the Pacific side. They are magnificent matrons, arrayed in voluminous cotton print skirts with tops of velvet or satin inlaid with gold braid or red stripes. They wear their long pigtails braided with blue ribbons, and they manage the business of the markets, etc., while the men slash away at the weeds in the fields with their cutlasses (machetes).

In the square there is a bust to the lifelong mistress of Porfirio Diaz, the dictator, Señora Romero. He gave her a villa and had the railway line diverted to run in front of the windows because she liked watching trains.

It is quite hot, so one seeks the shady side of the street. Yesterday I bathed, and the water was very warm, too hot. No cloud in the sky here. At Palenque it was pale English blue with white fleecy lambswool. But all the Englishness has gone.

How is Tim going – or has he gone? It is a different world here. In Los Angeles I sent a message to Julie Andrews, and she actually telephoned when I was out. I spent a lot of time with Elsa Lanchester.* Did I write and tell you? She is full of spirit – looks like a fat Pekinese. A bitter tang of truth in every phrase. Gave me a kiss and said: 'Never thought we should find so much to say to each other, or that I should enjoy it.'

Take care amidst the perils of an English spring, my dear. Shall be back some time in March, I hope.   David

28 February 1967   *Hilton Hall*

Dearest Sylvia, We got back about ten days ago in a wonderful flight from Mexico City, stopping only at the Bermudas and the Bahamas and being marvellously looked after by young Australian men. *Qantas.*

Unfortunately England is quite unreal to me: the United States and Mexico are reality. Perhaps it is because I had a bad throat – a quinsy – when I arrived and have kept too much indoors. It will be awful if this illusion goes on of England's unreality. Angelica enjoyed Mexico immensely: it was a great success taking her, and we enjoyed being together. She even skinned a snake which we found just killed on the road. It is seven foot six inches long. I am taking it to be identified in Cromwell Road tomorrow. . . .

Part of my difficulty is that I have been on the move for three months and can't get used to being static and sedentary. However, I am going to London tomorrow and hope a sense of reality will return in the wet London streets with the slithering traffic. Otherwise I shall be run over, and that will be that. Please write me

---

* Julie Andrews had starred in *Camelot*, based on White's *Once and Future King*, and so had become a friend of Tim and acquaintance of David. Elsa Lanchester, comedienne and wife of Charles Laughton, was an old friend.

a very terre-à-terre letter about bulbs and books and the selective employment tax. (Did you know you can reclaim it if you pay it for a daily woman, if you are over seventy?) I am seventy-five next week. I hope I keep going strong, as I want to visit India and Japan and perhaps an island or two, and time grows short. Not to speak of money. I spent all I earned in the United States and more on this Mexican trip. But it was immensely worth while. The Mexicans are very attractive, with their chocolate skins and black hair, and are always laughing. They eat iguanas.

Even my daughters are not quite real: they are visions of beauty, they hug me closely as in a dream and disappear like phantoms, which a moment ago were flesh and blood.

We brought back three hammocks – one for Fan, one for Nerissa and one for this house in the garden. Do you know that three-quarters of a million people in Yucatan are born, sleep, live and die in hammocks and never see a bed? I should think giving birth to a child in a hammock would be a nightmarish experience.

However, it is so, for we looked into several Indian huts – an earth floor, a heavily thatched roof and three or four hammocks. No beds, tables or chairs. Only a box for valuables.

I must stop this and think about England. The only news here is that the County Archivist has recut our Maze – wrong. He also said it was pre-Christian when it clearly states that Gulielmus Sparrow hos gyros formavit anno 1660. William has already made the Archivist very uncomfortable and will pursue him as relentlessly as a rat without a tail, but with perfect manners.

Love from   David

2: iii: 1967   *Goldhill House, East Garston, Near Newbury, Berks*
Dearest David, I am glad you are back; and I expect you will be real again just as soon as those antibiotics you took for your quinsy have worked out of your system. They're not called antibiotics for nothing.

I am sitting at a well-appointed writing-table with a black cat asleep on it, so I write on my knee the terre-à-terre letter you ask for. I would have written long before if I had had a Mexican address to thank you for the story of Porfirio Diaz moving the railway. It is of the Kingdom of Heaven. What happiness they must have felt as they stood side by side and he said to her – Now listen carefully. And the distant puff and rumble came nearer and the First Train approached, steaming like a dragon and blowing its whistle.

(The cat has now settled into a new attitude and gone to sleep with its head in the pen-tray.) The best bulb I can tell you about is also a book – *mine*. The White Life is finished, its last insertions and titivations over. You must at any rate read the last Alderney section (the rest you have seen), which so nearly cost me my life and reason. There was never such a flea market of ill-assorted material to be reduced and compacted into narrative. I have done it *extremely* well, the compacting, at any rate. He went on living till sundown, like a killed snake, and writhed wonderfully in Naples. . . .

I go home on Saturday, and on Monday the decorator comes, and all the books will have to be moved from Valentine's sitting-room and dispersed through a house where there are far too many books already. It will be a fine opportunity to read books I have forgotten we have, and even to find some I thought we had lost. Of course we should also see it as an opportunity to weed out books we don't want. Can you weed books? I can't. I discarded some Ruskin about thirty years ago and have often regretted it since. I don't know why exactly – but I know it was a mistake. I might have read it and liked it very much.

With my love   Sylvia

11 March 1967   *Hilton Hall*

Dearest Sylvia, I think your final part is wonderful – for me extremely illuminating. I think you have done it perfectly: telling us everything but not harping on details. Also, I think, by something like genius, you never allow the reader to lose sympathy with this man who was slowly being transformed into a monster, or the semblance of one, much against his will.

I am grateful to you for your quotations from my letters to Tim, and his to me. Because, although I saw very little of him in later stages, I was, I think, always important to him. That extraordinary telephone call from the hospital proved it. I am delighted by the way in which you have made Carol★ absolutely solid: she is three-dimensional. . . .

I am so grateful to you for coming clean about the Neapolitan boys, about which others only hinted but never made me realise.

The other great merit is its brevity. It would have been fatally easy to drag out his years of affluence. As it is they are kept in the exact proportion of their unimportance to the important years of creation and of growth.

I shall read these chapters over again. Today I rushed through them when my adorable week-end visitors were sleeping off the

★ Carol Stallings, née Walton, sister-in-law of Julie Andrews. She typed for T. H. White and managed his tour of America in 1963.

effects of summer time. Henrietta, her daughter Sophie, Frances (Ray's younger sister), a fellow grandparent of Sophie, and a delightful plump intelligent girl who helps herself to raisins from the cupboard after meals and when I offer her more looks shyly to see if I am making fun or not, but is reassured when I munch some myself.

So much love. To whom must I send the manuscript when I have read it again?

Yours   David

28 March 1967   *Hilton Hall*

Dearest Sylvia, I have been reading these last chapters again and am more than ever impressed by your sympathy and dispassionate judgement which go hand in hand – which wouldn't seem possible. . . .

I have relapsed into a complete vegetable since my return and doubt if I shall ever do a stroke of work again. It is partly because my two-day-a-week gardener is on the sick list owing to his neighbour jumping on his hand when he was on all fours. (His neighbour and he are at feud over a privy over which each claims sole rights, and each has padlocked it so the other can't use it.)

As a result I have spent the last month sowing early peas and beans, tomatoes (now in little pots), spring cleaning the bees, and reading *The Times* from cover to cover.

My real trouble is that I want to write a play and know I can't. Also while in Mexico I wrote a squib – so silly that I don't know what to do with it. Actually there is nothing to be done. But when one writes trash what does one do? You see for a long time I have abandoned my trash uncompleted. But this one got completed.

Perhaps if my gardener returns, I may start doing something. But there is at present every excuse. The potatoes have to go in. Also I am alone with William and cook our meals. And when I am not alone with him, the house is full at week-ends and I dispense drinks, etc. Well, all these excuses don't really wash, do they? I am lazy and mentally inert. That is the truth of the matter.

Very much love. Let's meet some time.   David

Sylvia commented on the injured gardener in a letter of 15: iii: 1967 (if the letters are not misdated, David must have mentioned the feud in an earlier letter now lost):

Was your odd-job gardener's hand stamped on with forethought malice? I can quite believe it. Even in dull-hearted Dorset the wrath that is kindled by village flower-and-vegetable shows is quite alarming. Cabbages inflame the passions. Do you prepare for sweetcorn by digging in all the household fish-heads, etc? I was assured the Pilgrim Fathers did, on Indian advice. For myself, I doubt if it makes much difference, but it is pleasant to have something of this kind to recommend to others.

4: iv: 1967   *Maiden Newton*

Dearest David, Thank you for sending back the last chapters of White – and for thinking well of them. I have spent a nightmare week going through the setting-copy; taking out the tacking-threads, trying to remember on p. 457 if I hadn't used the same phrase on p. 221, and at intervals sourly noting *stet text*. . . . The setting-copy was prepared by a very worthy attentive person who was inclined to know better than I what I meant. However, she had her uses. Her dunderheaded queries and suggestions showed me what readers I might expect, and I took out stumbling-blocks and put in explanations, and did a reading-made-easy in various places. . . .

My head still swims with concentration and boredom.

Do you know anything about a Perceval Gibbon who was a friend of Conrad's and wrote about South Africa? I have been asked if I do, and I don't. I am always ready to take trouble for others, which entails giving trouble to other others. If you had made an index to your autobiography I should not be troubling you.

I think you should send your squib to the *New Yorker*. It is becoming a public duty to mitigate their seriousness. I do my best; but it is too much for one frail old woman to attempt, I need a coadjutor. Besides, if you send it to them I shall ultimately read it and you will – long before then – have a resounding cheque.

Yes, let us meet. I would love to. I often talk to you in my mind, but as I can't supply the answers the talk languishes. Next month? In your boat? I am off to Carmarthenshire next week to eat Crêpes Suzettes at the Red Lion in Llangattock, a hideous village where a mysterious M. Pierre has chosen to napkin his talent. (They are the best I have ever eaten.)

With my love   Sylvia

7 April 1967   *Hilton Hall*

Dearest Sylvia, Yes I knew Perceval Gibbon fairly well. He was a dark little energetic man who must have turned up (but see the dates

118

of his novels) about 1910.* I think that he had a hand in the *English Review* about the same time as Norman Douglas.

One Christmas holidays I set off with the four Olivier girls and Maitland Radford to walk to Dover from Limpsfield starting along the Pilgrims' Way. We called in on Gibbon and his wife out of the blue, in the evening, somewhere in Wrotham and I think stayed in the village pub along the road. Gibbon allowed himself to show, rather unduly, the excitement that Brynhild Olivier's beauty had on him. I am not sure how many of us there were on the walk of about eighty miles in four days. (It was cold, and the days were very short, and we did rather well.) Nails came through the soles of my boots, and I finished in carpet slippers. Directly we reached Dover we took the train to London. The party certainly included Margery, Brynhild, Daphne Olivier, possibly Noel, Maitland and myself. I talked to Daphne most of the way, and we disagreed on almost all subjects.

I don't think my *Defeat of Pepsi-Cola* is at all the sort of thing the *New Yorker* would like. But I certainly might try them with something one day. To whom should I address it? Does one have to send it in quadruplicate so that all four editors can reject it simultaneously? . . .

Let me know when you come to London and come and eat a grilled sole on my boat.

Very much love   David

25: iv: 1967   *Maiden Newton*

Dearest David, Here is a person for you.

In our hotel in Breconshire there was a dapper elderly man with a light nervous gait and a puckish smile. He was with his wife and his sister-in-law, who completely despised him. He must have been a bore with his constant allusions to the 1914–18 war (he was probably heroic and regretted those days). Once I heard him assert himself. The sister-in-law said something about not seeing the moon from her window. 'You couldn't have seen it,' he said. 'It won't be here till Monday.' The two women laughed at his exactitude. He said firmly: 'I always know the moon.'

A long fidelity. . . .

I am feeling such infinite relief that I must tell you. After I'd done with Tim, and to tell the truth was feeling slightly oppressed by having done him so well, I began a story of my own ['But at the

* Perceval Gibbon was a South African friend of David's father who published (Gibbon) mainly stories but also novels and verse between 1903 and 1926. ∧

119

Stroke of Midnight']: on an almost impossible theme with nothing but myself to rely on, and so improbable that it had to be written with the utmost exactitude. Also it had to be very long. Far more taxing than the incest story. I finished it and sent it to the *New Yorker* – Bang! – and went off to Wales, knowing that this time I'd surpassed even their capacity to swallow me. I have just had a cable swallowing hook, line and sinker. Over ten thousand words – you'd make a novel of it! – dollars innumerable. But the relief is to find that I have been able to bring it off. It was not that I thought I would be hallucinated into writing like Tim: but writing like oneself is a precarious ownership.

Can't I see *The Defeat of Pepsi-Cola*? I'm sure I have been liberal enough in letting you see me. Dear David, now that it's all over bar the total silence I must thank you for your help and encouragement during these past three years. I would have often been at a loss without you, and it could never have been such fun without the thought of pleasing you.

With my love   Sylvia

29 April 1967   *Hilton Hall*

Dearest Sylvia, Thanks for your letter and all the things you say about my encouragement. It cheered me up and arrived at the right moment, as I had been depressed – There are reasons. But I think the chief one is that the weathercock on the dovehouse, which William has put up again, swings from north-east to north-west, and I curse the handsome bird. It has been like that for a fortnight. It once got as far as due west, but never south.

I have sent *Pepsi-Cola* and another rotten story I wrote some years ago to be typed. They are bad, but what is worse they are not saleable. I am delighted to hear about your story. Please let me know when it will be published. I look forward eagerly to it.

Did I tell you about Professor Hattori? He uses my books to teach his high grade students English, and the autumn before last he came to see me in France. I was alone there. I cooked him a wonderful meal, Poulet Celestine, and he fell asleep eating it. He had been standing in the corridor of the train all the way from Paris weighed down with cameras, tape-recorders. He has now published the first slim volume of my short stories. You will have read them, but I send you the book as a collector's piece. * I don't know if he will get round to doing another volume. Some of his notes are naturally

* *The Old Dovecote and Other Stories*, Apollon-Sha, 1966.

120

wrong. However, he got flea-bitten pony right. The French translator made it 'rongé de vermine'.

When are we going to meet? Why don't you, at least, come to lunch on my boat? I can give you a very good lunch – or dinner, if you prefer it. I might get Amaryllis or one of them to come.

Very much love   David

3: v: 1967   *Maiden Newton*

Dearest David, No, I had not read them all. I had not read 'The Lost Arrow'. It is beautiful, a flitting masterpiece, and most strangely moving, partly perhaps by its air of furtivity and being as casually knotted together as a hank of last year's bog-grass. It doesn't seem to be written at all. It flies over the whole process of making, and is. So I am much in Professor Hattori's debt – though more in yours.

I was interested to see that nationality is in the eye of the photographer. Professor Hattori has made you an austere hermit out of Murasaki, rousing like a snake from his stone hermitage and coiled meditations.

I curse your handsome weathercock with you. Last night there was no wind, so this morning there was a lid of ice on the water-bucket. It is curious to see the landscape becoming greener and greener in this wintry air – and faintly disquieting as if a force of nature had got out of hand. Reasoning with chattering teeth I tell myself that every year I expect spring to be warm, to be as I think of it in winter; and then it isn't, and its east winds are as shocking as the heartlessness of the young, and I feel ill-used and defrauded. But we are as silly as sundials; we only record the unvexed hours.

Was it you, dear David, who prodded the Royal Society of Literature into inviting me to be a fellow, or was it alphabetical order? A friend of mine who heard of this wrote to say: 'I believe Coleridge had something to do with it.' Had he?★ I can't see him inviting the patronage of George IV. But to be honest, I can't see Coleridge at all. I can't follow his stern. Probably I am wrong in supposing he had a stern at all. A vast sponge, with poems darting through it like fishes, and then shrivelled and desiccating in Highgate. . . .

With my love   Sylvia

★ The Royal Society of Literature was founded in 1820 under the patronage of George IV and partly at his instigation. The King agreed to pay an annual sum of a hundred guineas to each of ten 'Royal Associates' of the Society, and Coleridge was the first of them. But ten years later the royal maintenance ceased abruptly on the accession of William IV, whose circumstances were too straitened to allow more than a 'Half-Crown-ation', and Coleridge felt the loss of income severely.

Dearest David, I adore *The Defeat of Pepsi-Cola*. It is brilliant, it is solid, it is a manual for young anarchists, it is as cunning as the Old Serpent, and only you could have written it. Are you sure it can't be published? Why don't you disguise Amaryllis as a literary agent and have her take it to the Higher Publicity Bureau of Pepsi-Cola, explaining that it is by one of Britain's most distinguished men of letters and just what they need, published with wide margins, etc., as a form of publicity which would win all hearts and black the eyes of all other soft-drink firms. She could use the word sophisticated.

Or they could issue it as a serial in the advertising pages of the *New Yorker* or some such. Nerissa could do the illustrations. The introductory heading could run – Pepsi-Cola Inc. does not need to praise its products. Today it proudly inaugurates The Newer Advertising.

You would make so much money and so much réclame that you would never again have to bother about being an Author in Residence or a lecturer.

And Pepsi-Cola Inc. would be as a strong tower to you. No Government, no Administration, would attack a Pepsi-Cola author. I can see it all working out a charm. Twenty per cent when it does, please. . . .

Here they are. It grieves me to the heart that Pepsi-Cola must die a virgin.★

With my love   Sylvia

Dearest David, . . . A slip of paper found in the letter-box of his apartment in New York by a friend of mine began:

While you were out your exterminator called.

My love   Sylvia

Dearest Sylvia, . . . I have just made friends with a local figure – a small greengrocer, beekeeper, agent for beehives, etc. I made friends with him at the Hunts Show, where I took second prize for

---

★ It was eventually published as *First 'Hippy' Revolution* with illustrations by
Nerissa by San Marcos Press, Cerillos, New Mexico, in 1970. David sent
Sylvia a copy at Christmas 1970, inscribed 'Sylvia Townsend Warner with love
from David who wrote this story drunk with dislike of Coke, Pepsi and Root
Beer'.

granulated honey. I ordered various oddments. When he delivered them a swarm had come out and settled on an apple tree.

'Oh, I'll buy them. Fine swarm and a beautiful bee, Italian.' He brushed them into his skep with a handful of twigs. 'They can sting, too.' He then began gathering a bunch of stinging nettles with his bare hands. 'I'm an old-fashioned beekeeper. I always put a bunch of nettles where they clustered to stop them going back. Bees don't like nettles.'

Coming back through the garden he saw my Grosse Blonde Paresseuse lettuces. 'I'll have half a dozen of them – pay you sixpence each. I'm a greengrocer when I'm not a beekeeper.'

His bill for the appliances was £5:12:0. 'What will you give me for the swarm?' He was a little disappointed. 'Thirty bob – and two bob for the lettuce. That makes a round figure.' He was a small round figure himself – a bit like H. G. Wells.

Well, much love   David

Angelica, like Ray, was found to have cancer of the breast, and went into St Mary's Hospital, Paddington, for an operation.

2 September 1967   *Hilton Hall*

Dearest Sylvia, I believe Angelica wrote you a letter about your biography of Tim. She was carried away by it, and it was so good her having that to read while she was in the hospital. I think and hope they have done what ought to have been done when the same thing happened to Ray.

She came here from the hospital for about a week and then went for a few days to Charleston and now has set off with Duncan and Nerissa driving to the cottage in France. I am afraid it will be very exhausting. I follow on the 15th. I am terribly hadden doune by my bees (though I love them). The trouble is so much honey – about two hundredweight of extracted honey and about sixty sections. Now the honey-flow is over they start robbing directly a hive is opened and they smell honey.

Michael has asked me to invent a title for the White/Garnett letters. I told him it was a pity I wasn't illegitimate in which event my name would have been Black and *The Black and White Letters* would have been a good title. However, last night a title came to me. What do you think?

Letters between a Wild and a Domesticated Gander.

A Record of the Friendship of T. H. White and David Garnett. 1936–1963.

William says nobody will understand it. But I think it sums us up. I thought of pairs of birds of different kinds – owls and goshawks – pelicans and geese. Then I realised we were birds of a feather but with opposing philosophies and habits.

Curious how summer changed into autumn on a single day. It would be awfully nice if we could meet. But I shall probably stay in France until the end of October. It is a good place to write, and I shall be alone all that month – if I find I can write I may stay there. Then the winter. It has been a good summer – until this thing of Angelica's cropped up. I went to Stratford on Avon and saw Amaryllis on Wednesday last. She is curiously close to me. Forgive this drivelling letter, but I'm tired.

Love from   David

5: ix: 1967   *Maiden Newton*

Dearest David, I think a hundred times better of my book if it was a comfort to Angelica in hospital. (She wrote to me about it, such a convincingly praising letter that I put it by against rainy days.)* I am so distressed for you both – for your present estate; because I have strong hopes that the future may turn to the better. Medical science has more sense in it now, more expedients and many more recoveries to its credit. I know of several among my friends, so no doubt do you. But one does not easily remember this at three a.m.; and the shock and anxiety must have been terrible for both of you – for you, mon pauvre chat échaudé, with the past called back, for Angelica, the guiltless caller-back of the past, beckoned into this present. Give her my love, my good wishes, my best hopes.

Damn your bees! I shall be thankful to think of you setting out on the 15th.

I think you have found the perfect title – but failed to recognise it. *Birds of a Feather.* You are by no means that domesticated gander you put on to be – nor was Tim so entirely feral as he sometimes assumed. This Sandford and Merton antithesis isn't true, a title implying it would be entirely misleading. Leave your readers to see the disparities for themselves; but don't set them off with a false idea.

I am delighted that the letters have settled into a book – and even begin to believe it.

Alyse Gregory once said to me: My heart puts up a godless prayer. That is exactly what mine is doing, my dear.

Love from   Sylvia

* It has nevertheless disappeared, like so many others.

Dearest David, I shall be spending next week-end with the Howards, so I hope to hear what title you finally settled on for the book of letters. It will be a rather haunted week-end.* I went to t'other Finborough, Mr Pettiward's Finborough, to strike a large gong during Tommy's play, *Tom-Tit-Tot*. Gongs are acoustically unfitted for outdoor theatricals. Like preachers, they need a nave. So after the first flat thud I changed my technique and rubbed it into a roar. Whether this would obtain with preachers –

I am thinking of writing an article for the *Times* Woman's Page, headed 'Are your house-plants house-trained?' I saw an alarming one in my dentist's antechamber. Long tenuous filaments grew out of the potted plant, with lesser plants at their tips, and these floated about the room seeking for someone to strike root in; some unsuspecting person absorbed in reading *Country Life* or the *Geographical Magazine* might have been a victim for life.

When we were driving home from Scotland I noticed 'LANGAR' on a signpost.† So we turned off on a visit of piety. It is a big handsome church, far too good for Theobald. The rectory would have been a distress to Christina. It is Georgian red-brick, large, square and worldly. Christina would have had doubts as to the possible salvation of a child conceived and born in such a building. Not a cusp, not an ogee about it.

One of the things we were driving back from was Caithness, from Wick onwards it is a completely prose landscape, a plain statement of being such and such a height above sea-level – not a great height, but unremittingly level and unbroken. It is intimidating, but if I had found it when I was twenty years younger I would have tried to settle in it.

I have just realised why. It is a sounding-board for the wind. I would like to have a letter from you. That is really the gist of this one.

Love from   Sylvia

Dearest Sylvia, Thank you so much for your trivial letter which cheered me up. Nerissa, who is a wonderful girl, drove Angelica and

---

* Michael and Pat Howard lived at Little Finborough Hall in Suffolk. Tommy had a friend, Roger Pettiward, whose uncle, Walter Terry, lived at the neighbouring Great Finborough.
† The Rector of Langar had been Thomas Butler, father of Samuel and original of Theobald Pontifex in *The Way of All Flesh*. His wife Fanny was likewise the original of Christina Pontifex.

Duncan back to England a fortnight ago. Angelica was very exhausted here but has snapped back into great vigour on her return. She is flying out to New York to join —— with whom she tells me she is in love. They met last January in New York, where she spent four or five days on the way to join me in Texas before our tour in Mexico. . . .

It is, I think, rather marvellous of Angelica to tackle this sort of thing so soon after her operation. I really do hope it goes well, but I'm afraid it won't – possibly a mere dream. . . .

My feelings are naturally much more selfish than they sound. The thing is that I want a settled, peaceful existence and haven't had it for some time. So I think a parting, probably a divorce, would be a good thing. . . . So if this goes well, it will be better. If it doesn't I'm afraid she will take it hard.

All I have done since I have been here is to write a play. It is terrible, but there are one or two jokes of a literary kind that you would appreciate. It is about incest and whether it's better to know the truth if it upsets people. At least that is what I meant it to be about, but I couldn't get down to my subject but splashed about on the surface. I now know how not to write plays. I return to England early in November after two or three days in Paris.

Very much love   David

23: x: 1967   *Maiden Newton*

Dearest David, It is a sad set-out, and I am sorry it has happened like this . . .

It seems to me that her flight to New York puts her among swallows, cuckoos, wild geese; and bears – if it is bears who will travel for miles to a salt-lick. I think she is extremely courageous, and I suspect she is almost entirely intuitive. If cancer is an accessory of ageing, of becoming inattentive to one's bodily life, an impetuous love-affair in a different climate might be the very post-operative treatment she needs – a renewal and a reversal. I wish her well with all my heart. . . .

I seem absurdly hopeful, perhaps. But as I have never been a gentleman in courtly society, les maux d'autrui never afford me the slightest gratification.

I am reading Michael Holroyd's first volume about Lytton Strachey. It is a drudging peformance. He has included everything he could and should, and some of the ingredients are marvellous. And it is like a plum-pudding with the brandy forgotten.

I am in two minds about incest, and the question of your play.* I

* Sylvia had, of course, made incest the theme of her story, 'A Love Match' (see above p. 83), which goes unmentioned on this occasion.

think people should have some elements of private life they keep dark, and that incest could well be one of them. But I also think it a very bad plan that law, morality and all the rest of it should compel them to keep it dark. And I don't see how this can be amended till the world has grown better manners. Perhaps your parents, your parents poor Tim envied you so much, never said to you: 'Don't point!' Perhaps you never did point. But it is sound advice and should be given more often and to all ages. In a society which didn't point, the truth about a case of incest would not be all that upsetting and presently not upsetting at all.

When you are back at Hilton I steadfastly purpose to write again as you may need a little distraction over and above planting broad beans and clearing dead leaves from the gutters.

Meanwhile I shall think of you with a great deal of love. Sylvia

I ought to say that your letter has made me very proud – its confidence, I mean.

24 October 1967　　　　　　　　　　　　　　*St Martin-de-Vers*

Dearest Sylvia, You will forgive me bombarding you with letters, but I cannot write my novel owing to a squirrel-cage condition, so I am reduced to writing to the people I love when I have nothing to say.

Just inside the door of this old posting house where they changed horses for the diligence for the pull up the hairpin bends to La Bastide-Murat, there is a built-in stove, covered with tiles, with three small iron grates let into it.

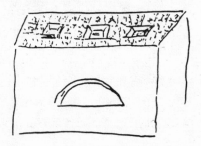

Nobody thought one could use it until Nerissa arrived this year and taught us how to. You fill one of the little grates with glowing charcoal embers from the fire, put your gridiron on top and proceed. I have just cooked an evening meal of lamb's liver, and eaten it. Prepared like this: Alternate lumps of liver with sage leaves plastered against and between them and onion – transfixed by *two* skewers. Thus:

127

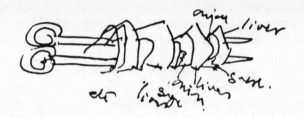

You use two skewers because if you use one the bits of liver slide round when you try to turn them over and cook the other side. The result is beyond the dreams of the greediest gastronome. The onion is half-raw. *That makes it infinitely better.* The flavour of sage is wonderful. (You have to pick the sage leaves off the liver before you eat it.)

This method of cooking is equally good with escalope de veau or beefsteak. Only you don't use the skewers. You oil them with olive oil and instead of sage leaves can use torn up bay leaves, which toast and impart their exquisite flavour to the meat.

Well, I have become so bitten with this method of cooking that I decided to build myself such a stove at Hilton Hall – possibly in the big fireplace. Then I realised that the little sunk grate of cast-iron wouldn't be easy to reproduce. So yesterday I went and asked the advice of an old ruffian at St Cernin who made me the table here and came chasing half round the canton looking for firedogs with me. He sent me to the Chiffonier. Not knowing French as well as I should, it did not occur to me that this was the rag-and-bone man, and I accosted a wealthy agent for tractors with the question, 'Êtes-vous le Chiffonier, Monsieur?' Which of course led to hearty handshakes. The Chiffonier himself was obviously a gipsy, rendered sedentary by owning a hundred tons of scrap iron. His wife was a bold girl with elflocks. I began to explain, and of course at the first word he understood, and led me through mazes of fire-backs and wrecked motor-cars and rusted-away sewing-machines to where he produced three charcoal braziers – portable – perfect in all respects.

But deeper than I've drawn them.

I bought two and went back today for the third; five francs each for the first two and four francs for the third – a bit cheaper than an electric grill – and the flavour of the charcoal makes all the difference.

Well, will you come and eat a meal off one of them? I forgot to say that they grill mackerel to perfection. In fact they can probably do all sorts of cooking I haven't thought of. Obviously muffins and crumpets. Probably you think this letter unduly occupied with food. So let me tell you about last Sunday. For the first time I was asked to have lunch with M. et Mme Vinges, our nearest neighbours and closest friends in the village.

M. Vinges is a retired roadman of about my age, living on his foreman's pension. His wife is exquisite – always a trifle regretful and retreating. She takes one's hand and presses it between both of hers. They look after this house when we are away and have the use of a quarter-acre field of lucerne in exchange. On arrival I found a granddaughter and her husband and three well-behaved little brats had dropped in unexpectedly. The granddaughter was in a mini-skirt – very smart and very pretty with big dark eyes – the husband (a mechanic in Toulouse) also terrifically smart with black almond eyes and side-whiskers. We drank sweet port and they went off.

Menu
Bouillon de boeuf with vermicelli.
Ending with the ceremony of the *chabrot*, i.e. pouring half a glass of red wine into the last few spoonfuls of soup, then tipping the soup-plate up and drinking it. *Very good. Try it.*
Hors d'oeuvres. – Paté de Canard truffé.
(bought at vast expense)
Tomato salad, salami.
Green french beans boiled and fried in butter.
Boiled beef.
Roast poulet-de-grain with green olives in a delicious caper sauce.
Cheese. Cherry cake. Fruit salad of oranges and bananas. Coffee with brandy.

Conversation was as good as the meal. Really it was wonderful. Vinges was taken from school before he could read and write to be a shepherd boy, but taught himself and then taught himself arithmetic. He was a prisoner of war in 1918. He has a large family, who have all done well. One son got over the Pyrenees in 1940, was starving in a Spanish prison, but was swopped by the Spanish to the British for food – spent two or three years in Glasgow and came back with the Free French.

Plenty of goodwill there.

Angelica is in New York, and I don't suppose I shall hear how things have gone with her until I get back to England on Guy Fawkes' Day.

Apart from the horror of telling people like the Vinges that we are divorced, I am really happy, particularly if she is. But, as I say, the squirrel-cage folly persists – round and round and over and over, knowing that even if there were anything to do I wouldn't want to do it.

Well, forgive me for writing a Tim White letter to you.

Very much love   David

On the back of the envelope:

Just heard from Angelica that all has gone well and she is very happy in New York with ——.

29: x: 1967   *Maiden Newton*

Dearest David, The flash on the back of your envelope is one of the best placed sentences you have ever written – and I think of how you must have enjoyed putting it there. I am so glad that Angelica's happiness should have arrived with such promptitude, with no draughty delays blowing cold on her project. It would seem that your wife has only to leave you for another for me to begin to esteem her. But esteem her I do; though I deplore her taste.

You must feel infinitely relieved. A stretched-out solicitude is torment, and all to no purpose. One can't believe in its efficacy oneself nor expect its object to believe in it either. A boot thrown across a room conveys concern far more convincingly than the most genuine, most anxious solicitude hovering round someone who isn't there and is incalculable by being absent.

I suppose there was a halcyon ten minutes when the squirrel-cage stopped dead; and then, I suppose, it went into reverse. I speak from experience of my own squirrel-cages. Perhaps you have more control over yours. But by the time you are reading this (for I can't catch you at the Ancienne Auberge before you leave for Paris) I hope you will be safely out of it, giving yourself a lick and a shake and feeling as happy as Ulysses under your roof of slates with fine Parliamentarian rockets going up all round. How lovely they must look falling through your elm trees.

Yes, indeed. I look forward to your feats with your grill-boxes. Pigeon spatchcocked would go well, I imagine, perhaps with a little fumigation of juniper berries. I admired the menu of the répas d'honneur those charming people gave you. It was so well assembled, with the one sauce coming just where it was needed to corroborate the hors d'oeuvres.

I must take back some of my injurious remarks about that life of Lytton Strachey. I still think the opening drudges, but it improves towards the end, and I look forward to the second volume – where I hope there will be fewer sisters. What a hideous lot to be accompanied wherever he went by a sister. But did he rather like it?

Have you ever been proscribed for indecency? I have. A mild woman who lives nearby and depends for books on the Dorset County Library asked, several times, for my last book of short stories. Her last application was pettish, and came back stamped: Not acceptable. I suppose it is the incest story, though it could as well be several of the others. The book is dedicated to you, remember. I'm afraid you are now a marked man.

I wish you a happy unregenerate winter selfishly devoted to writing your novel.

With my love   Sylvia

29 October 1967   [St Martin-de-Vers]
Dearest Sylvia, . . . I wrote a poem this afternoon, after saying goodbye to the Vinges who came in, and as I sent you an earlier poem in French, I thought I had better send you my second effort. I fear there are grammatical mistakes. Angelica was always able to correct my grammar. I could enlarge her vocabulary.

Fols is intentionally archaic. But what the hell. . . .

Very much love   David

Le Défi

Heureux d'avoir vécu dans la vieille auberge
Je pars, comme d'habitude à cette saison – mais cette fois pour
      toujours,
Heureux, mais fier, d'avoir acheté la vieille maison,
Solidement construite, les pierres mêmes se fendaient,
Les poutres tombaient en poudre
Chevrons vermoulus, tuiles brisées,
Avant de l'habiter notre maison était en ruines.

Sans soucis, cerveaux pleins de projets
Fols d'imaginer une vie nouvelle en France
Nous cherchions les châteaux imaginaires partout.
Elle m'a abandonnée.
Sans le savoir je tombe en poudre. Mais heureux.

Heureux avec les souvenirs d'une vie impossible à réaliser.
Je me moque de la poudre qui me tombe sur la tête.
Je retiens mes illusions.

29 octobre 1967

7: xi: 1967   *Maiden Newton*

Dearest David, Here is a copy of the book you have been so fostering to. Tim did me a great service when he became a go-between between us.

Yesterday I got a letter from a Canon of Norwich Cathedral who had seen a Cape announcement. He told me that when he met Tim during the Stowe period Tim said how dearly he would like to be a country parson. Too late for me, but perhaps you can use it?

I was pleased with the book till I opened it on p. 166 and saw that the printer in a little hiccup all his own had inserted that nonsensical hyphen. I would not have minded if it had not been hiccupped into a sentence about Ray. Now I am sullen about the whole book.

I hope you found your bees well. It has been discouraging weather for any right-minded bees.

With my love   Sylvia

10 December 1967   *Hilton Hall*

Dearest Sylvia, I have been alone here since Thursday, as William and Nerissa went up to Ridley Stokoe and are probably snowed up there in the hut. However, they like that sort of thing and get on well together. (Both the twins adore William.) I went out today to post letters and met the Hobsons, who came back with me for drinks. And tomorrow I am setting off driving through the snow to visit Quentin Bell and his wife and family near Lewes and then going on to Charleston to see Duncan. I hope I get there. Quentin is now a bearded Professor of Art at Sussex University with three children [and] a wife who is the daughter of one of the Oliviers (my oldest friends). Quentin is a Victorian paterfamilias with anxious eyes.

I got a very nice letter from Angelica this morning which cheered me up, and I wrote a very nice letter back to her. It is so easy to be grudging or surly. The thing is, in my situation, one runs through a whole gamut of emotions. If you ask: 'What do you really feel?' no truthful answer is possible because all possible emotions are latent – and they succeed each other. So it is very important to write when one's emotions are loving and friendly – which they always are after

132

getting a letter from her. It is when one hasn't been in touch that one begins to feel like a toad sweating under its stone. By the way, have you seen a toad or a frog lately? Frogs are extinct here, and I greatly fear toads are also. I love them both. Alas.

A lively and pretty American young woman appeared the other day. She is discovering the most fascinating things about Peacock's daughter Mary, who married Meredith and is the subject of *Modern Love*. (Some of the sonnets are wonderful.) The Victorian legend is that she ran away with Henry Wallis, a painter, then left him and returned from Italy broken in health and that Meredith and Peacock refused ever to see her again. This is true of Meredith. But she came back with child by Wallis (it was born in April 1858) and saw Peacock almost every day. Wallis painted Peacock's portrait in 1858 (when Mary was pregnant or after the child was born). She died unexpectedly and is buried in the village where Wallis was living, so presumably she was living with him when she died – Peacock was completely heartbroken. She is the model of all Meredith's emancipated women – very intelligent, tall, nervous and attractive. You can just see the horrible Victorians inventing her lonely outcast death – the Wages of Sin. Wallis brought up the boy as his own son (or daughter) – I am not sure of the sex.

I believed the legend and could never reconcile such behaviour with Peacock's character. It is a relief to know it wasn't true. I haven't done a stroke of work since Angelica left in September. However, I think I shall start in the New Year. Nerissa is going to spend Christmas here. The others plan to go to Duke Mary's and Fan to Skye. A Merry Christmas and a Happy New Year. Your book is being read and admired by all my friends.

Love from   David

21: xii: 1967   *Maiden Newton*

Dearest David, Thank you for telling me about Peacock. It is a comfort to learn that he behaved kindly and sensibly and did nothing Shelley's ghost could have taken exception to. But while I was rejoicing in this it crossed my mind that it is a poor state of things when one has to be relieved because someone behaved with common humanity.

When I was young *Modern Love* was a prig's pasture. It was explained almost with diagrams showing A, B and C. I thought, still think, some of the sonnets very fine; and improved by being sixteen-liners with more play. But it is what Mr Collins called Nature Subjects I remember best; except for a dreadful line I have never been able to shake out of my ears: My feet were nourished on

133 *Wallis painted Death of Chatterton with Geo. Meredith as model*

her breasts all night. Mid-Victorian sexuality is hard to take. I suppose marriage exacerbated it. I can't associate Meredith's feet with Skittles. And when it's *The Angel in the House*, and coy, it's worse. Do you remember how the gentleman filled Mrs Patmore's fair large ears with joy by asking 'Is this your little boy?' as if that were all to her?

You ask if I have seen a toad or a frog lately? We have plenty of frogs, they skip about in the strawberry bed. It is some time since I saw a toad. A number of toads are run over because they hunt insects on the road – as hedgehogs do. I love and venerate toads. I am sure Socrates had eyes like a toad. . . .

Here is a kitchen improvement, in return for Peacock. For roasting or basting a chicken, render down your fat or butter with cider: about a third cider. Let it come together slowly, till the smell of cider and the smell of fat are as one. This will enliven even a frozen chicken. . . .

I wish you a carefree New Year.

With my love   Sylvia

1968

For Christmas Sylvia had sent David a copy of *Two Conversation Pieces*, a booklet she had had printed with two of her stories about the misadventures of a family called Finch.

1 January 1968   *Hilton Hall*

Dearest Sylvia, A Happy New Year. You can hardly hope to produce another book as good and as universally appreciated as the life of T.H.W. but I am sure everything you do will be delightful. I must thank you for the Finches. I feel as though I had lived with them all my life – though perhaps I am glad I haven't. But I would give a lot to know Mrs Finch. 'As for Mr Finch – I want nothing about his character – it is my own,' as Tim wrote about someone rather different.*

I have spent a very – indeed unusually – happy Christmas and end of the year. Amaryllis, Henrietta and Nerissa were here with William and me. Fan had gone with her lover to camp in Skye. Richard and Jane and their boys had Christmas dinner with us. And on Boxing Day Rosemary Peto and Renée Fedden, both of whom I am very fond of, came to lunch with Renée's daughter Katharine . . .

Yesterday we found crumbs and grapestones on the breakfast table, and some time later Fan and —— appeared from the drawing-room, where they had gone to sleep after arriving at three a.m., having driven from Glencoe, where they had been camping. They had hot baths and then played music or sang without pausing, except for meals, until six, when they set off for Fittleworth in West Sussex, where they live in a wood. The energy of the young astounds me . . .

Ben Richards also arrived for two nights and left this morning. Now having washed up everything I have to face the New Year with a feeling that life is so fascinating that I never want to stop watching it. I must stop now to make a curry with that terribly tough leg of lamb-bone.

All my love   David

* Sir Walter Raleigh!

Dearest David, I have just heard, via the Powys grapevine, that
Gamel Woolsey★ is dead. Probably you know this already – a hale
old age is like being an artichoke, stripped leaf by leaf.

Our end of the grapevine is Lucy, the youngest daughter. She is
like a threadpaper Theodore to look at. She is diffident, nervous,
timid, full of fears and apprehensions. But whereas Theodore's
fears were rooted in him, Lucy's fears are floating and dart through
her like minnows. She still lives at Mappowder, where she settled
during Theodore's last days and flits for long country walks where
he paced. She is full of Powys piety and quirks ('eggs do not agree
with us'), the bouquet is unmistakable, but with much less body.
This may be because she married when she was a girl and the early
bottling took her off the lees. . . .

I enjoyed your letter about the crumbs and the grapeskins on the
breakfast table. Please write again. I have had influenza . . . not
badly at all but enforced by antibiotics which don't agree with me;
and I need *Pleasure*.

With my love   Sylvia

27 January 1968   *Hilton Hall*

Dearest Sylvia, Pleasure! Well, one gets it sometimes – I get it
unexpectedly – more, alas, from places than people. However, last
week I was driven down to Oxford by Rosemary Peto (ex-wife of
that neighbour of yours, Mr Victor Montagu of Mapperton) and
we took Dr Enid Starkie and Mrs Lane out to dinner and then
stayed at Mrs Lane's for the night. Do you know Enid Starkie? She
is an Irishwoman, about sixty-five or so, writes about Rimbaud and
Flaubert (a good book just out). She has that Irish vivacity and
determination to dominate the conversation. She always used to
dress in red, but since she has been given the Légion d'Honneur, she
has to wear a blue jacket to show it up. She never stopped blowing
her own trumpet. Hearing about her honorary degrees was quite
entertaining.

However, I quite lost my head to Mrs Lane, née Miriam
Rothschild. She is a dominating matriarch with lots of children and
adopted children, dogs, cats, bush babies and birds reared after
falling out of the nest. She had found a snared fox-vixen the
previous day, her son had wrapped it in his jacket, carried it home,

★ For Gamel Woolsey, see above p. 51. Sylvia's informant, Lucy Amelia
Powys, was the youngest of Theodore's sisters, born in 1890 and married to
Hounsell Penny in 1911.

cut off the snare and let it go, getting bitten in the process. She is also a scientist and has recently made discoveries about the rabbit flea which I find fascinating (I spare you the facts, which you might find sordid or unpleasant). Also she flattered me very skilfully about my books, so perhaps that explains it. Next morning Rosie drove me back by lovely by-ways as far as Windsor and then by the usual motorway to London. And it was extraordinary to see places still as beautiful as fifty years ago.

I know about Gamel's death. Gerald writes a lot to Frances Partridge. Her dying had gone on so long – cancer – that one had got to feel she never would actually die. It must have been ghastly, Honor Tracy, who adored Gamel, and Gerald getting on each other's nerves and fighting over her living corpse.

I have escaped the influenza but had a bad cold which I stifled with capsules. Apart from my visit to Oxford, I lead a quiet life with William; most of my energies going into preparing meals, reading books, weeding the garden (which unfortunately brings on spasms of heartburn owing to bending down). My chief pleasure is in my daughters – particularly Nerissa – a marvellous creature. Amaryllis is so preoccupied with her future and acting, Fan with blowing the horn and love, and Henrietta lives a social flower-child life into which I dare not pry. But they are all most affectionate and all beautiful . . .

Very much love   David

8: ii: 1968   *Maiden Newton*
Dearest David, . . . please tell me those sordid, unpleasant facts about rabbit fleas. Poor rabbits! Their characters are always being impugned. Do you remember the old gentleman on Hampstead Heath who assured Tommy that all rabbits were syphilitic? . . .

You need not tell me that Nerissa is a marvellous creature. I saw it at a glance. I have never met anyone else so completely composed by Purcell.

The only time I met Enid Starkie – a long while ago – she wore a large floppy tam and was bloodcurdlingly like Rimbaud. Perhaps she is one of those people – like White assuming Hadrian – who resemble from piety. Was she looking like Flaubert when you saw her?

It is viperishly cold here. Probably colder with you. How did Mme de Staël with no protection between a turban and high girdle endure it? Horrid woman! I don't really mind her sufferings.

With my love   Sylvia

Dearest David, . . . Today my hairdresser said to me: And do you realise that on the longest day it will be dark at ten in the morning? He is an intellectual from the Midlands, it would not do to contradict him, so I shuddered appreciatively. He attributed all our misfortunes to de Gaulle – who I am old-fashioned enough to esteem. What godlike good fortune, for instance, to be shot at during that Te Deum in Notre Dame! That sort of thing does not happen to every public figure – and to get away with it.

The Howards were here a couple of days ago, and Michael told me that the White/Garnett letters are safe in proof. He mentioned it with a certain modest awe; as if he had not expected to land that salmon. Dear salmon, I am very glad you are landed; twice glad as I hope you will now be writing another book, perhaps the fourth volume of your autobiography.

With my love   Sylvia

Pericles has walked all over this letter but doesn't apologise for the paw-marks.

[ca 29 February 1968]   *Hilton Hall*

Dearest Sylvia, Did I tell you that I nearly wrote to *The Times* to say: 'I am backing Britain by staying an extra hour in bed and invite others to join me'?

However I thought at seventy-six, the joke would be on me.

I don't *altogether* esteem De Gaulle. I feel rather as I did about our half-Siamese farm cat Kidman, who rewarded the hand that fed him with serious bites. Fan still has a deep dimple on the wrist from one of his canines. We *respected* Kidman.

I rather admire Madame de Gaulle. Shortly after the General and Madame arrived in England, Michel St Denis was invited to dinner – a meal which lasted a long time as the General embarked on a long and tragic history of the Decline and Fall of France.

When the meal ended Madame rose and retired, saying gracefully:

'Messieurs, je vous laisse à vos petites affaires.'

I have been leading a social life, which has the immense merit of keeping me so busy that I have no time to knock my head against the wall. . . .

Sylvia had asked David for works on German literature, and he replied:

I enclose a list of prescribed reading for you. . . .

This list emanates from the German Department, University

College, *via* a Mrs Howells, who is writing a thesis on Gothic novels of horror in which she maintains that the English novelists of the 1800 period were more influenced by Shakespeare, Marlowe, Webster, etc., than by German contemporaries.

She identified the play that Mr Flosky receives by post while staying at Nightmare Abbey. He almost quotes Coleridge's review of it in *Biographia Literaria*. The author was Maturin.

Love from   David

3: iii: 1968   *Maiden Newton*

Dearest David, Thank you for the list of prescribed reading; and for the news that Mr Flosky's play has been tracked down. Very soon we shall know all about all the novels Miss Languish's Betty fetched from the Lending Library, and the plays Caroline Bauer acted in before she went to be comfort to Prince Leopold, and needed so much strong black coffee to sustain her in that rôle.

Fuseli, too. About a twelvemonth ago I had a letter from a lady in America who is writing a book to give him his long-last due. I'm afraid she is rather silly. Why she wrote to me was because she had read Titus's opinion of him in *Lolly Willowes*, took it au pied de la lettre as mine, and asked for more lights. A difficult letter to reply to. I advised her to go to Switzerland, where he is now ardently collected by the Swiss Government – the oils, not just the drawings.

Talking of slighted works of art, have you ever been in the underground of the Tate? A long time ago I lent the Tate a small William Callow, and in 1964 I felt it my duty to see how it was getting on. So I wrote to the Curator and was given an appointment. There was a proper person, who took me down in a lift, and led me through this extraordinary graveyard, crammed with marble nudes wrapped in sheets of cellophane, great furry seascapes and lowering landscapes, portraits of pop-eyed children, blessed damozels, Derby winners; and paused in front of a very incompetent late Victorian nymph clutching some shreds of muslin and made entirely of vinolia soap, saying, This, I think, is yours. There was a moment of black panic when I thought I should find myself obliged to make her mine. But in the end my William Callow was found in excellent condition, and quietly on show.

If you should ever feel inclined for a little Mortality, behold and fear, do go to the Tate underground.

I backed Britain by getting in several gallon tins of olive oil. Patriotism begins at home.

With my love   Sylvia

Dearest David, Forgive me for writing a distressing letter. It is my old habit of relying on your advice.

Valentine was told yesterday that she may have a carcinoma in her breast. It cannot be determined till there is a biopsy. Angelica seems to have made a very good recovery. Will you please tell me what was done in her case, and if she had post-operational radium treatment? The surgeon whom Valentine consulted looks on radium treatment as a matter of course. She is averse to it. So am I. I have seen so many instances of its backlash.

Forgive me for raking up old sorrows.

With love   Sylvia

8 March 1968   *Hilton Hall*

Dearest Sylvia, I'm so sorry. Angelica had the whole breast removed. They then made an examination (histological) of the tissues they had removed and decided on the strength of that on not having radium treatment.

They then – a fortnight after the operation – had a second operation removing the ovaries. As Valentine is much older than Angelica (forty-nine) there may not be . . . any reason for the ovary removal.

She had a room in St Mary's Hospital, Paddington, where everything but the food was good.

It is much too soon to tell whether it will recur with Angelica or not. It often doesn't for a number of years, but I believe there are fewer recurrences nowadays than in the thirties when Ray had it.

Very much love to you both.   David

Dearest David, Michael sent me an advance copy of *The White/ Garnett Letters*. It came this morning. I had the astonishment and delight of finding your dedication.* I pinch myself, but it is still true. Thank you very much, my dear.

And thank you for your letter. It was as supporting as I knew it would be. Various people who had to be told have replied with instances of theirs who have had a breast amputated and have never been so happy and thriving as they are now. Such unanimity, such a

* 'To Sylvia Townsend Warner who in her biography has given us the real man'.

dawn-chorus, is bloodcurdling. You can judge how gratefully I read your plain statement.

Very much love   Sylvia

Dearest David, While Valentine was in Guy's Hospital (the surgeon said he was well satisfied with the operation) I prowled about Southwark Cathedral. And there I found something I believe you would be interested by. At the east end of the north aisle is a book labelled Petitions (it lies on a slab or a tomb or some such). And the petitions make the queerest reading. They are mainly by children or old people, people of the neighbourhood, I would guess. They are in the nature of Complaints or Suggestions to the Management – the Management being God. They are so practical, so irreligious, that I had the sensation that Defoe was reading over my shoulder and making notes for his own purposes. Except for one or two gentry aspersions on the Church of England by Anglo-Cats or Cats *pur sang*, I saw nothing that was not a straightforward expression of a straightforward wish.

Do go and read this. It is so very odd and plain and timeless.

There is also a very enjoyable effigy of Lionel Lockyer with an epitaph stating that he would always be remembered for his virtues and HIS PILLS.

You know everything. What were Lockyer's pills for?*

I have seen quantities of frog-spawn – I remember you were concerned about the frog population. And is the cow parsley as superb in Hunts as it is here? I have never known it in such a toss and foam of splendour.

With my love   Sylvia

I answer all my fan letters from the USA telling them how much they will enjoy *The White / Garnett Letters*.

Dearest Sylvia, I am so relieved to hear all has gone well with Valentine's operation. You must have had a hellish time wandering around Southwark. It is the one marvellous thing that Hemingway wrote in *Farewell to Arms* – wandering around while the person one loves is in hospital, in danger. One is being flayed alive without

---

* Lionel Lockyer (1600?–1672) was the originator of Lockyer's Universal Pills or Pilulae Radiis Solis Extractae, which he prescribed for everything from Fits of the Mother to the Pox.

realising it. Well, I don't know about Lockyer's Pills, although a faint faint voice seems to tell me that there is a reference to them in Russian literature – e.g. Gogol. We must find out. I should quite like to enter my own suggestions to the Almighty if I thought he looked through the Southwark Cathedral volume frequently.

My life has been rather social lately: and also complicated by the presence of Chuck Sachs, who is trying to put on a screen version of *Aspects of Love* – raising money, etc., beguiling actors. He is at all events paying me enough to live on for six months.

Angelica has returned to England, and I have seen her twice. Her situation is not very happy . . . Oddly enough it no longer hurts me to see her. I simply enjoy being in her company. . . . But I can't help. To make up for this she is wildly generous – a great blessing as nothing is more stupid than quarrels about pillow cases.

She seems to think that by resigning her claims on everything, she can somehow make up for the situation. I am no longer in love with her, but I would do anything to make her happy – only that is impossible, and I am the person least able to attempt consolation, as all my motives are suspect. . . .

Then I have been leading a social life – and have made a conquest of a whole family – mother and two lovely daughters. I send you my warmest love, dearest Sylvia. Have I sent you a copy of *White/Garnett Letters*? I can't remember. Please tell me.

Love and very much of it. David

[15 June 1968] *Hilton Hall*

Dearest Sylvia, . . . There was an agreeable review in the *Guardian* yesterday. The writer said that in his last stage Tim was more like Trimalchio than Thoreau.

I have been invited to go to Corfu and have accepted. I hope you don't think me wrong.

My hostess is a sworn enemy of the Colonels. I shall be away for July.

Angelica is back in London, but I don't know what her plans may be. My wretched bees swarm all the time, it was the bitter cold of May which prevented me rearranging the combs on the Snelgrove system. . . .

Much love David

18: vi: 1968 *[c/o Margaret Manisty, Morleys,] Mayfield*

Dearest David, I shan't be able to tell you if you sent me a copy of your book until I go home next week. People unfailingly forward bills, circulars and specimen copies of *The Canadian Dog World* – but not so, parcels.

Your letter did reach me. And I have been grateful ever since for your summary of 'being flayed alive without realising it'. Now that we have a reasonable prospect of the end of the wood I am beginning to feel the result of that process. I am a vacuum with a few remaining lumps of fortitude knocking about against my ribs.

I hope the *Aspects of Love* film will come to something. It could make a very good film, if the producer gets the swirl of the book. Indeed, the swirl, the current of events, *could* be better conveyed in a film medium, where the unlooker is carried where a reader makes *on* his way. Anyhow, six months far niente is a cosy thought. . . .

We are still in Mayfield while Valentine finishes off her radio-therapy. Five minutes a day; and it is astonishing how five minutes can eat the heart out of twenty-four hours. Mayfield is a riot of good taste. However, in the alleyway of its old oak-timbered hotel is a notice reading

LADIES
GENTLEMEN AROUND CORNER.

This props my mind. And last week I learned that I am now an Elected Daughter of Mark Twain.

With my love always   Sylvia

20: vi: 1968   *Mayfield*

Dearest David, Your present of *The White/Garnett Letters* was sent on to me today – thank God. Thank God not that the copy was, etc., but that it exists to be sent. I remember my uneasiness when you declared you would not do the book.

My first act was to look at the dedication page to see if it were still there.

I liked the *Telegraph* review which said White was Philoctetes. He wasn't; but it is a rather noble waving feather, and I imagine he would have stuck it in his cap with satisfaction.

I hope you will have a happy holiday in Corfu, enjoying scandals about the Colonels and forgetting your wicked bees.

My love, very dear David   Sylvia

13 August 1968   *Hilton Hall*

Dearest Sylvia, I have just read your contribution to the Nancy Cunard book.* I never guessed that you knew her and protected

---

* *Nancy Cunard: Brave Poet, Indomitable Rebel 1896–1965* edited by Hugh Ford (1968).

her. My knowledge, as you can see, was intermittent and superficial – perhaps fortunately.

How are you and Valentine?

I have returned ten days ago from a month's holiday in Corfu, to
which I was invited by a rich woman who seems to like me and
fascinates me. As a result I have got burned brown in patches, have
lost seven pounds weight, have swum more than I have done for
years – once in a really rough sea – and temporarily became at least
twenty years younger. Since returned to England I have relapsed,
alas, into the old dodderer. Perhaps because I was alone here for a
week watching the puddles fill fuller. William is now back, and I
have an excuse for cooking meals. . . .

My beloved daughters are scattered about: all with their agonies
and problems.

I wrote this just now:

> We are seldom face to face. But he is always there,
> Skulking behind every truck and car,
> Gaining ground with each day that passes.
> But he is no longer an enemy: no longer feared,
> But a protector. He will announce, and no one can gainsay
>   him:
> 'Whatever David has left undone: Hearts unreconciled,
> Books unwritten, children left to fend for themselves,
> All that is over. Now the weeds
> Can grow freely: the Dovehouse crumble.
> Those that needed him must look elsewhere,
> While all goes on in its spinning, million might.'
> And with his quaint humour he'll announce:
> 'What's his name? That about to be forgotten fellow
> Was not unique – only a few months or years
> Ahead' – and grudgingly admit: 'Yes. He loved life,
> Which goes on much the same, in spite of me.
> What he felt millions of other men have felt,
> And millions unborn will feel.'

I don't know why, my dear, I should inflict these clichés upon
you. Actually I feel like a lion – but one which resents getting wet.

Love to you both   David

17: viii: 1968   *Maiden Newton*
Dearest David, Selfishly, I am pleased to know you are back.
The knowledge somehow secures my mind – though you need not

144

fear you will find me on your step weeping bitterly with only one shoe.

But how miserable to come home feeling like a lion to a cold kitchen and a soused garden and the obligations you quitted still dangling. . . .

I was pleased to meet you in the Nancy Cunard book. It is a beautiful phrase about her eyes.★ I loved Nancy and esteemed her. She had no vulgar faults: did not backbite, bear grudges, whine or flirt. Once or twice she brought some queer followers down here with her, but they were always devoured with dignity and candour. You have got a word wrong. We didn't *protect* her (I think she was unprotectable). If anything, she protected us, saved us from the mental slovenliness of provincial thinking in wartime, aerated us, scratched the mildew off our manners. And she had another rare merit. She parted so cleanly. Went off like a swallow.

I think she must have been George Moore's child. She had a particular easy ceremoniousness with her village neighbours at Lamothe which was *A Story-Teller's Holiday* to the life. I don't think that came to her from Leicestershire or from the U.S.

Valentine is still hampered by post-operational strains and subsidences but people assure me she looks much better – and, in flashes, she is. The cats are catnip to her. We have a stair-carpet, wonderful in our eyes because it is a very handsome stair-carpet (like clipped sheepskin), and because we have never had a stair-carpet before. Both cats think it was installed for them to sharpen their claws on. Shooting at them with a water-pistol is a good deterrent, but one cannot spend one's life lurking on a stair-head with a water-pistol. So today she is trying a new expedient, and the stairs are trimmed with discommoding objects: a hammer, a torch, a tin of boiled sweets, an alarm clock, a pair of candlesticks, etc. To us, of course, the reason for this is perfectly clear.

How lovely to have swum in a stormy sea! I would envy you to the point of hatred if I had not in this last fortnight written a stormy story – the first time I have been able to write since the New Year. It was a dreadful interim. I thought I would never want to write again.

With my love   Sylvia

Now you have got all this fine lined paper† to write a poem on, please do. I like your poems.

★ 'the long eyes like glimpses of the sea, and the voice like seagulls'.
† Unused at the end of Sylvia's letter.

145

Dearest Sylvia, . . . Your cats are bold indeed. I bought a reindeer's skin (a beautiful thing, but I don't know what to do with it), and our cats are frightened of it. But I suppose they don't realise your stair-carpet was once a flock of sheep. . . .

I am afraid the poem I enclosed in my last letter is the only one I have written since I wrote a couple of French ones last October. But if I write more I will send them you. You and the wastepaper basket share them between you.

I have cheered up because Nerissa came for the week-end. She is going out to St Martin in about a week, planning to live there alone. I shall go out about three weeks later and spend a fornight there, and I hope my friend . . . with whom I stayed in Corfu and Italy, will pick [me up] there and drive me home.

She is living in a house in Tuscany with her married daughter, son-in-law, three unmarried daughters, a boy-friend of one and a girl-friend of another, and she complained of loneliness.

I can imagine what she means, but I don't mind loneliness – only emptiness. And at the moment I am luckily not feeling empty, but full of warmth and excitement.

But I could talk about this better than write about it.

I read a review of a Penguin Heine – German with prose translation beneath each poem – which quoted some of Heine's sayings:

> 'If thy eye offend thee pluck it out.
> If thy hand offend thee cut it off.
> If thy brain offend thee
> Join the Catholic Church.'

Rather apt for the times.

Love to Valentine (don't tell her, but I am a little shocked by the water-pistol).

Love from   David

PS. Do you know that Henry James once killed a cat in his garden in Rye?

Dearest David, . . . Titus grows lovelier, bolder and more loving every day, and thinks nothing of the water-pistol. It is a very mild water-pistol. We had a much larger one once, black and perfectly lifelike. This was got to deter our poodle from barking our heads off. One calm summer's afternoon I heard her barking on the doorstep beyond my endurance. I took the water-pistol and opened the door silently and stealthily. She was barking at the new parson who had come on a conjectural visit. I rearranged my expression and invited him in. But as I was brought up on the axiom, Never explain, never apologise, my lips were fastened. We meet from time to time in the post-office.

I can tell you what to do with your reindeer's skin: You can polish leather with it – boots and bookbindings. The skin of any deer is supposed to be sovereign for this, but no doubt a reindeer skin would be better because an animal in a cold climate would secrete a better oil in its bones.

I can now die happy having told you something you didn't know. But I won't do it yet if I can possibly avoid it. . . ?

I suppose you are now at St Martin. Your kind neighbour there will be pleased to see you back. You will be reading the local paper, I hope. Can you understand, at once, those contracted advertisements with no vowels? That's the test. I can't, not on and on.

I have harvested my garlic – a splendid crop. I have made rowan jelly, from which proceeds grouse – a promising grouse casserole simmers in the kitchen. Red Admirals loiter about the garden, and a mole tunnelling under a path obligingly sends up heaps of the best potting earth. I wish it were always September. Even apart from Keats this is the time of year I am happiest in – though I only discovered why this very morning. Spring is rather a bitch. It insists on being waited for, keeps one at a stretch, stings like a young nettle. Autumn just arrives, and embraces, no fuss, no proclamation. It is like being looked at by Ray.

Do you know that one can now smell the sweet peas which Keats smelled? A seedsman called Unwin has rescued them, seeds from unprogressive gardens, from Latin America and Provence and Mexico. The stems have a thousand tendrils, the flowers are small, sharp-coloured like hundreds and thousands, and the scent is ravishing. Half-a-dozen flower-heads will scent a room. And as no one has improved them they are extremely hardy and flower incessantly.

I hope you are very happy in your French home.

Love from   Sylvia

4: xii: 1968   *Maiden Newton*

Dearest David,

No, dear. I won't write eight hundred words on Tim for the *D.N.B.* (How pleased he'd be to know he'd made it.) Nor, I hope, will you. You charm as appealingly as a lapwing, and all the time

147

you are protecting your own nest. I am delighted you have a nest. I hope you will have a happy winter writing, and that it will extend into a happy spring and summer. So write to Mr Williams and tell him you won't, and add that you have consulted me and that I won't either. The English-speaking world is full of deserving young men panting to write for the *D.N.B.* supplement. One should give the young a chance. It might be the foundation of a career. Ten pounds, however, is mingy.★

I wish Nerissa joy of her kittens. Are they hard or soft tabbies, silk or tweed? Pericles has just brought in a moorhen. It was unharmed and went away swearing like a Christian.

We were in Wales in October, Snowdonia. I fell in love with slate pavements and doorsteps. Dolgelly in rain was sleek as caviare. We stayed for a while at Portmeirion for a little luxury, and the first thing we saw was Clough Williams-Ellis wearing bright yellow stockings and *beautiful* breeches, all majesty and agility.

Here are the Keats sweet peas and some poems.

With my love   Sylvia

Please go on writing.

The poems that Sylvia sent David were a copy of her privately printed *King Duffus and Other Poems*. In his next letter he refers to her poem about King Duffus, who was bewitched and exclaimed:

> I sat among poets and philosophers,
> Carving fat bacon for the mother of Christ;
> Sometimes we sang, sometimes we conversed.
>
> Why did you summon me back from the midst of that
>   meal
> To a vexed kingdom and a smoky hall?
> Could I not stay at least until dewfall?

14 December 1968   *Hilton Hall*

Dearest Sylvia

Thank you very much for *King Duffus*. If Tim was Sir Walter, I am King Duffus. While in France I was bewitched: my glass ran with a decent Bordeaux or Bourgenil (spelled wrong) and I certainly helped a Madonna to a pâté more delicious than our local pork pies. And now!

★ White did not in fact make it into *The Dictionary of National Biography* for 1961–1970, perhaps as a result of David and Sylvia's reluctance to write the article, but in the volume of *Missing Persons* published in 1993 there is an article on him by Richard Ingrams.

Everything that I have been shirking descends on me – and now fog and frost and King Winter knocks at the door – and what a lot of *work* there is in this country.

Self-pity is despised – but let me please give way – and despise me to your heart's content. My young birds are all fledged: I have seen them fly out of the nest. All duty is over. Yes *duty*. But what has that got to do with it? One can't stop loving as the barn owls do in October – or as the cats feel towards their mature kittens. . . . And now – well, I'm supposed to rewrite a film script in the coming week and buy Christmas presents, and when Christmas comes I shall have this house fairly full with William, Amaryllis (and she has problems), a girl called Nicky, her son aged four months called Beccalalis (husband absent in Paris) and possibly Henrietta, and I shall cook all the meals from Friday till Thursday. Roast turkey and all the fixings – and will a ham or even a brown calf's head hold out? All I have laid in so far is a splendid bough of mistletoe.

Well, Sylvia, my trouble – and I think yours – is that we love life. How extraordinarily happy they must be who hate it! What a good wicket they are on! In ten years' time – universal nuclear destruction of the populations, animal and vegetable, of the earth. So in the season of Peace on Earth, I wish you a Very Merry Christmas and Glorious New Year.

I start writing a film script on Monday.

Love and more love   David

[Postcard] *17: xii: 1968*   *Maiden Newton*

A little prematurely, the Holy Innocents
Are slaughtered and hang head-downward.
Geese, turkeys, capons, ducklings, pheasants –
And King Herod must cook them all.

1969

6: iii: 1969   *Maiden Newton*

Dearest David, I come crawling out into the morning sun to ask
how you are. When you wrote last you were putting on a kitchen
apron to cook for a family party; and after Christmas you were
going to write. I'm sure the cooking was exemplary, but what
happened about the writing? Like Tim, I long for another volume
of autobiography.

As for Tim, he is being reprinted all over the place. Cape is doing
Farewell Victoria and the Bestiary, Chatto is doing the first Aston,
sans Aston.* A plea has gone to Collins for a reprint of *Burke's
Steerage* – on my prompting, but I doubt if anything will come of it.

Do tell me some scandals. I haven't heard any for months. A nice
fresh green scandal is what I need as a pick-me-up. In exchange, a
recent grand London wedding of some local gentry was devastated
by the bridegroom's best, most fashionable, aunt going totally
bald in the course of one week, just previously. Wigs, tears, etc.

I am trying to write a short story without a word of explanation.
Actions only, watched by a not very speculative signalman from his
box at a branch line country station.†

With my love   Sylvia

10 March 1969   *Hilton Hall*

Dearest Sylvia
    You ask me for scandal. Really you must imagine that I live in the
great world and a half a century ago. I don't think scandals exist. If
everyone is beyond the fringe how can anyone infringe? . . . .

A small scandal is omitted.

Well, well. I was seventy-seven yesterday but shouldn't know it.
I spent a very happy week-end taking a friend to see Trinity College

---

* White's first novel, *They Winter Abroad*, was published under the pseudonym
James Aston, and was now being reissued under his own name.
† This story, which sounds curiously like an earlier one called 'The Level-
Crossing', was not published and may not have survived.

Library and King's Chapel and Sir Thomas Malory's fifth possible birthplace and Little Gidding. And I cooked her a meal of venison with honey sauce and brown lentils.

These are the only scandals near home – and until I go abroad I can't think of others. Really financial scandals are more fun. I am going to select and edit Carrington's letters. They are marvellous and fully illustrated with charming drawings.

Someone used that phrase, 'Keeping up with the Joneses', to me the other day, and I snapped out angrily: 'I'm ahead of the Joneses.'

So we áre, my dear.

Love   David

18: iii: 1969   *Maiden Newton*

Dearest David, I am delighted to think you are going to edit Carrington's letters. I heard this from Michael Howard last week and was delighted then; but I can put more belief in your statement (what doesn't one say to publishers?), so I am now more delighted. I long to read them. *Please* have them ready in time for my closing lines, and don't be swept away from them by swarms of bees. She was so respectable and animal in that distempered Zoo of a book [Holroyd's *Lytton Strachey*] – she and your sister-in-law, Frances. All the others snuffled and ran at the eyes: in the book, I mean. I don't believe it was a true picture. No, Duncan didn't snuffle. But he was considerably moistened by them. . . .

Did you see this in *The Times*? – over the window of a booking-office in a country station:

> Ayez l'obligeance de me parler avec douceur sans élever le ton et sans me contraire en aucune manière. Chez les gens de mon âge le bruit et la contradiction provoquent des hausses brusques de tension, de l'hyperacidité gastrique, des troubles cardiovasculaires et je deviens très rapidement désagreable. . . .

With my love   Sylvia

4: viii: 1969   *Maiden Newton*

Dearest David, How are you? Where are you? Are you going to France? How are you getting on with Carrington? Did the old-fashioned Keatsian sweet peas come up well, and do you like them?

Did you read of the village of Galliciano whose church was destroyed during the last war and, despite many requests, has never been repaired? The parishioners are now declaring *en masse* that if nothing is done they will all become Protestants.

With my love   Sylvia

Dearest Sylvia, It is wonderful to find a letter beginning How are you? Where are you? Well, I'll take you at your word and try and answer. But perhaps facts first and states of mind, if any, afterwards. The facts are that William has just got married to a delightful, quick-witted girl of twenty-eight. She is small, dark, with eager eyes, laughs a lot and plays the clarinet and has just qualified in the new science/art/fashion called music therapy. We had a wonderful party here: a great many of her relations came – her father has nine brothers; he is a mechanic,* they come from Islington. So did most of our other guests – including Angelica. All my daughters here – Richard, Jane, etc. A lovely night. The party was planned for about thirty, but about a hundred turned up. Six dozen of wine was drunk and two dozen beer.

It was a good party – young people and I myself splashing into the pool. Angelica came and was dancing 'Knees up, Mother Brown', while an Islington uncle played and sang lots of songs like 'You're the only girl in the world' – and outside on the terrace the more sophisticated danced to Beatley records. William and Linda left for France at 7.45 next morning. But there were twenty to lunch that day, fifteen to dinner and twelve to lunch on Monday. Then I was alone to rejoice and clear up.

William and Linda plan to live in Swaledale. This means that I shall let this house if I can, preferably to an American professor. It's only eleven and a half miles from Cambridge. I have the builders in, painting and renovating plaster, and I am putting an advertisement in the *New York Saturday Review of Literature*.

Meanwhile I am working hard at the Carrington Letters. That is another subject.

William and Linda came back from France last Sunday, and left for Yorkshire, house-hunting on Tuesday.

Well, so much for facts. But what about the emotions and states of mind which result? For as you know these can be various and contradictory.

I can't live here alone (a fact). But I see that my life is uprooted and at a turning-point. My chief occupation here is waging war

---

* Linda's father, Fred Burt, was actually a metal-worker with three brothers and six sisters.

against asparagus beetles (I have killed 340 this year). There might be better occupations. But few happier. Routine is over: i.e., garden, cooking and week-end parties. Adventure begins at seventy-seven, and I embark on it somewhat doubtfully. I have taken a cottage with studio attached belonging to Alec Penrose's daughter Angela Derville, who married a Frenchman called Joe and lives in a marvellous ancient château built against the English in the fourteenth century. Nerissa encouraged me to take it, but now wants to live in Spain – or to explore it. So I shall have this cottage (perfect in all respects) on my hands for two years from 1st January 1970.

I don't intend to live there all the time. How can I live *entirely* alone – without asparagus beetles? But the fact is that the woman I love most lives too hectic a social life for me to share it permanently – even if she wanted me to. And I feel a little bit as though I had agreed to fly the Atlantic solo.

Wildly exciting – but?

Carrington – the book is wrecked by the amount of material – enough for ten volumes.

Yesterday I read for seven and a half hours xerox copies. *All worth publishing*. It will be a volume of samples, and the joy of following up detail inevitably disappears. Well, forgive this egotistic letter, but you asked for it.

Please write me an equally long letter about your life, and let's meet before the grave claims us – not all that time left.

Love   David

9: viii: 1969   *Maiden Newton*

Dearest David, Well!

I dare say it was a slight surprise to William too. I hope he will find his house in Swaledale, be very happy and have a daughter to whom he can transmit his resemblance to Ray.

I cannot hope so compactly for you, my dear. You have not left, nor let, Hilton Hall yet. Circumstances grow fins, as John Cowper Powys remarked. It might become necessary for you to remain. A deserving couple from Hungary (with incendiary tendencies but otherwise very agreeable) might need a roof over their heads; you would have to stay with a fire-extinguisher at hand, and for a change be cooked for. You might find yourself irresistibly drawn to an American professor (entomology, var. beetles). The English-Speaking Union is said to be a good place for letting houses by. It distresses me to think of you in a cottage, *perfect in all respects*. You would be more lonely in fewer rooms, and far more oppressed by a

153

routine that has to be learned anew. It is not in your character, dearest David, to come down in the world. Should you not consider going to a city? I believe there is very agreeable society in Aberdeen; if one lives behind granite walls one does not feel the cold; you would have fishermen and professors and new acquaintances. Or Dublin, if you can stand the Irish for more than a week. I think new acquaintances are very important. It renews one's vigour to be taken on one's merits, without all the strings and accustomed notions which age fastens on one.

I think you should advertise for an American author to rent your cottage. You forget to say where it is, but I so much discount it that I don't care. No doubt it is fully rural.

I would ask if I could rent Hilton Hall, but it would be too much of an undertaking.

I live in a narrowing noose. Valentine had a second operation at Christmas. It pleased the surgeon, but she has been unwell ever since. Now they are snuffing round cancer of the lung. She has been put on a hormone treatment. It is tantamount to a suspended sentence, really, for all they say of it.

I feel for you about the material in Carrington. I had the same trouble with White. In the end, I fell back on *form* as the only tolerable expedient. Oddly enough, once I was vowed and sternly pledged to form, I found it possible to fit in a great many details which had scattered like quicksilver before.

I wish we could meet, but for the present I don't see how. And I send a great deal of love and true concern along with all this good advice.

Always   Sylvia

As far as I am aware, I have not killed one asparagus beetle. Do they eat it?

15 August 1969   Hilton Hall

Dearest Sylvia, Thank you for your letter. I am so sorry about Valentine. I know, though I would not remember, just that.

Leonard Woolf died yesterday. I was very fond of him – saw him last summer when he gave me lunch and talked about E. M. Forster's relations with him. It is a relief he is dead, as he had a stroke and couldn't bear not being able to look after himself.

He asked me to be his literary executor years ago, but I hope he has made another will, as it would take me the rest of my life to go through his papers.

If he hasn't, I shall force Quentin to do the job and promise to rubber-stamp what he does.

Forgive me writing such a stupid letter: I don't often have moods of self-pity – as it would be absurd in such a lucky individual.

The cottage is near Montcuq between Cahors and Montauban . . . at the end of a cart track through a copse and looks south over a steep valley. I have been reading seven hours a day for a week xerox copies of Carrington's letters and feel like a ferret emerging pink-eyed from a rabbit-warren. Also living in the past of one's friends seems to make everything timeless. I scarcely know in which strata I am. She wrote immensely long letters to her lovers almost every day and frequently twice a day. She could be very good – after a quarrel – 'You haven't written. I am an actor without his cue. Are we acting *Othello* or *As You Like It?*'

Dear Sylvia – I send you all my love and sympathy.   David

1: xii: 1969   *Maiden Newton*

Dear David, Valentine died on the ninth of November. You will know too well how I have felt. Like Ray, she had the solace of dying at home.

I intend to stay here, alone. No bread is better than half a loaf. This not to say that I would not be delighted to see you. Perhaps when a transatlantic tenant has stuck to your new paint you might include me in a Western Tour.

With love   Sylvia

8 December 1969   *Hilton Hall*

Dear Sylvia, I send you my love.

I love the visible world so much that it consoles me to know that it is going on: however much we mess it up – day and night, high tide and low tide, summer and winter: forever – and that we don't.

But such reflections are no help for pain and loneliness: for that there's no cure, my dear.

Well, all my love   David

1970

Dearest David, . . . If it is a weight off your mind, then I am glad you have let Hilton – though the thought of an extra floor on the Dovehouse embattles every drop of Tory blood in my veins; and all for an Irish peer, too, you sorry slut! Your tenants sound detestable. I suppose your books will be safe with them, as I don't suppose they can read: except Jones. Jones may be literate; and a Taffy, too. Jones is the danger.

I liked Lot (I think Montcuq is in Lot?). We were there when the tobacco crop was being gathered, and the gatherers walked with vast bunches of tobacco plants, stems upward, in each hand and looked as if they were walking in farthingales. There were affiches in two languages: French and a dialect rather like Catalan. And I remember a small stone manor-house, empty except for a quantity of poultry, who squawked, flustered, strutted in and out, coupled and kept up an incessant conversation; and as I was watching them I realised that this was the nearest I should ever get to the Versailles of Louis XIV.

How old we both are, my dear. Alike in that, if in nothing else. In a way, I am more like the Sylvia you first knew, for I have reverted to solitude. I live in a house too large for me, with three cats; and when the telephone rings and it is a wrong number I feel a rush of thankfulness. I was grateful to you for your letter after Valentine's death, for you were the sole person who said that for pain and loneliness there is no cure. I suppose people have not the moral stamina to contemplate the idea of no cure; and to ease their uneasiness they trot out the most astonishing placebos. I was assured I would find consolation in writing, in gardening, in religion, in tortoises, in tapestry, in doing another book like the White biography, in keeping bees, in social service (the world is so full of misery); and many of these consolers were people whom I had previously found quite rational. Your only runner-up was Reynolds Stone's wife, who said, whiskey.

But when one has had one's head cut off –

Please, if only for my peace of mind, outlive Michael Holroyd. For my pleasure too, come to that.

There you are with your enormous hearth, your refrigerator, £1000 p.a., the days drawing in: you are ideally circumstanced to write to me from time to time.

With my mortal love   Sylvia

[Apparently incomplete: September 1970]   *[Le Verger de Charry,*
Montcuq, Lot, France]

I have just finished a short novel which I started five years ago and got stuck in [*A Clean Slate*]. It is about a woman of forty-seven, in love with a boy of seventeen . . . If there is one thing I am sure of, it is that all my friends and the reviewers will shake their heads in dismay over the book and regret that Bunny – once so talented – should have published it. But I *shall* publish it, because, though I think it is imperfect with rough edges and lapses (which I cannot smooth or fill in), there is a lot of psychology which is of interest. *I have written it entirely from the woman's point of view*. Very few men have succeeded in this. Not many have attempted it. Tolstoy did partly in *Anna Karenin*. Women are much better at writing about men than *vice versa*.

Anyhow Cape rejected it, and Hamish Hamilton have accepted it. I go to New Mexico on the 26th I believe, and return within twenty-eight days.

Love to you my dear and stroke each of your cats for me. I have no cat now.

David

14: xii: 1970   *Maiden Newton*

Darling David, When I read *Carrington* I decided you would have had your belly full of letters and that I would not write to you for a while – incidentally, how love declares itself in the style: no one reading those letters could doubt that it was Lytton she loved; the others she only enjoyed being in love with.

But now you have sent me that irresistible Pan, that nobly easy-going Aphrodite, *and* an address (I had been asking myself, Is he in France, is he in New or Old Mexico, has he gone to the Lofoten Islands for a change?). So I can wish you a Happy Christmas and an unexpectedly merry New Year. . . .

I am as dark and sad as (I think) any Fate could require. But to see the assiduity with which I avoid falling downstairs, catching colds, suffering from malnutrition, insomnia, insolvency, you'd suppose I was bent on survival. It is not so; I am just bent on keeping away from doctors and the Welfare State and preserving my existence as a

157

Moping Owl, with my three loving sensual unregenerate cats about me.

I wish you had a cat, better still a brace of cats, dear David. They are worth a waggon-load of disinterested well-wishers. . . .

Love from   Sylvia

1971

Dearest Sylvia, I don't know when I last wrote to you, but it was a long time ago, perhaps when I was living here alone – as I am at present, though I have [had] a lot of visitors in the last month: William, his wife and his son Merlin aged eleven months, Henrietta, her Sophie and friends, and Nerissa and two Americans.

The summer has been very changeable, and there was a hailstorm with hail-stones as big as bantam's eggs which has destroyed the crops of my immediate neighbours – grapes, maize, tobacco, sunflowers, melons – all stripped of their leaves. Luckily it was very local and did not touch the vineyards in the valley of the Lot. But it will be a bad vintage, and so I am bottling as much wine of the 1970, which is good, as I can find bottles for.

My news is good. The long novel [*The Sons of the Falcon*], 95,000 words, which I wrote here in the winter has surprised people and is being published by Macmillan on my eightieth birthday next March. It is, as I no doubt told you when I last wrote, full of bloody murders – set in the Caucasus about 1868, a few years after the Circassians had been driven out of their valleys by the Russians and had taken refuge in Turkey.

I have also a very short novel published about a fortnight ago in a very unpleasing jacket by Hamish Hamilton. It is very sexy, and I use the word cock a good deal. The book has a good subject really: but I was suffering from that terrible passion for economy of statement – sometimes a great virtue – but in this case I think the reader will hardly know what I am talking about. I have seen no reviews and heard of none. It will probably be treated as an attempt at pornography, which it wasn't. I am giving Hilton Hall to my grandsons. My houseboat is being put into a steel box which will cost £1450! Nerissa is living in it. I shall probably stay here at any rate till Christmas. Please write to me.

Very much love　　　　　　　　　　　　　　　　　　David

Dearest David, How comfortable it sounds – to be alone bottling wine. I wish I could come to twirl the corks in sealing-wax, as I did so long ago at Hilton.

You did not tell me the name of your Hamish Hamilton book. It is Low and Mean of him to scramble it out at this time of year – unless he had his eye on sales at the Pop Festival in Essex. Perhaps you made thousands there which he hasn't troubled to disclose.

The Revd Thomas Boston, preaching against pinning hopes on death-bed repentances said it was improbable that a man would leap from the harlot's lap to Abraham's bosom. Your leap to Macmillan after Hamish Hamilton seems much the same. I hope Abraham's bosom will be profitable. How many publishers have you now frisked through?

I, a model of steadfastness, had my last book of short stories published by the Viking in April, and the English edition comes out with Chatto in October. I will send you a copy. One or two of them are less short than usual and better – or so I think. It has a good title: *The Innocent and the Guilty*. Do you remember Chekhov writing so unkindly and wisely to a woman novelist whose name I don't remember, telling her her style was growing middle-aged? Those words are ever before me.

On Saturday I shall be having my yearly treat: some musicians I know will come and sing madrigals to me; *two* counter-tenors last year, could anything be more delicious, as the mice said of the passages greased with bacon-fat? We borrow the church for the occasion, and I am the only audience.

I had to jaunt to Aldeburgh, where I went to help hang pictures by John Craske★ for an exhibition, and stayed on for part of the Festival. Ben Britten and Peter Pears were very kind and loving to me, and gave me *quantities* of the best asparagus I have ever eaten; and another pleasure was soles straight out of the sea. I thought I would never eat a *tough* sole again: these were tough as Old Diggory. The audience at the Maltings was a permissive spectacle, varying from County Ladies in satin and tiaras to heights of fashion in short tarpaulin skirts and brilliant cross-gartering – and I've never seen a finer array of whiskers and lovelocks. I am still of your great-grandfather's opinion (or rather, his Circassian's) about unhairy chins.† Being kissed by respectful whiskers makes me sneeze.

★ See above, p. 52.
† Actually it was his grandfather, Dr Richard Garnett, and the relevant lines from 'The Fair Circassian' are:

> 'Let the man that woos to win
> Woo with an unhairy chin;'
> Thus she said, and as she bid
> Each devoted Vizier did.

> From the beards a cord she made
> Looped it to the balustrade,
> Glided down and went away
> To her own Circassia.

For the rest, I contrive to be a moping owl. And I look forward to your bloody murders.

And I send you very much love   Sylvia

Darling David, I have asked Chatto and Windus to post you my book of short stories. I hope you are still in France with time to read it before you go off to Mexico or wherever. It will not take you long.

I envy you being in France where, if you turn on the radio, you will be safe from hearing an Ulster accent. It seems impossible that people who make such repulsive sounds could do anything but hate each other. It has sent me back to the *Decline and Fall*. No doubt the Fathers of the Church also yelled and screamed and *bored* – but it is soothing to have Gibbon's quiet voice retailing them.

I had forgotten that when he was young he was, from the neck down, slender as an elf.

There is an interesting exhibition of legal costume at the Law Courts: I realised that gaudy costumes are connected with slaughter. I know the woman who was responsible for arranging it. There was a difficulty about the tailor's mannequins, all so young and smirking. But a theatrical dresser was invoked, and I cannot tell you what a villainous set of Tom-Harpies he contrived, how stupid, sadistic, *sly*, he made them. All his life he must have harboured a grudge against the Law – and heaven sent him this blameless opportunity to express it.

The B.B.C. sent a reporter into the street to gather opinions about Hirohito's visit to London. One woman said. He's called Hiro-shima, isn't he?

With love   Sylvia

1 November 1971, 9.50 a.m. our time
  (i.e. summer)   *Le Verger de Charry*

Dearest Sylvia, There is a faint nip in the air, but the sun is hot and the sky cloudless blue. No wind. I am sitting under my oak tree. Your set of delinquents arrived. It is odd, but the two not published in the *New Yorker* appeal to me most. I think 'Two Children' is *perfect*, and perfection is the rarest quality. Have you ever read 'His Red Mittens' by Stephen Crane? It is also about a small (but smaller) boy's need for manliness. 'Bruno' is very moving but perhaps a shade too much of a moral tale. As for 'Oxenhope', I keep going back there myself – although I never lit the Marsh Gas T. S. Eliot or

Frank Morley told me he had been at school with a boy who could set light to his farts – I was with them both and can't remember which one told the story. 'Truth in the Cup' is almost perfect, but I feel a shade of doubt – his exit is a little contrived. What a brilliant writer you are Sylvia! So fertile, and so various and almost too amusing.

Well, I must boast a little, and I really have something to boast about. Last winter, as I have no doubt told you, I wrote a long novel, which Macmillan are going to publish on my eightieth birthday next March. Their General Books Editor (to use an Americanism) inquired when I was coming back, as he wanted to meet me. I replied I had no plans for returning – whereupon he, Alan Maclean (brother of the famous defector), flew out. I met him at Toulouse airport, drove him back here, dined but not wined him, as he won't drink (ex-alcoholic) and put him on a train for Toulouse at Cahors at midday next day. Now isn't that the height of grandeur? I like him. He wanted to break to me his plans for selling the book. One of Miss Christina Foyle's literary lunches! Have you been the object of one? Or attended one? I went to one given for Betjeman when Lord Samuel gave a long speech. He, Samuel, is what the Stracheys called a death packet, and I dozed off to find Stephen Spender, sitting next to me, on his feet and majestically walking out in the middle of his Lordship making an attack on the poetry of Dylan Thomas.

Well, will you come? I would rather have you beside me than any other writer I know. It is a good deal to ask. A nasty business. But Maclean thinks he is going to make me some money. I don't suppose he is right but don't want to discourage him.

You lie in wait for dogs with a water-pistol. I trap mice and creatures called lérots (garden dormice in English). They are the size of half-grown rats and have a black stripe across their faces, and they gnaw holes in any unoccupied bed, in the mattresses, and also play football with walnuts in the attic. The obvious thing would be to keep a cat – a fine ponderous tabby tom is what I want. But conscience forbids, because I should have to leave him when I came back to England. I have just heard that there is an unfledged owlet at the château in the grenier. If I bring him and put him in my attic, will his parents find him and feed him, and will he settle there?

Because if they don't I shall have to feed him twelve times in the twenty-four hours. I can't hope to trap twelve mice a day, so I shall have to snip off my white elflocks and wrap a little bit of beef in each locket full of hair and then persuade him to swallow it. Owls must have 'roughage', and this seems the only way. But I hesitate to embark on such an adoption. Particularly because I don't want a tame owl sicking up pellets of my hair, but a wild owl policing my estate and sleeping in my attic. They are said to snore, but the lérots and rats make as much noise as a football crowd over their game and indulge in a lot of rough play, judging by the squeaks.

11 a.m. It is now so hot that I have had to take off my pullover, and the butterflies pretend it [is] still summer.

I have just started another novel and, like your stories, it will be a moral tale, but the horrors will be a lot cruder than those you describe.

By the way, have you ever known anyone with an appalling disfigurement?

I know a man with – is it lupus? – over half of his face. He is a rather authoritative beekeeper who seems quite unaware of his appearance. One of the things about leaving Hilton is that I don't keep bees any longer. It is a relief. As I get old I find I don't want to be trying my strength all the time, and the bees were always a test of my morale. I liked it when I had succeeded – say in picking out and catching a queen – but beforehand I always felt as a policeman must feel when he walks calmly into a gang of roughs and makes an arrest, knowing that it is a nice thing as to whether he is set upon. Of course I loved the bees, which the policeman probably doesn't.

Well, forgive this maundering letter. I used to think the verb maunder was derived from the Rev. Maunder's *Dictionary of Universal Knowledge*, but the *O.E.D.* says I am mistaken. A pity.

Very much love, dear Sylvia   David

1972

Dearest David, I love you very much. I am profoundly indebted to you for that introduction to Chatto and Windus. I constantly re-read your books. I am glad you are an octogenarian and wish you many happy returns of the day. I hope this new book will be a creditable and profitable child to you. I would be made very happy to see you again

BUT

(dearest Bunny)

I will not come to that Foyle luncheon. This is not ingratitude. If I thought I would enjoy it I would come like a shot. But I shouldn't. I should see you immersed in sociabilities and think wistfully of how happily we dined together on the evening of our day in the Essex marshes.

What a lot of books we have written! This is borne in on me because I have carried basketsful of them out of this room into the next, where they will sit patiently while my tobacco-coloured walls are washed rather cleaner by Mr F. Palmer, Builder and Decorator. While that goes on, I shall be in Denmark. And when I come home, full of Scandinavian energy, I shall rearrange them on an improved system. They seem to have been arranging themselves, for I am sure I never put *Les Malheurs de Sophie* next to *Psychopathia Sexualis*. The little bitch looked very smug and snug there, it must have been her designing, her machination, her thirst for self-improvement. Unless it was Madame de Genlis, who was looking smug near-by.

What a pity you'll be too lazy to get the current *New Yorker* (January 27th). It has a story by me in it totally unlike anything the *New Yorker* has ever had before and more short sentences to the square inch than you would believe possible.★ It is also a very fine and inflexible narrative, I would show it to Defoe without shame.

What did you decide about the owlet? Did your grey elflocks agree with it? I dare say it would have eaten chopped hard-boiled egg (I've never known a bird that wouldn't) garnis ou non.

You could borrow a cat – a cat with a missionary spirit. But

★ 'Something Entirely Different' in the *New Yorker*, 22 January 1972 (not the 27th, as Sylvia says).

perhaps your lérots have left off wanting to hibernate in your mattresses by now. (N.B. If woken untimely, they die, so be careful and walk your attics in stocking-feet.)

Very much love   Sylvia

15 March 1972   *As from Moby Dick*

Dearest Sylvia, Really, you write me such letters that I don't know what to say or where to look. It is a real comfort and reached me when I was in the worst stage of 'flu. A really bad raw throat, bronchitis. I am well now except for boneache and tremble.

Yes – it is extraordinary and splendid that we are both alive and working. I am halfway through another book but don't know if I shall solve the difficulties that lie ahead.

You ask how I wrote *The Sons of the Falcon*. Well, the story about the icon being hidden in the child's body was told me years ago by Basil Kouchitachvili.* I told it to a friend and then began to think and ask myself: 'What kind of man does such a thing?' And the answer came with Prince Gurgen. I started writing just after Christmas and finished the first draft by April. Then I came to England and read a few books on Georgia and Transcaucasia. The worst bore was changing everyone's name to a genuine one. Not only a bore but terrifying lest I should miss a Nikko, which was Valeri's original name.

I was obsessed by the book and often woke up with a new idea in the middle of the night and had to write down something so I should not forget it. Also I thought of extravagant things and asked myself: 'Why not?' and put them in. There is no proper end to the book – but then there isn't in life.

The characters I like best are Iriné and Foma. They are both very real to me.

---

* He recorded it in *The Flowers of the Forest* (1955), pp. 217–18:

> The Kouchitachvilis had an ikon in the family which had worked miracles: it was their chief treasure. But the family split up and the ikon was claimed by a cadet branch which had become more powerful than the senior branch. One day the family was taking the ikon on its annual pilgrimage to a local shrine when scouts that had been sent ahead came rushing back to report that the junior branch had laid an ambush to rob them of the ikon. The head of the family reflected; then he drew his sword and thrust it through the body of his youngest child. He then hid the ikon in its belly and the party went on its way as a funeral procession, the women keening their dirges. The ruse was successful and the ikon remained in the possession of the senior branch . . .

It is early yet to say whether the book will sell on the best-seller standard. But already it has sold five thousand and much more than repaid the advance. That is a solid comfort.

23rd: I wrote this when I was in bed. I've been told you are in Denmark, but send it all the same. I go north for Easter to have a look at my new granddaughter – William's – called Romany. He has a son called Merlin, who is not quite two.

All my love   David

24: iv: 1972   *Maiden Newton*

Dearest David, . . . I hope the bone in your elbow will come out quietly and that you won't miss it too badly and that it is in your left elbow.*

Bassoonists are hard to come by. William's best chance might be to look about among teaching institutions; or he might haunt dance halls. Indeed, the latter might be better since there would be a more hardened standard of professionalism. (Unhardened bassoonists can be a liability.) But more to pay. Trumpeters should be easier in his brass band locality. . . .

I will risk being a Dame, dear, rather than forsake you. Last month, I was momentarily singed by the honour, for the U.S. Ambassador's social secretary introduced me to him as Dame Rebecca (she and I were there to be made honorary partakers of the American Association for the Advancement of Literature, and Mr Annenberg had to make a small party for it). Earlier partakers attended, and *quantities* of total strangers in long white beards remembered meeting me. As for me, I was much as if I had been on a peak in Darien. Can I really have forgotten them all?

I liked the Ambassador. Such a cosy man.

With love   Sylvia

Tell me the result of the elbow.

5 May 1972   *Moby Dick*

Dearest Sylvia, I have returned here after an absence of eleven days to find your letter. I went for a day's fishing on the Itchen, but my cousin Dicky said: 'We can go to Wales!' So we drove off, each in his own car, down an incredible stretch of concrete called the M4 and in no time had crossed the vast bridge over the Severn and were

---

* Many years before, when carrying a bottle of wine in each hand down stone stairs to a party, he had slipped and fallen on the tips of his elbows, chipping off slivers of bone, which were now playing up.

safely in the twisty dandelion-fringed roads of Wales. We lived in a caravan together for five days. I read an ingenious novel by Iris Murdoch called *Flight from the Enchanter* – when I was not standing knee-deep in the river in a howling gale. I caught nothing, Dicky a sixteen-pound salmon. Dicky makes a pot of strong Indian tea – Typhoo Tips – six and sometimes seven times a day and drinks 'a dog's nose' – a double gin with half a pint of beer. (A mug before getting up. Tea for breakfast – luckily, as his coffee comes out of a tube – a mug of tea in the morning before lunch. A mug after lunch. Two mugsful at teatime, a mugful before going to bed. Sometimes a mugful while waiting for dinner after the dog's nose.) We ate better than you might suppose, as I did the shopping. The place – Dan-yr-Allt – might have been invented by de la Mare.

Forty or thirty years ago the big house was burnt down, the eight gardeners were dismissed, and the park and gardens left to themselves. The ruin stands on high ground overlooking the river Tywi . . . There is a mile of river with sewin and salmon, and one finds otters' footprints in the mud. A pair of buzzards are nesting in the park. The first rhododendrons are coming out. Narcissi flower through beds of nettles. There are wide stone steps leading to impenetrable thickets of bramble. The wind was bitter. It rained in spiteful showers. Everything was lovely. I walked back purified and trembling with fatigue. Whisky never tasted better.

On Monday we said farewell, and I set out to explore and drove past Lampeter to Trigonin [?Tregaron] and then took a mountain road only wide enough for one car with scoops at intervals where one could wait. The mountains are as splendid as Yorkshire or the Pyrenees, and the Forestry haven't spoiled much as yet, though they are hard at work, and ewes and lambs are doomed. It was a real discovery. Many are so steep and made of rock, so the conifer will never grow. At five o'clock, after a stupendous drive on the only fine day, I reached – where do you suppose? Boughrood Castle, of course.* I was welcomed with open arms by Michael, kissed tenderly by Pat and given weak China tea with lemon in it. Very different from the brew of Typhoo Tips. The castle has come on a lot since last June. There are no workmen on scaffolding embarrassed by catching sight of me in the bath – had they been hoping for Pat? The great stairs are free of scaffolding. Michael has his kitchen fully equipped. We dined in the dining-room.

But somehow – put not you trust in possessions – Michael would

* Michael Howard had retired from active publishing in 1970, left Little Finborough and moved to Boughrood Castle, Llyswen, Brecon, which he planned to make into a retreat where writers and artists could rest and work.

be happy, I think, though he must know he is digging his own grave. But I don't suppose he does – sometimes a faint cloud passes over his face as he tries to recall the two and twenty things he has forgotten.

Pat occasionally looks almost demented with sorrow – at other moments boasts about the hens. She gave me six large eggs at parting, and I have just made my supper off two of them boiled. London eggs aren't safe to boil.

They are very proud of your tapestry, which hangs above the fireplace in the great sitting-room. It seemed to me that it was the night sky – the darkness of night embracing pussy – though I'm not sure I would have dared to call that creature Puss.

William has found his bassoonist and his horn player, whom I called a trumpeter – ignorance, Madam. So now I have to arrange with the châtelaines of five châteaux for performances. . . .

Michael and Pat long for you to visit them. But the carpets and the curtains aren't yet quite ready for you. I hope I shall live to see your name in the Honours List.

Very much love   David

8: v: 1972   *Maiden Newton*

Dearest David, . . . Your account of Boughrood bears out my forebodings. Too large to be lived in by themselves; and how exhausting to be shared with a miscellany. They will be like that unfortunate character in the Psalms who was scattered abroad among the beasts of the people. After the two hundred and twentieth reference to Kilvert they will die raving. I am so sorry, because it is a magnanimous design, and I am fond of them both.

Kilvert sweeps me to *Munby*.★ Have you read *Munby*? It is enthralling. For one thing, he seems to be a perfectly honest diarist; for another, he has set me off on a speculation as to whether do-gooders are in fact pursuing an intuitive policy of being done good to – a fulfilment of that *Drang* towards the dark, the threatening, the forbidden, which they felt as children, those dark alleys they weren't allowed to explore. That raises a further speculation about class distinction in Victorian philanthropists. Children of the poor grew up in those alleys, felt no gentry *Drang* to explore them, and if they grew on into philanthropy, just plainly wanted to demolish them, as savagely as Florence Nightingale. Do read *Munby* and tell me what you think.

★ *Munby: Man of Two Worlds: The Life and Diaries of Arthur J. Munby 1828–1910* by Derek Hudson (1972).

Last week I met Christopher Sykes – whom I meet from time to time and always with pleasure: he is that rarity, a Man of the World. He told me how after the fall of Berlin he had to investigate post-Hitler high society – it was in good condition and radiant with whitewash. At a party of the whitewashed was a rapscallionly Rumanian, who had the effrontery to refer to his participation in pre-1945 doings. There was an appalled silence. Then the white-washed tried to restore the tone of the party, disclaimed all knowledge of, disbelieved rumours, wondered how on earth anyone could have been so misled, so misguided, etc.

'*Someone* had to join the Nazis,' said he; as one might say 'Someone had to go to the Jones's garden-fête.'

I am glad I have you to share this with. Altogether, I am glad I have you.

Very much love   Sylvia

18: ix: 1972   *Maiden Newton*

Dearest David, Thank you very much. I shall be delighted to appear in your book of short stories.★

I remember 'Purl and Plain' as clearly – and admiringly – as if I had written it myself. It came out in *Vogue* during the benign dynasty of Miss Todd. . . .

I can boast to you: at our age boasting is out of place, but you are a crony and I can boast to you. In the first quarter of this year I wrote four short stories, and with as much excitement as if I had never written a short story before.

This is a sad time of year. The garden is a blaze of beans and full of earwigs, and I have had influenza. Not a fig. But as I love you I hope you are battening on them.

Have you read *Munby*?

Love from   Sylvia

When does *Purl and Plain* come out? I shall expect an advance copy.

2 November 1972   *Le Verger de Charry*

Dearest Sylvia, . . . I don't think I have told you about Tiber. He is an entire tabby tom, now eleven months old. I got him from a . . . lady who lives under the church spire visible on my horizon. She is difficult to approach, as her lover is an Italian stone-mason of prodigious strength and no brains, and legend has it that he attacks any males on sight and that she embraces them all, so that

★ *Purl and Plain and Other Stories* was dedicated to Sylvia.

169

there is some foundation for his jealousy. Rumour brought the news that among her herd of felines was the cat I wanted. I drove there, found she was washing her hair and returned twenty minutes later to find a plain body of fifty to sixty with an incomprehensible accent wrapped in towels. I came straight to the point. 'I want you to give me one of your cats.' 'You're welcome.' Tiber stalked in among a crowd of grey and parti-coloured siblings – heroic, terribly lean. He was caught, put in a carton and driven home. He has turned out to be handsome beyond belief, affectionate – he loves to lie in my arms, purring – he has different purrs, eats voraciously, drinks milk, walks me every day to the château – half a kilometre away – to fetch the post – understands quite a lot of what I say to him – more than I do of his delicately nuanced mews – answers to his name, of course, and sleeps outside at night. He made a puddle in my bed three times in the first three weeks. Then I beat him within an inch of his life and six inches of my own, and he has not done it since. I am, as you may imagine, his slave, but he is a kind master. He has put on weight prodigiously and will soon be as much as one can lift with one hand. He is a dark tabby with a golden spotted belly, a little off white under his chin. He loves to sleep with his head upside down, and his appearance of innocence would then deceive St Peter. With any luck he may outlive me, as there are no cars and roads to run him over. Have you read Colette's *La Chatte*? It improves as it goes on. I am now reading Gide's *L'Immoraliste*. I rather like two aphorisms I have found.

'Regrets, remords, repentis, ce sont les joies de naguère vues du dos.' And 'On ne peut pas être sincère et le paraître.' . . .

Love from   David

7: xi: 1972   *Maiden Newton*

Dearest David, I was delighted to hear about Tiber. I have known for a long time that what you needed was a maître-chat; and plainly he needed you. He could not have associated with a family, human or feline. The latter would have involved kittens, and he would have had the trouble of killing them.

When you collect this letter he will be with you. When you open it, please give him my love and esteem, and tickle the off-white patch under his chin and administer a long firm stroke from his nose to the tip of his tail (quickening in speed and fervour as it comes towards the tail-tip) on my behalf. And finish it with a flourish, as if it were the end of a violin concerto.

But roads and cars are not the only danger to cats. Please have him inoculated against feline enteritis. Epidemics of it are Nature's

way of controlling a spreading population of rustic cats, like the
herd belonging to the lady you got him from. . . .

    With love   Sylvia

Does Tiber like roast chestnuts? My three batten on them.

1973

Dearest David, The house is not my own. The kitchen floor was
rotting away, two strong men are hacking it out and replacing it with
gangplanks, everything is either mislaid or put somewhere else, the
new acid-blue paint is not the colour I chose, I can't get at the larder,
a Pit lies between me and the refrigerator, the herb-bed is covered
with shavings; it will all be worse before it's better. I wanted a
change of scene, a change of mind. And I remembered *The Sons of
the Falcon*, and thought that might do. A fantastic landscape, a
rational society – O, my dear David, what a good book it is, and
what good it has done me. I kiss your honour's hand, my due first
act on rising from the dead.

How is glorious Tiber? Before long he will have young grass to
walk on, and soon after that fledgling birds to eat. And he will be
the first-ever cat to know these joys.

I spent a long Christmas at Boughrood. I admired a great many
things about it, but most of all their slates: considerably thicker than
my two thumbs and the size of old-fashioned table-napkins.

Rosamond Lehmann came to dinner one night (her son lives
nearby): plump, suave, diamond candelabras swinging from her
ears, smiling with indifferent benignity, an Indian God.

Your friends the [Hugh] Cronyns were there too for most of the
time, with his portrait of you. It is a good likeness and he has caught
the smirk of creation; but not a good picture, I thought. You
overbalance it by falling out of the frame.

That's all I have to say – except to exclaim and bewail about
tigers. Did you see the Wild Life figures? When the last tiger is dead,
nothing can ever reillume that beauty and glory. Tiger will be over.
Tiger will be extinguished.

And the global population increased last year by seventy-four
millions.

But the purpose of this letter was to thank you for *Sons of the
Falcon* and to send you my love.   Sylvia

Dearest Sylvia, How dreadful about your floor. With me it is my roof. The Roman tiles let heavy rain through which drops on to the floor of the attic, which is my wooden ceiling, and comes through in a large puddle – luckily in the centre of the floor. It is partly the effect of the sonic booms, the tiles jump apart or huddle together. However Angela Derville says she will have the roof lined during a dry spell.

I am so glad you re-read *The Sons of the Falcon*. I agree with your praise. It has pace and freshness. But your letter is very timely for after all that praise you need to hesitate to tell me what a jumble sale rag-bag my collection of stories is. You should have got your copy a few days ago. I got mine this morning.

not ?

I have just finished my novel about a French village in the 1914-18 war. I may call it *Plough over the Bones*. I set out to write a different book but discovered that I could only keep to my original idea by falsifying the character of my hero. So the book now carries a diametrically opposite message to the one I intended. The people in it are real but not very interesting. My hero is a very heroic French peasant boy. It is about the village where I worked with Francis Birrell in the Quakers' War Victims Relief Organisation in 1915. It isn't perhaps a whole – good bits, though.

Tiber has been an anxiety. Sexual maturity has hit him hard. He was badly mauled in two fights with the Wood Cat. Both arms bitten severely and what are called superficial wounds all over the front. He went off for thirty-six hours and returned yesterday morning hungry and disposed to rest. Before then he was restless and would not eat. He has to lead his own life. It's like my children.

Last night the Cronyns, who are here on a short visit, came to dinner. I gave them:

Soup. Bayonne ham and salad. Paella and red cabbage sweet and sour cooked in wine with apple and onions, Chocolat Angelique, cheese. Chocolat Angelique is made with 2 oz butter, 2 oz grated chocolate, 4 tablespoons of sugar, ¾ pint of milk – boiled down to a thick cream – then 3 tablespoons of rum stirred in.

I am going to Venice in April. I shall drive there and back, which will be an immense pleasure. In fact it is my chief pleasure in recent years – exploring by-roads, crossing mountains, seeing birds and different kinds of people.

I am eighty-one in a few days' time and must say extraordinarily well for that age.

It is a blessing not to be in England. I found it so emotionally upsetting when I was there a year ago. And I haven't a telephone here.

I would suggest your coming here for a change of scene, but I think you would be too cold at this time of year. Yesterday morning it snowed. Today it has been baking with sun and blue sky. But you must come in the summer or autumn.

Very much love   David

6: iii: 1973   *Maiden Newton*

Dearest David, 'The Wood Cat'

Oh!

But I am sorry for Tiber – sorrier than he is, I dare say. Do you grow catmint for him?

There was a hangman in Germany who had mistaken his profession, and could not bring himself to perform a hanging until he had eaten a catmint root.

Tell Tiber how much I esteem him for all his wounds being in front.

Love   Sylvia

On 27 April David learned that Amaryllis, who had been living on *Moby Dick*, had been found drowned in the Thames.

6: vi: 1973   *Maiden Newton*

Dearest David, I have only just heard about Amaryllis. I grieve for her, I grieve for you.

It is hard to be a stoic in one's old age.

With my love   Sylvia

13 June 1973   *Le Verger de Charry*

Dearest Sylvia, Thank you for your note of sympathy. What is so hard to bear is that Amaryllis might have enjoyed another fifty years of the happiness and beauty of daily life, which is what I appreciate more and more.

Can you explain how and why cats make love to us? Tiber will come, if I am reading or writing or lying on my bed and will 'tease tow' with his claws. Then, coming closer, will gaze into my face, suddenly dig his pointed muzzle under my chin once or twice, retreat, roll on his side, inviting my hand, turn his head dreamily to one side, passive and luxurious. Then he will turn on me almost fiercely with a burst of purring, and so on, and so on.

But is this, as I think, reserved for human lovers? With a female cat I think he displays no such graces but is fiercely practical. It is more like the love that was shown him by his mother when he was a kitten. And naturally it is shown most strongly before and after I have fed him. But the luxury of his furry love is very beautiful.

He fights continually with the Wood Cat – a savage beast that has run wild and supports himself in the wood by hunting, flying from man. He is more versed in battle, and Tiber is continually appearing with his scalp furrowed by the Wood Cat's claws, paws bitten through and lame, ears bleeding. He has just recovered after some days of lameness when his paw was swollen like a boxing-glove. I keep him shut up at night to save further fights, but now he can put his paw to the ground he will go off to fight again.

We had a terrible storm yesterday evening, with all the artillery of Heaven and hailstones like large lumps of sugar bouncing all over the carpet from the chimney, and today the leaves are torn and many barley fields laid flat and peasants half ruined. Every room was flooded – except the bathroom.

Very much love from   David

18: vi: 1973   *Maiden Newton*

Dearest David, . . . Tiber makes love to you for the good reason that he loves you, and loves making love. Cats are passionate and voluptuous, they get satisfaction from mating but no pleasure (the females dislike it, and this is wounding to the male), no voluptuousness; *and no appreciation.* Tiber has the pleasure of being pleased and knowing he pleases in his love-making with you. I am so glad you have each other. Does he roll on his head? Does he fall asleep with an ownerly paw laid over you?

We had a dark grey cat (Norfolk bred, very Norfolk in character) called Tom. He was reserved, domineering, voluptuous – much as I imagine Tiber to be. When he was middle-aged he gave up nocturnal prowlings and slept on my bed, against my feet. One evening I was reading in bed when I became aware that Tom was staring at me. I put down my book, said nothing, watched. Slowly, with a look of intense concentration, he got up and advanced on me, like Tarquin with ravishing strides, poised himself, put out a front paw, and stroked my cheek as I used to stroke his chops. A human caress from a cat. I felt very meagre and ill-educated that I could not purr.

It had never occurred to me that their furry love develops from what was shown them as kittens. I expect you are right. The ownerly paw is certainly a nursing cat's gesture.

You should encourage Tiber to sleep with you. He might come to prefer it to midnight battling with the Wood Cat. Come winter,

175

he certainly will. I am afraid of the Wood Cat's claws, still more of his teeth.

Were your hailstones blue? We once had such a storm here, with lightning ripping hail from the sky; and the hailstones were hard as marbles, and blue as aquamarines. And there was another storm, after a long drought, when the lightning was green. It was strange to see the bleached fields, the rusty trees, momentarily sluiced with the look of spring.

I have been spared acquaintances who might have explained to me about blue hailstones and green lightning, so I can enjoy them with simple pleasure.

> Earth, that grew with joyful ease
> Hemlock for Socrates –

The longer I live, the more my heart assents to that couplet.
With love   Sylvia

23 June 1973   *Le Verger de Charry*

Dearest Sylvia, Thank you for your most delightful letter – especially about your Norfolk Tom. I reply at once lest I forget to tell you what Pierrette said yesterday. I told her that I had difficulties with Tiber. When I cooked a chicken for myself he refused to finish up the lights I had given him.

Pierrette comes for two hours a week to mop down my tile floors and polish the furniture. She is the wife of a peasant farmer; a tall lean woman with blue eyes who enjoys her life. When I told her about my disputes with Tiber I added: 'Quelquefois il est plus fort que moi.' Pierrette laughed and said: 'On n'a jamais le dernier mot avec les animaux.' That gave me insight into their farm life which delights me.

I received a book yesterday for which I have been waiting for six years. It is by an American woman friend of mine called Diane Johnson, and the book is called *Lesser Lives*, published here by Heinemann. It is the result of her researches into the relations of George Meredith with his first wife, Peacock's daughter Mary Ellen.* . . . I am asking a bookseller to send it to you and hope it arrives.

I love Peacock, and if only I knew Greek and Italian and the literature of those countries, I should think myself rather like him.

* See above, p. 133.

176

He died at my age, eighty-one. I have had a happier life. He was married to a mad wife for thirty-six years.

Work on my studio renovations may soon begin – plumbing, a wash-basin and bidet to be installed, a floor of hand-made tiles. In addition the roof of this cottage will be removed in August, a layer of asbestos laid down and the Roman tiles replaced. At present it leaks like a sieve. Luckily the storm flooded the library at the château, and my landlord decided something must be done. He hates anything later than the sixteenth century, and I have been searching in vain for a sixteenth-century letter-box! The result is, if a shower comes on between the postman's arrival and my collecting my mail, the ink has often run and letters are indecipherable. These are minor troubles.

Yes, I've seen green lightning but never blue hailstones. Very much love to your current puss or pussies and to you   David

2: vii: 1973   *Maiden Newton*

Dearest David, I thought a great deal about your sixteenth-century letter-box. Poors-boxes go back some way (what are they in French? un tronc?). Sheridan refers to them – true, that is not sixteenth-century, but he would not have made them a simile for a lady's smile if they were not already current objects. I think we could safely call them seventeenth-century. I dare say there are quantities of poors-boxes in decaying churches in your diocese, you might be able to steal or buy one. Or you might consult the Curator of the Musée Arlaten [in Arles] – only a step in a good cause – where they have *everything*. He could show you a fine specimen, and you could have a replica made.

True, the slit will be on top, so the rain will still get at your mail. But this could be overcome by having the box sideways. This is the best I can suggest at the moment. If I have any more good ideas I will write to you.

I have been having letter-box trouble myself. The newsagent's man is lame and cannot walk up to the house, so I have *The Times* put in a lidded wooden letter-box at the end of the drive. But a blue-tit incontinently laid eight eggs in it, it had to be respected till she had hatched them and sent the fledglings into the world. (She did, all eight.) Meanwhile *The Times* had to be left in a *low cellophane carrier* dangling from a willow, and usually arrived damp. And I have not a butler to air it for me. All very inconvenient. On n'a jamais le dernier mot avec les animaux, as your Madame Pierrette observed.

I am glad you have a Pierrette. I am amazingly lucky in mine, *she is a Cockney,* with a splendid vocabulary. She gets me a weekly rabbit for the cats, and one of them was left on a doorstep, and her neighbour's cat bit off its hindleg, and she brought it down to me protesting that I should not pay the full price for it. After a great combat de générosité I got my way: later in the morning she referred to it as 'that abdicated rabbit'. Apropos of a row at a local funeral she said: 'I could see she was a fanatic. She had an umbrella.' You and I write very well; but we can't match this. She and I are waiting to hear the upshot of a village clash of opinion. There is a young woman who is a convinced atheist, and when she had a son she had it registered as Pagan (Christian name, not denomination). It is a splendid name, she should be satisfied with that; but she is determined to have it christened; and so far hasn't found a clergyman broadminded and submissive enough to agree. With each refusal she becomes more anti-clerical, more of a militant atheist. I expect it will be carried to the Bishop before long.

Lesser Lives has come. Thank you very much. What a tissue of vile nonsense! It is all of a piece with that odious Mrs Humphry Ward persecuting Aubrey Beardsley. I am filled with admiration of Mary Ellen because she didn't condescend to repentance. A little repentance at that date – and respectable connections – could go some way towards rehabilitation. Not all the way, but some way, because public opinion felt there was something dashing about running a little way with the hare.

Yes, you *are* like Peacock, my dear: like Peacock in having lived on into an age of uncongenial Faith. I suppose people have to be believers. The object varies, but the devotees are much the same. I sit appalled at the sheepishness and credulity of the present iconophiles, who believe that every irregularity of mind, such as genius, can be ironed out by People who know Better, psycho-analysts, sociologists, psychotherapists, qualified social workers.

All faiths are worldly. Do you agree? – means for getting on, rising in the world, social insurance.

Pericles, Titus and Moth send their best regards to Tiber, and so do I.

And I send you very much love   Sylvia

3 July 1973   *Le Verger de Charry*
Dearest Sylvia, I write this letter, though it is doubtful when you'll get it if English postal sorters continue to think they can save Humanity by refusing to handle mail from France.* French generals don't have English mistresses.

* They were protesting against the French nuclear test in the Pacific.

Thank you for your most enchanting letter. It came at a time of great anxiety. For about three weeks Tiber has got steadily thinner. Suddenly I realised he was desperately ill. Then he was a bit better and disappeared, then came back and could scarcely walk – but took himself off again. I looked for his corpse all day, and in the evening saw a dark patch in the field below. My field glasses showed it was Tiber. He was lying on his side – but still alive. I carried him back; it was too late for the vet. He drank milk which he sicked up again. I gave him water which he drank. He was alive, but only just, in the morning. The vet came and gave him two piqûres – told me to buy a hypodermic and go on.

By evening he was looking up. Luckily the daughter of an old friend and her husband – both doctors – came, and this morning he gave the injections while I held him. Tiber is much better and would like food – but I have only got boiled fillet of cod, and he refuses it. He drinks water: is hollow as an empty bag. Tomorrow I shall buy a chicken and some veal or else *rate*, spleen. He likes that. The vet told me not to give him milk. He has been angelic, very stoic, only sticking his claws into the table when the needle went in. Then a curious sound when I stroke him, a third growl, a third purr, and a third complaint. I talk to him a great deal, and today and yesterday he showed no signs of going off alone to die in private, but sleeps most of the time but now asks for food.

Later. He looks at me royally: sure of himself with one front paw stretched out: he came and climbed on to me and when I stroked him gave a high-pitched purr. He is a bag of bones and tendons. The flesh has wilted. And he won't look at boiled cod!

He is only one of my immediate problems. The tiles for the floor of the studio have to be fetched and laid before the plumbers instal lavabo and bidet. Then curtain rods put up, curtains made, etc., etc. . . But the immediate thing is the carting of the floor tiles here before the lavender is ripe for cutting, as that will take priority.

Peace and quiet, my dear, in retirement. I feel like a field marshal conducting a campaign without *intelligence*, general staff, or Medical Corps, and only mercenaries who may leave the colours and go on an annual holiday! Well, Tiber is alive, and everything will be All Sir Garnet, as the old regular army said in 1890.

By the way in a catalogue of twentieth-century fiction being displayed in Texas Gamel (photographed with Llewelyn Powys) is labelled Garnet Woolsey – a curious slip for Americans to make.

All my love   David

179

Dearest David, Your letter has just come, with the story of Tiber's rising from the dead. I am so thankful, for both your sakes. Henceforward, you will love each other more deeply, more appreciatively. He must have been miserable, feeling he would die, he will love you for having rescued him, cherished him, restored him to raw stewing steak and the joys of the living: and for *talking to him*.

Now is the time to encourage him to stay in or about at night. A regular *en cas de nuit* of raw meat will make him methodical, and sleepy. Would *you* eat cold boiled cod?

If he should ever be so ill again, remember brandy butter. They will lick it off their chops even if they can't swallow, and it is as restorative to them as it would be to us.

As for plumbers, wrong-headedness is inborn in them. The tiles must be laid so that they can take them up before they instal the pipes, and so that they can relay them and break a few while doing so. But Tiber is alive, you can mock plumbers.

This is only a cry of joy, for now I have to pick beans and make a salad for my cousin's lunch. He is intelligent and greedy, so he is worth it. Besides, I shall share them.

My love always   Sylvia

Pour my love on Tiber and my congratulations to him for holding on so stoutly against She'ol.

11: x: 1973   *Maiden Newton*

Dearest David, How are you, how is Tiber? Is he growing a thick coat against the winter? Do your new tiles keep out the rain?

Tonight there is a frost – the first frost. It has immobilised every sound, and if the sun shines tomorrow I shall see all the leaves begin to fall as if they were drilled to do it – filing off like a regiment. I feel as if the frost were watching me.

Some friends of mine have just come back from Russia – from Tashkent, where the mosque is being trimmed with gold-leaf, where there is a bus service to Samarkand. This was striking – so were the women passport officers in Leningrad. They all wear hats. Not uniform hats, ordinary bourgeois hats – to look reassuring, I suppose, for no other hats were seen. But in the Gos-shops in Moscow, magnificent wedding-dresses, white and swan-like. They came back, full of excitement and admiration, and have had a hard time ever since, trying to overcome the stalwart local belief that everyone on one-sixth of the earth's surface lives in misery.

I have a charming screech-owl in the garden, who takes her little owlets for educational flights. Her voice when she talks to them is gentle and melodious; and they answer her by repeated staccato 'pip! pip! pips!', going off all round like small squibs. It is a pretty concert, flute and pizzicato fiddles.

What else have I got to tell you from your native land? Robin Wordsworth visited his country church for Harvest Festival. In the middle of the altar was a wrapped loaf – the kind known as Mother's Pride – ready-sliced in a cellophane caul. A young couple I know, having got married, had to decide on a honeymoon. They blued their resources on a night at the Ritz.

It gets colder and colder – it couldn't get stiller. I shall go to bed. Write and tell me how you are.

Love from   Sylvia

17: x: 1973   *Maiden Newton*

Dearest David, I am no more than halfway through the Sommeilles book [*Plough over the Bones*], but ever since the first pages I have been wanting to kiss you on both cheeks. David, it is triumphant. The people are as living as if one knew the feeling of their skins, they bear down on one, slightly larger than life-size, as if they had come out of a mist suddenly. You set out on the narrative at a stride as if you were going to walk the length of Hadrian's Wall – and world, you are so compelling that at intervals I have to break off and gather myself together for what will happen next. I am so happy and glorified on your account. I hope you are happy and glorious too. My God, you should be. I feel like Sheba writing to Solomon: a fortunate Sheba, who has known Solomon for a lifetime.

Please, dearest Solomon, write me a little inscription which I may stick on the scarlet page. And even more *please plea[se]*, tell me about how you wrote the book. How long have you been nursing it up your sleeve? Was it latent when you wrote about Sommeilles in your autobiography? Did it leap on you out of a common bush?

How did it feel to come back to time present?

I send you my rejoicing love, and a fond stroke to Tiber, that big and handsome tom cat   Sylvia

31 October 1973   *Le Verger de Charry*

Dearest Sylvia, Your letter [of 11: x: 1973] has been forwarded back from Italy where it missed me. I was away for exactly a month, driving altogether four thousand kilometres. . . . On the whole Italy is not a good country to drive in: there are too many cars, too many people and no lonely lovely roads. The towns make up for it.

I drove myself back over the Maddalena pass to Barcelonnette. The Italian side is dull, but the French side astonishingly beautiful with forest – leaves scarlet of dogwood, gold of larch, ruddy beech and deep green of pine – reaching up to the snow and rock.

I brought home a lot of loot: that is I bought myself a clockwork spit for roasting in front of my wood fire, four kilos of mountain honey, a huge bit of Parmesan, a big bottle of oil and a cotton bedspread of green and red pattern. On my return I found all well. I had lent my cottage to an unknown man to act as a cat-sitter and he had done well by Tiber, who however had a new lot [of] scars and healing wounds. . . .

How symbolic is the wrapped loaf on the altar! I see Patrick White has been given the Nobel prize for literature – another wrapped loaf for worship. Michael [Howard] gave me an advance copy of his latest novel: *The Eye of the Storm*, and I ploughed through its six hundred pages during my holiday. The plot, the characters, much of the psychology, is remarkable and deserves great praise. But the writing! What do you make of such passages as: 'As light as unlikely probably as painful as a shark's egg the old not body rather the flimsy soul is whirled around sometimes spat out anus-upwards (souls have an anus they are never allowed to forget it) never separated from the brown the sometimes tinted spawn of snapshots the withered navel string still stuck to what it aspires to yes at last to be if the part the dream life will allow.'

Nor can this old Blimp approve of the constant use of 'like as if'.

There is an Indian summer here. I write this sitting in the sun – much warmer than indoors.

I shall, I think, be alone now for some time and so may be forced to do some work: but as I can't write about shark's eggs anus-upwards I am trying to write the complete story of what happened to Puss in Boots after he had married the Miller's Son to the Princess, palming him off as the Marquis of Carabas.* I don't suppose I shall succeed, it is *like as if* I had forgotten how to write English.

Very much love   David

14: xi: 1973   *Maiden Newton*

Dearest David, *The True History of Puss in Boots* has been on my conscience – my human conscience – ever since your fragment in the Chatto and Windus Calendar.† This time, do face it and finish

---

* Published in 1974 as *The Master Cat: The True and Unexpurgated Story of Puss in Boots*.
† 'From "Puss in Boots" ' in *A Chatto and Windus Almanack 1926*, in which a cat explains that in the story of Puss in Boots 'you may read the history of how

it. You have had a long interval in which to face the wickedness of man: you can have only an incomplete picture of it compared with Tiber's; but with his help you should be able to make out. One of the things cats find hard to stomach is human silliness. I have seen mine look at me with almost despair.

At the moment my three noble creatures are fossicking with the trash-bin. There is nothing in it worth having, as well they know: two egg-shells, some chestnut husks, coffee grounds, grenadilla's rinds, potato peelings. It is an abstract pursuit of knowledge they carry out.

The man – is he called Gallix? – who wants to do a thing on Tim, and translate *The Goshawk* wrote to me too. I advised him to hunt you down. I mentioned you were very hard to catch: however, he has done it. He seems a straightforward fellow. He began his letter by telling me his age.

Did you know that one can walk under the Thames? There is a footway from Greenwich to the Isle of Dogs. Next week I shall be doing it, as I am going to stay in Greenwich with a cousin. She tells me the Isle of Dogs is called so because Catherine of Braganza kennelled her dogs there. I find this hard to believe: it is so exactly like the things I say myself: a blood-lie.

Next month I am being entertained on my eightieth birthday by Chatto and Windus and assortment. I said, when asked, that you are one of the people I'd like to meet. But I'm afraid there's no hope. Nor would I tear you from Tiber and your winter woods and your book. It was only if you happened to be in England. I dislike *being* anything, and generally I dodge it very neatly: but pig gangs aye to the wall till ae day. Then I am being taken off to Boughrood. If Michael gives me Patrick White's six hundred pages to read I will smile falsely and say I've read it already, you lent it to me because you admired it so much.

Very much love. Enjoy Puss.   Sylvia

David did not go to the birthday party, but arranged with Michael Howard to send her a dozen bottles of sherry.

19: xii: 1973   *Maiden Newton*

Darling David, They sit, those dozen bottles, like jurymen, and I cannot really believe them. Not that I don't believe in your affection

cats first came to distrust men'. But it stops short of actually telling the story. In 'The Castle of Carabas' in *The Cat's Cradle-Book* (New York, 1940; London, 1960) Sylvia had told her own version of the sequel to the Puss in Boots story.

183

and your capacity to sweep me off my feet: but did you really mean them? Or did Michael misunderstand you? If he did, please tell me the misunderstanding, and I will set it right: to the extent of six bottles. I won't be more upright than that, as I am very fond of dry sherry, and would be sorry to wrong your kindness by under-estimating it.

Dear David, I am, in plain honesty, very grateful and touched and pleased.

I felt envious of Michael when I heard he had seen you so lately, and seen Tiber, I don't feel he is as worthy of Tiber as I would be. His mind is given to his five pampered jades of Asia. Pat has a wider outlook. I suppose it was they who told you about my birthday, for I cannot suppose you sit reading *Who's Who* by your winter fireside and I don't see how else you could have known. It was a *very* fine party. I have seldom felt less like being eighty on a birthday. The next morning I went off to the Chinese exhibition where by far the loveliest thing is a seated woman as self-contained as Ray, and very like her. If I had been Paulina, I would have called her to life.

Then the Howards drove me to Boughrood. No one else there: pleasant for me, but sad for them. I am worried how they will manage for visitors while everyone is fussing about petrol and England's extremity.* Do you know any rich person with good taste who could be directed to Boughrood? Any one who would like to fish in the Wye? Or write a book on Welsh heraldry? Or sonnets to buzzards?

As for England's extremity, I would like to knock their heads together. The Government can only play poker and the Opposition can only play soccer and the only aspiration the combatants can make is to get together round a table.

How are you and Tiber getting on with Puss in Boots? I have been waiting to read that book for fifty years. Does he throw in a touch of Stendhal here and there? *Henri Brulard* was obviously written by a cat: there is the same photographic memory of where everybody sat at dinner; the same registering memory by which cats find their way back to Land's End from Duncansby Head, infallibly recognising what they cannot possibly have seen through the walls of their wicker hamper.

Happy Christmas, darling David! Prospering New Year!
Love   Sylvia

---

* There was a fuel crisis, both in oil from the Middle East and in coal and electricity at home. The 'three-day week' had been announced to begin in January.

Dearest David, You have put me in a quandary. I have you all together, in order, in a bookshelf which nicely holds you and T. F. Powys (and a Bible to keep Theodore in a good state of mind); *and* your grandfather. But when I came to put away *Plough over the Bones* and *Purl and Plain* there wasn't room for them. By taking away your grandfather there was room. So I took him away. I have been uneasy ever since. So tonight I shall take out two of your *Net for Venus* period books, and restore him.

That is my New Year's resolution. When I first read *The Twilight* I was so young that I read them au pied de la lettre, as immensely superior fairy stories. I have loved them ever since, I have added veneration to love but love came long first. Learning and felinity.

My only other New Year resolution is to go to bed earlier. But that is statutory. I make it yearly and never keep it.

Were you involved in those floods I read about? I hope not. The damage floods do is negligible -- and rather exhilarating (there go the refuse bins! and the old potato basket!). It is the aftermath which gets one down, the rich deposit of mud and the bluebottles which gather to the stink.

Yesterday I went out to lunch, and on either hand I had a printer. The left-hand printer asked me if I had known Charles Prentice. I said I knew him very well, and in a moment they were off, praising him like Cherubim and Seraphim; and knowing what they praised.

'And I shall smile, though underground.'

It was you, dear David, who showed my poems to Charles, and established me in that kind receptacle. My birthday party seemed incomplete without the pair of you.

I still write poems from time to time. Here is one.

> Learning to walk the child totters between embraces,
> Admiring voices confirm its tentative syllables:
> In the day of unlearning speech, mislaying balance,
> We make our way to the grave delighting nobody.
> Thus the wheel turns in the bright implacable river.

. . . Happy New Year to you and Tiber. Scratch him behind his ears for me.

Sylvia

David also wrote poems from time to time. Here is one written at Charry:

L'Étranger Hedgehog

Sans nous saluer il entre dans la maison
Par la porte ouverte du jardin.
On se rencontre au fond du couloir,
Et le petit bonhomme se crispe, voulant se cacher.
Je lui apporte du lait dans une soucoupe,
Et le hérisson projette le nez.
Oh quel nez! Sensible, pointu, efficace.
Il hoche les épaules comme une vieille,
Allant á la messe, prise par une rafale ajustant son châle.
Il tourne pour mieux regarder avec ses petits boutons noirs.
Nous le laissons avec la porte ouverte.
'Bonne nuit, le petit.'
Il ne répond pas, il ne dort non plus.
Le matin il est parti sans nous dire adieu.
Il sera heureux de ne plus revoir des étrangers.
Nous sommes heureux qu'il ait bu le lait,
Et de lui avoir dit bonsoir.

1974

Dearest Sylvia, I was woken this morning at a quarter to nine (to eight by your time) by a knocking by the old man who brings Express letters and telegrams. It was your letter of 17 October last which had been sent to Italy – arriving after I left. Typically —— left it lying about for two-and-a-half months and then, conscience-stricken, forwarded it Express. You must have been thinking me an oaf not to reply to your wonderful paean of praise of *Plough over the Bones* – far more than it deserves. But it makes me happy that you believe in my people. My villain was invented, and so was my anarchist Étienne. But Georges I knew very well – like a speckled toad – but he actually had raked out the remains of the soldier who was thrown into the burning house, put them in a bucket and buried them in the cemetery during the German occupation. He had that innate sense of propriety which is so deep in the French. Eglantine, Old Émile (who was looked after by the young village girls) and particularly Pierre Lanfrey were my friends. I thought of writing it while I was finishing *Sons of the Falcon*, because I am living in France, and the months at Sommeilles were when I got to know France and the French well. Old Conduchet is also someone there I knew, and he was actually torn in two by the desire to be the open-handed benefactor of his neighbours and to get the better of everyone.

The woman enjoying doing a man's work cutting up trees in the forest lives in a farm just across the valley here. I am burning wood – oak logs one metre long – in my fireplace now which I bought from her husband. She was so happy when I found her working in the forest that I wanted to kiss the sawdust off her cheeks.

I have just finished *Puss in Boots*. It is not an agreeable book, no more suitable for children than *Gulliver's Travels*. But it needs tinkering with: it is perhaps a bit too crude – in that way like life. Incidentally it has led me to a Shakespearean discovery, perhaps known to many already.

If you look up Cats in the index of Frazer's *Golden Bough* you are referred to a horrible account of how cats were collected in wicker baskets and burned alive on St John's Day and how Louis XIV set fire to such a bonfire and danced round it wearing a wreath of roses. Why were they burned? Because witches could turn themselves into cats, and if you burned enough cats you were pretty sure to burn a few witches. Old and young women who loved their cats dared not protest for fear of being accused of being witches. But the millers, the corn merchants, the farmers who suffered from rats and mice in their granaries, did protest, saying that their cats 'were harmless necessary animals', and Shakespeare echoed their adjectives, which are not ones which would occur to you and me – though true enough.*

Tiber is in good fur, but he coughs as though he might be going to be sick, but doesn't actually vomit. I thought it might be worms in the stomach and have wormed him, but perhaps it is a ball of fur?

I am going to the Canaries – or rather to the Isla de la Palma – invited by my cousin Dicky, whose wife died a few weeks ago. I shall drive myself down to Malaga and then fly to Grand Canary or Tenerife, and after that take a small plane to his island. He says there is hot sun, bathing and masses of wild flowers on land and fish in the sea.

There is no cat-sitter in sight, but there are generous friends who will take Tiber in. I am uneasy, as they have a playful dog and two neutered cats as well as ducks, chickens and rabbits (the latter shut up in hutches). He will undoubtedly fight the male neuter cat, but he may go off in a dudgeon and not return. Though the French no longer burn cats alive, they shoot stray cats in the woods.

'Hodge shan't be shot,' said Dr Johnson, and I wish I could say the same of Tiber. I can't take him with me, as he hates being driven in a car. When I drove him to the vet he peed all over the dress of the charming girl who was holding him. When we got out of the car she pulled it off and improvised a dress out of a very large handkerchief in which she looked like Diana. I have decided to be cowardly and drive down via Barcelona and Valencia – country now ruined by seven-storey blocks of flats and notices in English and German informing one of Real Spanish Dancing Girls and Flamenco. Two years ago I drove through the centre of Spain and was very nearly done for in a snowstorm between Toledo and Avila, by a miracle managed to turn my car round and go back to a village with a bar with angels who dried my clothes and gave me a bit of fried cod and an apple for supper. A rich man, i.e. he wore leather shoes and a tie, had also taken shelter. He had a weighing-

* *The Golden Bough: Balder the Beautiful*, ii (1913), 39–41, confirms that cats were burned as creatures whom witches might turn into, but the millers' complaint is David's own extrapolation.

machine, brand-new in a cardboard box. They spread a newspaper so as not to soil it, and everyone weighed themselves. Then they called in the cook – a woman like a short barrel. She was overjoyed, very proud indeed because she weighed more than anybody else, 116 kilos – 256 pounds, eighteen stone odd.

There was universal joy at this result.

Well, how wonderful to get your letter this morning!

Your affectionate   David

1: ii: 1974   *[Maiden Newton]*

Dearest David, I am grateful to the old man who woke you at 8.45 because you then wrote me a letter I was very happy to get, and sent an inscription which I shall stick into *Plough over the Bones* with love and pride.★

I write a scurvy stingy Blue in haste, to ask, if this reaches you in time, what will be your address in the Canaries and how long will you be there.

I have several things I want to say and, now that you have finished *Puss in Boots* and I shan't be interrupting you, I would like to send you specimens of how I am writing now – a new vein which has possessed me during the last year. I think you might like them: they are factual about the unreal. I grew tired of the human heart.

I drink your sherry and bless your name. I have never seen so much sherry in my life. I am like the old sailor who came into Father Divine's heaven on 158th Street, looked round at the angels carrying in trophies of ice-cream, and said 'Such abundance – such abundance!' and could say no more. Did I ever tell you about that heaven? A match for your Bar with Angels. Whatever they have done between Barcelona and Valencia, they can't have obliterated that *prose* landscape.

I hope Tiber will be satisfied with quelling the dog and the neuter cat and eating a few ducks, and will not go off to the woods. After all he is a cat who knows the world.

Love from   Sylvia

9 February 1974   *Gerona*

Dearest Sylvia, I am so glad you like the sherry. I have been in Spain for five hours and haven't tasted a drop. I am on my way to the Canaries – or rather to the Isla de la Palma – driving to Malaga, and

★ 'For Sylvia whom I have loved and whose work I have loved and admired for over fifty years David 1923–1973'.

flying from there. God knows when I shall get there – the young woman in Toulouse gave me the wrong ticket – to Las Palmas, and I have to try and change it.

Yesterday I parted with Tiber. I let him out to do his business – and he ran off. I pursued gently. And as he suspected something dreadful (I had rolled up the carpets) I should never have caught him had it not been for his decent inheritance – he had to rake leaves and soil over his excrement. He goes to some friends with a half-witted young dog, a ten-year-old neuter male and a seven-year-old neuter female. Not what a sexually vigorous young tom hopes for. But such is life.

Actually (to get rid of the cat subject) a large unmistakable Siamese stalked across my road in the foothills of the Pyrenees at least a mile from the nearest human habitation. I stayed last night in a little town called Limoux and all today drove by tiny roads through the French foothills of the Pyrenees – sun – blue sky, patches of snow and then the impossible ranges of snow mountains . . . against the sun.

I went out of my way to Cerét to see the Museum again – wonderful painted bowls – the insides painted – by Picasso, and many many other things.

I drove smack though into Spain without having my passport or green card looked at. A customs man gave me a wave, and so I drove on. Here I sat on the Rambla, where the inhabitants parade, for three-quarters of an hour. Everyone was happy. Parents with prams. Quartets of lads brave enough to have grown their hair to their shoulders. Girls in Royal Stuart Tartan kilts or mini-skirts – or fur coats and trousers – and so many whispered nothings, and such eagerness, that I began to like the Human Race. It was weak of me – but I hope a pardonable weakness.

Well, are you alive? Is there peat to be dug on Egdon Heath? I hear the miners' strike is in full blast and probably flying pickets are preparing to blow up whatever goes on at Winfrith nowadays. I shall be back at Charry by the middle of March. Write and tell me your impressions of the Revolution.

David left this letter unfinished and enclosed it with his next.

21: iii: 1974   *[Maiden Newton]*

Dearest Bunny, I never regret my decision to live on alone, and most of the time I manage very well. But tonight I am quite alone; for I am going away a few days tomorrow, and as the cats can't keep house by themselves, I took them to their luxurious Hilton Hotel (O derisive and injurious name). And being alone I suddenly became *afraid of being alone*. Casting about for some prop to my courage I remembered *The White/Garnett Letters*, pulled it out, read the dedication and the last sentence, and was no longer a vain shadow.

And I ought to tell you this and you ought to know it. Please know how much our long affection means to me.   Sylvia

28 March 1974   *Le Verger de Charry*

Dearest Sylvia, Your little note to say you were afraid and lonely without your cat, came today, as I was meaning to write to you. I enclose an unfinished letter which got mislaid, written as I was setting out. Since then – well, I have swum in tropic seas (the Isla de la Palma, the smallest of the Canaries, is just in the tropic of Capricorn or Cancer). Don't go to the Canaries. In Tenerife the notices are all in German, *Echt Bayerische Kuchen*, and at the restaurant the diners have got so fat they can barely reach their knives and forks. On the Isla de la Palma (nothing to do with Las Palmas on Grand Canary) the sands are coal black, and there are fields of coal black lava extruded in 1949 on which nothing grows. Actually getting back through the Atlantic breakers left me very breathless, and I realised I was an old man.

Then a week with Gerald Brenan and the lovely and intelligent girl who lives with him. I read his *St John of the Cross*, published by the Cambridge Press. Very well written and a revelation of the horrors of sanctity. Owing to the most trifling differences they flung each other in gaol, and beat each other – But when at last he died, suppurating from sores, crowds broke loose about his corpse and someone bit off one of his toes – clever fellow to get an authentic relic. I spent a delightful fortnight with Janetta [Parladé], married to a Spaniard who is so charming and gentle and amused and who talks perfect English. I was rather proud, as I introduced Janetta, who is an almost professional cook, to a way of cooking squid or cuttlefish which she did not know and is the best way there is – stewed with aubergines and tomato in red wine. There were oranges on some trees and others in full blossom and bee-orchids and tiny wild daffodils.

I took five days driving back across the central plateau. Before Avila the snow was banked high on each side of the road, but the road itself clear and the snow mountains very beautiful. But it is a country of red mud and mules and ancient shepherds frozen by the wind or burned black by the pitiless sun. No wonder the saints lifted their eyes to heaven and rejected the world.

And then when one gets to the Pyrenees and France one finds

oneself in a land of cowslips and primroses and beechwoods, and for the first time I could eat my picnic lunch outside the car – and then I heard the cuckoo!

And the fields pale lavender with lady's smock, almost my favourite flower.

When I got back I found a telegram nine days old to say Macmillan are pleased with *The Master Cat*, my story of Puss in Boots. But we have to find an illustrator who can draw things simply – like Ray's woodcuts.

However, it is good news for me and rather surprising.

All my love   David

8: iv: 1974   *Maiden Newton*

Dearest Bunny, Nothing will induce me to go to the Canaries to lie on coal-black sand. I am glad you got to shore – though to such a Stygian shore, black and barren. And I am glad, though envious, that you have heard the cuckoo. Here it is still a hopeful identification with barking dogs. We are a poetical nation: at any other season we know dogs for dogs.

I am slowly going out of my mind trying to find a French equivalent for 'A little bit of bread and no cheese' or some similar bird-song tag. Except for 'coupe lui l'cou', for the cuckoo, everything else is farmyard. Please ask your dear Daily, whose name I have forgotten. It must be a wild bird.

When you were driving through the Pyrenees did you come upon a derelict lieu de pélérinage called Bétharram? It has a church filled with votive tablets *c.* 1825–35. A girl fell in a brook, a beautiful lady stood on the rim, handed her a twig, hauled her out by it, and disappeared. The interesting thing is that Bétharram is in the next village to Lourdes. It seems improbable that Bernardette did not hear the story from the other side of the mountain.

I did not know about St John of the Cross's toe. As you say, what promptitude. I can imagine the watershed of mind when the kiss turned to the bite. Fine indomitable teeth, too.

M. François Gallix came to visit me (like the King of Spain's daughter) to talk about Tim White. He is charming: young, shy, enthusiastic and serious. A Burgundian by birth. He brought some of the translation of *The Goshawk*. I thought it was good. He manages to get some of the limberness, and almost some of the rant, of the original.

I hope you found Tiber well and not too downcast by that mixed society. Of course he ran off when he saw you roll up the carpets.

They do it as a demonstration of damn-your-eyes. It is a token of love. I will be too tactful to ask if he behaved himself as an evacuee.

Yesterday I draped a counterpane over the garden seat to air. It made a tent, and Pericles and Moth spent the morning playing hide and seek underneath it. It is a formalised sport. Cat 1 hides. Cat 2 approaches, goes round the tent, snuffing and snuffing. Cat 1 rushes out, Cat 2 pursues him, they roll on the grass, decide to sever and begin all over again. The snuffing is completely artificial.

Would to God I knew an illustrator who can draw things simply – like Ray. I have a very fine Siamese cat, in appliqué, which Pat Howard made for me, but I doubt if her *drawings* would have the massiveness for your story, though the appliqué is a hammer-blow statement, the hammer in a velvet glove. You finish your stories outrageously fast. But I can't complain, since I hope to read it before I die. For all that, I implore you to be exigent about the illustrator and to keep Macmillan dangling till you are satisfied. A breath of fancy could blight the whole book.

With my love   Sylvia

27: vii: 1974   *Maiden Newton*

Darling David, Michael Howard said you have finished *Puss in Boots*. Do I congratulate or condole? A finished book is a brief glow, for me – not always a glow even; a farewell on a rainy day. When Valentine was alive it was a reason to go to bed and drink champagne. Now there is a moderate incentive to tidy the larder.

Plough over the Bones was returned to me yesterday, and I have for once a complete house of Garnetts. But it won't last. The returner of *Plough over the Bones* wants to borrow *Pocahontas*.

François Gallix lunched here last week. I like him very much, though he should not be going bald at his age. He told me that there are very few nursery rhymes in French. My heart assented that this didn't surprise me. I thought of replying politely that we have very few rococo confessionals in England. Do you know those blue and white penitential *alcoves* at Isle-sur-[la]-Sorgue? But I refrained, because I am not invariably delighted when Americans know every tower in Suffolk and every teapot in the Bowes Museum.

I stayed in such a house last month. Its name means "The Cry of Anguish in Battle," and all around are mountains out of the Mabinogion. The house was built on the side of a mountain, and its builders applied it, so to speak, to an outcrop of slate which with a little hacking and chiselling they made a newel stair out of. So I learned to climb a piece of Welsh mountain to my bedroom. No rail or rope or such-like amenities, just one's natural ape. The ground flooring of large black slate flags was like walking on black butter.

How are you, my dear, and how is Tiber? I wish you would walk in and eat my white raspberries and my white currants. First they were scorched, then they were drowned. It seems to be the exact treatment they require.

If you do your own cooking – I think you do – by now you might like to try my new way with courgette. Scrape it and slice it as usual and put it with two-thirds of well-flavoured vegetable stock, one third olive oil, just enough to cover it. When it begins to cook add a handful of garden-mint, chopped roughly, and let it simmer on till it has absorbed the oily stock.

I turn my mind from the thought that in five months' time I shall be cooking Brussels sprouts. They are such spinsterish vegetables. I thought I'd got the better of their virtue by roofing them with fried bread covered with mustard and brown sugar. . . .

Love from   Sylvia

5 August 1974   Le Verger de Charry

Dearest Sylvia, I was so glad to get your letter. It was a bitter disappointment not having time to come and look in on you in Dorset when I was in England. The reason was that I am planning a new novel, and it was essential to drive up to the East Coast of Scotland, because I cannot draw it from my head when it is well known to so many and the novel is historical.* The visit was actually rewarding, and a fisherman – the only one left – gave me three magnificent crabs. If I had only been in Cornwall Dorset would have been on the way, but I started from Wales.

I posted the proofs of *The Master Cat* back this morning and am very pleased with it – my daughter Nerissa has drawn exactly the right illustrations – though they had been put in the wrong places. But that will be put right. And Tiber has helped – as you will see when you get the book, he is the only French cat to have set his mark on a work of English literature. So we are both puffed up.

21 August. This letter was interrupted and got shoved away, so I continue it with an anecdote about Einstein which I got third-hand. In America he went to live in a suburb which was not 'lilywhite' and had an educated Negro family next door and greatly in awe of him. Their daughter, aged four, was not, and she and Einstein became friends. She asked him to her birthday party, and he accepted.

* *Up She Rises*, based on the adventures of his Scottish great-grandmother, Clementina Black.

194

However, he was aloof and silent. Suddenly he asked his hostess if she had an upstairs bathroom. She led him to it, and he remained there for an hour. She was urging her husband to go and see if he had been taken ill, when he came downstairs, very gay and social, and was the life and soul of the party for the rest of his visit.

When they went to the bathroom later, they found a long mathematical equation written in child's chalk on the wall. He had been taken short with it and had gone to the bathroom to relieve his brain, not his bowels. It meant nothing to them, but they fixed a piece of plate glass over it to preserve it, and the man who told Hank's informant had seen it. It is borne out by Valéry asking Einstein if he carried a notebook to put down his ideas. 'No. Ideas are so rare.'

Maynard [Keynes]'s description of Einstein is: 'Charlie Chaplin with the forehead of Shakespeare.' I once stood directly behind him. Where? Where he was sitting in the House of Lords, at the Opening of Parliament.

Well, we had some hot days here, 93° in the shade at six p.m. I have had constant visitors, the last being my darling Nerissa and her lover, who has had a wonderful effect on her, bringing her back to her old self and banishing the belief that it is a moral duty to épater not only her bourgeois parents but the whole of humanity. Tiber felt the heat.

All my love, dearest Sylvia   David

20: viii: 1974   *Maiden Newton*

Dearest David, Does Tiber leap up on to whatever you begin to write and rub his head passionately against you? That is what Titus is doing at this moment. It is too wet for him to go out and hunt moles, and he has to express himself somehow. Please congratulate Tiber on his addition to English literature, which is much too bedogged, though its cats are distinguished, from pensive Selina onward. I long for your book and Nerissa's illustrations. It is very obliging of you to be such a rapid producer. I don't have to think I shall be dead before I read another work by Garnett – while I despair of ever setting eyes on George Painter's book about Chateaubriand,★ at long intervals he sends me extracts from Chapter One.

Which bit of the East Coast? I know it only at either end: Berwickshire, with towers of herring guts along it and armies of gulls flying round the towers, or that very handsome and sinister coast of Caithness; and a snatch of Perthshire where inland there is a

★ Eventually published in 1977.

beech hedge twenty foot high: fastigiate beeches, plaited and clipped into a wall. . . .

I have been having visitors too. One of them was Peggy Ashcroft who summarised the plight of ageing actresses by saying in a smouldering voice. 'Now I have only Volumnia left me.' . . .

Yesterday I was given a hunk of farmhouse Blue Vinney. This afternoon a friend will be bringing me a basketful of figs and English peaches. I am not doing too badly. And the *New Yorker* go on paying me enormous cheques.

I wish all our friends were as fortunate. Boughrood is in a bad way; very few people paying to go there, and Michael wanting to wash his hands of it. I grieve for the rescued house and garden as much as for Pat and Michael who put so much hard work and hard hope into it.

The swallows are gathering (they take off from Maiden Newton station, it is on a hill with a quantity of useful wires), my cats are growing heavy coats, the hawthorns are covered with berries, all of them already crimson. There is every sign of a mild winter.

Referring back to my cheques from the *New Yorker*, I don't think you show enough interest in my writings. I intend to send you galleys of a recent story – a great weight of galleys, for it is almost a novella. I *intend*; I don't go so far as to say I will.

My love to Tiber (have you a photograph you can send me?). My love to you   Sylvia

15: ix: 1974

I wrote 46 so carelessly that my letter was returned stamped Voie Inconnue – like an alternative title to *Le Grand Meaulnes*.

22: x: 1974   *Lower Frome Vauchurch, Dorchester*
      (This new address has been forced on me, God knows why.
                                                    T'other still serves.)
Darling David, I was at Boughrood last week – an old engagement and they wanted me to keep it; so I can tell you my impressions. Pat has gone ahead and bought a cottage. . . . *

Michael is walking in his sleep. If he could find a job – if he could find a house. He goes up to London and comes back with neither. *He looks much smaller*, has the sad meek expression of a lesser

---

* The scheme to use Boughrood as a haven for writers and artists had totally collapsed, and they were trying to sell the house. Moreover Michael had fallen in love with another woman.

carnivore, which is the expression of being consumedly in love. . . .

I think he misses your support – your worldly wisdom and your intrepid control of hornets. There is a *Boy's Own Paper* quality about him which is very touching. I could do nothing for him; and was sorry.

As for Boughrood, the leaves were falling all round, and lying in lakes of shining wet colour: and the saplings, with seedsmen's labels still round their necks, were growing and thriving. The rooms are emptier – things being put away – their proportions lovelier and statelier than ever. It was as though the house were unleafing.

I did not think there was so much regret left in my old bones.

I hope your rheumatism is better – sciatic nerve? – and that you will be able to go to Spain and winter there happily.

My love to you, and to Tiber. Michael says he is as handsome as a Lord, and has a beautiful relationship of owning you.   Sylvia

1: xii: 1974   *Lower Frome Vauchurch*

Dearest David, It is the kind of night and the time of year to listen to a story. I have come to Tiber's Mark, and add my own to it. The narrative is so beautifully *paced* – with such variety and cunning. The studious moment of Chapter XVII came in the nick of time to remind me I was reading a work of art and must control myself.

And then I came to the picture of you and Tiber, and sighed with approval to see you both so happy in each other. I remember writing somewhere in my voluminous works that the expression of love is stern. That is how you are looking at Tiber, and he feels the force of it, and responds with possessive paws laid on, to show he can love seriously too. He has a lovely mask with his languishing slitted eyes and the critical tip to his nose. Handsome Tiber! I am so glad you have got each other.

As for Peter Pendrey,★ he ought to be clawed till he knows better. I wish Nerissa had done the front of the jacket. 'O puss, you sleeping mass of fur' – I have three sleeping masses round me as I write. The two Siamese had their claws snipped shorter this morning by a visitor. They purred falsely while it was done. When she drove off this afternoon they followed her, and watched her settle in her car with civilly blank faces. When the engine started they turned and walked briskly back to the house.

Where are you, my dear? At le Verger with Tiber or freezing in the winds of Spain? And *how* are you? It is one of the bores of old age

★ The artist who designed the book-jacket.

197

that it makes one distrustful of oneself. But I have never regretted my decision five years ago to live alone.

Love   Sylvia

The Times of 17 December carried a long obituary of Michael Howard, saying that he 'died suddenly', with no indication that it was suicide.

20 December 1974   *c/o Señor Don Geraldo Brenan,*
            Cañada de los Palombas, Alhaurin el Grande, Malaga, Spain
Dearest Sylvia, I saw about Michael in *The Times* yesterday – by chance someone had brought a copy.

I would like to know the circumstances if you know them.

Perhaps if there hadn't been a postal strike and I hadn't gone to Spain I could have helped. But probably not.

I have recovered from 'flu and am going today to Gerald's and shall probably stay in Spain around here till the New Year. So if you wrote at once I would get a letter.

Strange, two such different men we both loved – publishers – and destroyed by love: Charles and Michael.

Take care of yourself, my dear, dear Sylvia   David

28: xii: 1974   *Lower Frome Vauchurch*
Dearest David, How ever deep you are in Spain, you will have heard that Michael Howard killed himself (peacefully with an overdose of barbiturates). It was a planned thing. He wrote several *faire-part* letters to his friends and relations, and arranged that his sons should go to Boughrood to look after Pat. She had been away for a couple of nights and came home to find the house full of policemen.

I grieve to know he is dead. The more so that he was so handsome, so limber, so much a graceful animal. And I think of his young woman, left on the outskirts of the tragedy. When I was at Boughrood he went to London for twenty-four hours, and returned bringing Pat a scythe. A grim gift, in hindsight. If one put such things in a book, they would seem very false and painstaking.

I know you will be sorry, and I send my condolences.

With love from   Sylvia

1975

Lower Frome Vauchurch

Dearest David, . . . How are you, my dear? And Tiber? Are you back with him? I was so glad to have his picture on the jacket of Puss. You were both very becoming to each other.

In February/the Third did a performance of *Timon of Athens*. It has been totally misunderstood. It is a savage contemporary satire on the toadies and turn-coats between old Elizabeth and new James. Timon is a pretext for speaking out his mind: Alcibiades reproaching the Senate for neglecting an old soldier says: 'My wounds ache at you.' I am wild to see it produced in the clothes of that day – those balloon breeches, thin beards on starched ruffs, shoe-roses and walking-canes. If I were ten years younger I would insinuate myself into Stratford on Avon and get it done properly.

With love   Sylvia

13 April 1975   *Le Verger de Charry*

Dearest Sylvia, . . . I may possibly come to England for a short visit in October. I don't want to, but not everyone is prepared to come out here to see me. Already I have had several visitors, and Tommy's nephew, Derek Goldby – one of Helen Tomlin's sons – is here at the moment and laughing over Julia Strachey's description of his grandmother. He is a tall young free-lance theatrical director who has just directed (we used to say produced) a play in the Théâtre Poche in Brussels.

Before his arrival a young Tasmanian woman, unknown to me, came and stayed nearly a week. I liked her very much – a biologist who had done work on the pollution of rivers. She was twenty-five, and there seemed no age barrier between us – only her pronunciation of many words and my deafness.

Before she came I had a short visit from my friend Diana Gunn, who gave me a novel she was writing [*Ella's Dream*] to read. I read it. I liked it. I thought it very good – and now less than a month later I cannot remember what it was about – terrible. Did I tell you to read her essay on *Anna Karenin* and Tolstoy? (I think it is very good – called *A Daring Coiffeur*.)

I was a long time recovering from my visit to Spain, where I was ill and was taking some dreadful pills advised by a chemist against rheumatic pains. They turned out to be cortisone and made me feeble and inert. Luckily I got 'flu badly – the doctor was horrified when he saw the pills. But it was emotionally painful, as I discovered that though warmly invited, I was not wanted. I spent most of my time with Gerald Brenan, who is [in] a good condition and reconciled to the girl he has lived with chastely since Gamel's death having taken a lover. I like her very much indeed and what I saw of the lover. Tiber is lost for good, but a red squirrel comes every morning – eats his breakfast of acorns outside my window. His table manners are exquisite.

Well, very much love. Please write again,   David

8: v: 1975   *Lower Frome Vauchurch*

Dearest David, If you come to England in October it would be very good and kind of you to visit me. Or I might hoist myself up to London to see you. I was there briefly last month, and watched a very fine blizzard *terrifying* Whitehall, dwarfing and bleaching it. I had been visiting Ian and Trekkie Parsons, where I met Quentin Bell and his very handsome and stately wife. She sat upright, well back into her chair – not a fidget in her. I think she is descended from one of those Oliviers you played with as a child. I liked her very much, and felt she had been composed by Gluck.

I am very sorry about Tiber. He and you looked so happy and pleased with each other in the photograph on the dust-cover of *The Master Cat*. I think your stars must be in a bad quarter of the heavens. Tiber gone, and you nearly destroyed with cortisone. Horrible drug: if it had not been stopped in time you might have developed a moony round face and gone bald. . . .

Are your woods full of nightingales? The best orchestras of nightingales I ever heard were in the woods round Aubeterre. They sang in rivalry, but the rivals were massed choirs. Another pleasant thing I remember at Aubeterre was an old man who had moored a shallow boat to the riverbank (Dronne), filled it with earth and grew salads in it.

My deep-sea–diving, *cum* naturalist, *cum* stone-mason friend, who long ago was our garden boy, took me for a drive last Sunday. His car was full of rattles and squeaks, and he remarked thoughtfully that it was like a wood at night.

What are you writing now? I wish it may be another book of your autobiography – provided you don't rush it.

I have grown so old that I actually go to bed before eleven. I must go now.

With my love   Sylvia

29: vi: 1975   *Lower Frome Vauchurch*

Dearest David, Since you ask to see what poems I am writing, here are a few: I write very few, anyhow.

I agree about Michael. It was Boughrood, that miscarried love, reinforced by that papa he never managed to shake off his back. Boughrood is still in the market: those intending buyers who had signed and sealed renegued at the last moment. Pat goes there from time to time and dusts it.

If you have been forbidden salt, get a bottle of anchovy sauce. It is better than salt in any cooked food: and the secret of Melton Mowbray pies.

I am in the burning jaws of a drought. It reduces me to short sentences, but otherwise I am enjoying it. I will write and tell you when it rains.

Fond love   Sylvia

i

Experimentally poking the enormous
Frame of the Universe
This much we know:
It has a pulse like us.

But if it lags for woe,
Quickens for fever,
Or calm euphoria measures it for ever
Other astronomers must show.

ii

has already been quoted on p. 185

iii

On the heels of Easter when the sun dances
To flute of birds and thrum of sap rising
Comes the bitter surprise, the Blackthorn Winter,
When hailstones clatter and skies darken,
And the lamb forlorn
Cries out, 'Why was I born?'

iv

Fish come solid
Out of the sea,
Each with its appropriate
Measure of majesty.
The purposed sprat
Knows what it would be at;
The skate,
Twirling in its death-agony,
Is the embodied
Wave that flopped down
On the fisherman's coble and left him to drown.

v

Night after night I say
'I may die before day.'
Why should fate interpose
This tedious cadenza
Between my music and its close?
Would I were away!

1: ix: 1975   *Lower Frome Vauchurch*

Dearest David, I shall be here the first week in October and
delighted to see you. Shade to shade may come rather drowsily.
You grow deaf, I mumble; but at least we shall be in each other's
presence. May I give you a meal, will you spend the night? . . .

I must catch the post, so no more now except Welcome – and
have you heard that Pat Howard is happily married?

Love   Sylvia

29: ix: 1975   *Lower Frome Vauchurch*

Darling David, I will expect you on Monday 13th (the 12th is
tethered to Another). Won't you come to lunch? Will you stay the
night? I will repeat the carrots in chestnut sauce which first endeared
me to you.

I too am filled with horror in Polite London. But yesterday I was
driven from Greenwich down the Old Kent Road and could love
London again. The population has darkened, but there are still
terraces and terraces of the old mild brown brick.

Unless you counter-order me I will expect you to lunch on
Monday 13th.

Love from   Sylvia

From Sylvia's letter to Bea Howe of 16: x: 1975:

David came last week, and I gave him brandy with his coffee, and some admirable fillet steak. I watched his start of delighted surprise when he sank his teeth into the first mouthful.

After the first mutual shock of seeing ourselves so much changed for the worst, we found we had not changed so much after all, and it was a happy visit. Nerissa was with him. She had been driving him all over England, visiting William in Grisedale, and a cousin in Wales, and a cousin . . . in Somerset – and so on. I asked after Hilton. Hilton he gave to Richard, Richard has let it to a model tenant. The model tenant is devoted to lawns. The lawn is like an advertisement, smooth grass paths have been cut through the orchard, there is not a nettle left. Bunny seemed pleased. I listened in woe. I detest the thought of lovely sombre untidy Hilton turned into a stockbroker's bijou.

Nerissa was charming, and *extremely* beautiful, and very like Vanessa [Bell]. She wore *large* scarlet boots, and lives in Bethnal Green, in a house divided into flats for the new generation by the L.C.C. I suppose the indigenous inhabitants are put away in some High-Rise horror, or transferred to the new outskirts.

19 November 1975   *Le Verger de Charry*

Dearest Sylvia, A kind American has sent me a sheaf of pages of the *New Yorker** – the text very oddly illustrated. The stories are terribly disillusioning: I shall never want to live in Fairyland again: I would sooner live on Beverly Heights, where there is surely less protocol though no doubt just as much jealousy among the lovely ladies.

(Did I ever tell you about my friendship with an Ex-Miss United States? She has lived incognito for seven years and keeps an Art Gallery.)

Well, you have certainly created a world. Those Welsh fairies on Plynlimon were just like the four Olivier Girls and Rupert Brooke and Békássy, and I should have fitted in admirably. My father wanted to call me Hobbinol after the dwarf in *The Faerie Queene*, in which case I should probably have been stolen and castrated by those loathsome Bretons. I would rather live in our world [of] bombs and bureaucrats! And the terrible thing is that you are right. So was Shakespeare.

* Containing some of Sylvia's stories about the Kingdoms of Elfin.

Well, I am back here – my life shared by a Tasmanian biologist girl who studies the pollution of rivers.

I went to my French doctor yesterday, who said (in those words) after listening to my heart, etc.: 'You are HO.K., Monsieur Garné.' One of the few words he knows of our language.

Life goes on: rain, fog and today sunshine.

On the 13th December a kind friend is taking me to an International Cat Show in Toulouse. I am not sure that I shall enjoy it. I prefer to admire in private. But Rachel Devas wants to go, and I am trying to persuade her to enter her cat Tigger, who is a lovely grey tabby with tiger's stripes, and the legend

Frère utérin du celèbre Tiber.

The only new thing in my life besides Vicky Thorp of Tasmania is a box for smoking sausages, fish, fowls, etc. You sprinkle oak sawdust below a tray and a grid on which your trout or sausage rests and put it over a fire and the results are marvellous. My steel box is too small. I should like to smoke a turkey and only smoke half a chicken. Do write to me occasionally. I haven't written a line and am horribly indifferent to my delinquency.

Very much love and regards to your Orientals.   David

12: xii: 1975   *Lower Frome Vauchurch*

Dearest David, . . . I hope you are still HO.K. in spite of the International Cat Show. I have only been to a very minor specimen, and thought it agonising. Cats should never be constrained, nor exposed to envy and jealousy – and passed by for another cat. My three live in amity, but that is because I am careful never to differentiate – like my cousin's wife, who explained, when I commented on her three children being so affable and uncontentious, 'It's simple. When one offends me, it is slaps all round.'

I envy you your smoke-box. I do rather the same sort of thing in an oven, but it's not so reliable. At the moment I am flavouring everything with fennel. It is the redemption of ordinary white fish, and I have a large crop of miscarried finocchio and can't bear not to make use of its mermaid hair.

I am spending a truly Christian Christmas, giving a turkey to a large deserving family, and going out to lunch myself on a brace of pheasants. No cooking! No drumsticks days afterwards!

I was so charmed by your Nerissa when she came to lunch. She sat so elegantly patient while we were discussing what we ate in the twenties – sturgeon, and dinosaurs. I hope she will bring you again

204

my dear dinosaur. It was a pleasing astonishment to find how well you still knew me.

Goodbye for now. Please write some more of your ancestral story. . . .

Love   Sylvia

1976

Darling David, I wonder where you are – in Spain for the usual change, or coiled up at Le Verger; and if you are writing that family history novel you told me of when you were here with Vanessa [Nerissa]. I very much hope you are working at it; and not in too much of a hurry – I say severely – to finish it. I have been foolishly obliging and consented to have my Elfin stories booked. I held out against it, saying I have longed to be published posthumously; but then began to think of what posthumously might entail: my punctuation being tampered with and a preface by God knows who – say, Malcolm Muggeridge.

But I feel very lonely and deprived and *uninterested*.

Today I wanted to look up 'The Spartans on the sea-wet rocks' and took out Housman's *Last Poems*. And finding I was right about the Spartans I read on; to the last page. And on the last page was THE END. As you might expect. But I suddenly had a vivid sense of the goblin pleasure A.E.H. must have had as he wrote those words, in a neat scholar's handwriting, licking dry lips, slamming that noiseless door.

We had a gratifying fox-hunt here, last week. The Cattistock Hunt heard there were a great many foxes in Frome Vauchurch, so they set out, all shiny and expectant. They had scarcely found before another fox started up, with hounds after it. Then another fox, with other hounds pursuing. To cut a happy story short, so many affable foxes joined in that the hounds were completely disrupted, some tearing through gardens, others rioting in the graveyard, others holding up the butcher's van, all in a state of frenzied excitement and completely out of control. After an hour of this they were roared and tooted into houndly behaviour, and taken back to Cattistock, totally exhausted, gasping for breath, their tongues hanging from their chops. They had never run so fast in their lives.

Now write and console me for my chaste un-Elfined life.

Very much love   Sylvia

Darling Sylvia, It was delightful to find your letter in the box up at
the château. Such a good description of a fox-hunt!

Well, I have been living alone since early in the New Year. Soon
after Christmas we saw a black tom cat hovering around. I gave
him some milk, and after a little while he came in gingerly. Slowly
he became tame, but he likes biting one. I described him at first as
the kind of fellow that one would warn girls against if he were a
man. But we got to like each other – his feelings warmer than mine.
For a lady in Montcuq who had lost her cat heard that he was here,
and two young men appeared on motor-bicycles, squashed him
into a tiny basket and went off. The lady loves him. He was born in
Paris (perhaps that's what is wrong, I don't like Parisians). Well, she
kept him shut up for three days. Two days later he was at my
kitchen window asking for breakfast, having trotted out the four
kilometres. They have catnapped him twice since then, and he has
got back always in two days. Unfortunately it was raining hard,
and I left him indoors, and I went off for a long lunch. He had made
a mess on the bed in the living-room. I have washed the Mexican
blanket and the old eiderdown, and they were so dirty I think I must
wash all the others.

And then today he made a pool after his breakfast while I was
making my coffee. I beat him – but not enough – and washed the
floor with Eau de Javel. He tried all the morning to make up to me,
but I was cold, and now he has gone off. He will be back at the
kitchen window tomorrow morning.

Well, that is all my intimate life, but my birthday has led to social
contacts. A big joint birthday party with a huge South African
fellow who started life penniless – very poor whites – and now earns
his living as a builder and has a house on a Greek island. Twenty-
eight people sat down to lunch in the house he lives in, and I had a
cake with eighty-four candles on it! And now lunches with people.

I have got to the end of my book [*Up She Rises*], and I am now
going through it and patching the weakest places. I seem to have
forgotten how to write. Well – well – It is about 100,000 words
long. But being true to the facts, there is really no point to it. How I
envy you your elves! I write about steam-pumps and paddle-
wheels.

My daughter Fanny (Nerissa's twin) is coming here at Easter.
She is now a street musician in York and is superbly happy. If you
go to York and see a tall girl playing the trumpet put your fingers in
your ears and give her 10p. I love her dearly.

Very much love   David

PS. Oh, the weather. We had three weeks of sun, and I got one hand painfully sunburnt and had to wear a glove.

Daffodils and white violets everywhere.

Now the almonds and peaches and wild cherry plums are in flower and the weather is a blustering British day and rain.

I am very well but usually fall asleep after lunch. How are you and your cats? Much better behaved than my Parisian Apache, I am sure.

3: iv: 1976   *Lower Frome Vauchurch*

Darling David, I have just told a friend who is apt to go to York to look out for your Fanny. How splendid her trumpet must sound in the Shambles; or rebounding from the West Front of the Minster. Is she allowed to serenade the Minster?

I dare say you will be happy with a Black Tom Cat, once he has got you under his paws. In a manner of speaking he has eloped with you. You are already feeding him and doing his washing. The rest will follow. He will sleep in your arms and raid your larder, and you will entertain each other with tales of your conquests (pray mention me).

I have just painted a Leonardo – very convincingly. It was part of the cargo of a ship bound for the Duke of Orkney, diverted by the Elfins, of Elwick in Caithness, who lived by wrecking and pillage. I have also laid a hedge, raised a storm by witchcraft, eaten wild strawberries after midnight when they are chilled with dew, and enjoyed myself very much. After I had sorted and tidied the earlier Elfins to come out this autumn I forswore Elfinity and settled to a respectable human story. It was a pleasure to break my vow and go back to Elfindom.

I have nothing so spirited to tell you as the Maiden Newton fox-hunt, but here is a very beautiful example of piety; and of official persecution. My first glance at the headline led me to suppose that Berserk is another U.S.A. university. . . .

Cutting enclosed headed 'BERSERK STUDENT BITES 3 IN JET', 'An airport official said the man began asking passengers if they believed in Jesus, and then biting them.'

I am glad you had such a grand birthday. Please make sure you have another.

Your loving   Sylvia

5 May 1976   *Le Verger de Charry*

Dearest Sylvia, I have just heard and caught a fleeting glimpse of the Golden Oriole. He has a quite unforgettable whistle which I first heard in the summer in Russia in 1904. It is the perfect first moment of summer here.

My daughter Fanny . . . has been ill, so her visit here is postponed. She had starved herself and lay for four days with 'flu alone without anyone looking in to see if she was alive or dead – was given ephedrine by a doctor and became light-headed. However she has been rescued and is now back playing the horn and will come out shortly. I woke up the other day in tears – something which has never happened before – and wrote the following doggerel, which please don't show to anyone.

> He has been weeping,
> His face wet with tears.
> He has been reaping,
> His corn has no ears.
>
> His wife and he parted.
> His daughters go mad.
> But he's not fainthearted,
> He thinks good of the bad.
>
> The one he loved most
> Drowned herself in the Thames.
> Those who give up the ghost
> Are nothing but names.
>
> He does not look back,
> For his friends are all dead
> And white is as black,
> When all has been said.

Well, well, one feels like that sometimes.

I have sent off my long novel and may hear soon from Richard whether Macmillan will publish it. He has been in charge of the new edition of *Grove's Dictionary of Music*, which led to the discovery of the following letter to my great-grandfather. I have a photocopy in Italian but send a translation.

> To the Most Excellent Artist
> Mr G. Patten of London.
> Esteemed friend, The portrait which you have made of me is so extremely like that I can never sufficiently express my satisfaction. I await the copy with impatience. Such a gift will be a precious record to my posterity and Italy will behold with admiration the work of a British genius such as you are. Accept the sentiments of my highest

esteem, gratitude, and friendship with which I have the honour to subscribe myself, your sincere friend   Nicolo Paganini
    Paris 10th November 1832

The copy in question hangs or used to hang until recently in La Scala, Milan. The original belongs to W. E. Hill and Sons, the violin makers. I want to get a photograph of it. This is, I think, something to boast about. George Patten, A.R.A., was my mother's maternal grandfather.

A pretty girl here called Monique was married the other day to a peasant fruit farmer. The menu of the wedding feast contained:

> Cascades de Hors d'Oeuvres
> Princesses de la Bergelotte
> (small trout out of the local stream)
> Rendez-vous des Limaces   (lettuce salad)
> Selle des Causses   (saddle of lamb)
> Tentation des Souris   (cheese platter)

I have forgotten about half the dishes. But I like these bucolic jokes. The wedded couple were not left to themselves until 8 a.m. next morning.

    Very much love   David

30: v: 1976   *Lower Frome Vauchurch*

Dearest David, I hope by now your daughter Fanny has recovered and is staying with you. Did she bring her horn? Did it sound melancholy in the woods?

Your woods must be in great beauty now – beech woods – chestnut? That is the sort of thing I would like to know; when I love distant friends I want to know their background, and the prevalent quarter of the wind.

In a not-so-long-ago letter you wrote of washing. I found that the ideal method of washing is to do it by foot. I had an Indian rug which for years had been getting dirtier and dirtier, and which the local cleaners refused to handle because it was so frail. In despair I filled the bath with soapy water and dunked my rug, and got in barefoot and trampled on it. The sensation was charming, the dirt that flowed out ennobling.

The rug came out no frailer than before and looking like the late Mrs Milton. *See sonnet by her widower, Milton.*

The world is too much with me. A warm loving voice has just telephoned to say it will be here in fifteen minutes with some tobacco plant seedlings and its two children. It is cold as March and an iron drought. No prospects for seedlings. I must nurse them indoors. I have only myself to blame. I asked him to grow the seedlings for me. . . .

I must go and find some sweets for those children – something carminative. I must also go and find a warm jacket.

Do you ever feel the childishness of old age? I don't mean second childhood, but the particular childish excitement at being able to do things dexterously? – to pour out milk without spilling it, to put things back in their proper places, to be capable and responsible? It is a pure pride, as it was then. I only get it occasionally, and it lasts like morning dew. But for its moment it is delightful, and seems as natural as Mozart. . . .

This letter has been at the mercy of interruptions. I shall write again, when I am more of a piece.

With very much love   Sylvia

8 June 1976   *Le Verger de Charry*

Dearest Sylvia,

Your delightful letter has just come, and thank you. Well, I am happy and rational. Fanny spent ten days here, and there was not one moment of parental irritation. She is a splendid creature, and she enjoyed doing all sorts of important repairs for me: the woodshed door which had come off its hinges, the back door which would not open more than six dragging inches – and she finally cut down a large oak tree which threatened to fall on and obliterate the bathroom. That was exciting. She fastened a rope to the top and the other end to the car's bumper, and when it shivered and started to fall, we drove the car up the lane and the tree fell in the only open space, missing the roof.

You ask about the trees; they are all oaks, which don't grow large – but there are four big wych elms in front and one bigger oak. My cabin is built on a terrace facing south-east with a cliff behind. And in front a valley with a magnificent view of fields and crops opposite and the château above a wood.

Well, I am a bit at a loose end, as I have finished my book – accepted by Macmillan with most kindly words – £1000 advance of which £600 comes to me after agent and tax. Not much for two years' work.

No, Fanny is glorious. She is taking a course in Operatic Stage Management. She has been an assistant stage manager among other things. But it was extraordinary to discover that she loves me and tolerates me, and we talk freely.

Yes, of course I feel proud of filling the pot with ground coffee with trembling fingers without spilling it and of my cooking and remembering names – at which I often fail. Today I was asked who wrote *Little Lord Fauntleroy*. Now the name of Hodgson Burnett comes back, and perhaps wrongly. But I could only think of Ivy Compton Burnett and kept my mouth shut! It is hot here: Today 86° F in deep shade. Yesterday and the day before only 80°. The farmers cry out for rain while feverishly baling their hay. Even Puss feels the heat and comes to seek the cool of the living-room: usually he snatches breakfast and goes off for the day.

I thought today that the best companion I could have would be a python. The trouble is that I should have to keep mice or guinea-pigs for him to eat. But as they only swallow a guinea-pig once a month, it would not be too much work. And I could leave him curled up in a basket for a month when I visited England or Spain or Italy.

Perhaps I should be able to deliver oracular statements. I was visited by a snake-lover two days ago – a Clerk in the House of Lords who kept a python and a boa constrictor fenced in above his Aga stove.

By the way in southern Spain they sell figs in little round plaited baskets, and I think Shakespeare must have seen one. One of them would hold the worm which was brought to Cleopatra most comfortably. I should like to show it to you – and also to the next producer of the play.

Everyone tells me to write a fourth volume of my memoirs. But nothing is interesting except truth, and truth can be painful. At our time of life it is better to look forward to the pleasures of next week. So if I attempted a book a large part of it, all bitterness, hatred and unforgiveness would have to be left out and a very expurgated version of my heart produced. There's plenty of delightful material: Jersey cows, fields of ripened wheat. But I could not say that by farming I slowly lost Angelica and arrested the growth of William and was an unconscious tyrant and that it was extraordinarily short-sighted to give my heart to cows and wheatfields.

It was so hot today that I swam in a lovely pool. First I went to the market at Valence d'Agen and bought food and then back with my friends for a swim and lunch and then two games of chess with my host – of which I won the first and he the second. Then back to find my bees had not swarmed, thank goodness, and your letter. You envy us our sun. I envy you your river. Oh, and red and white currants, for which I searched the market in vain.

Very much love   David

It is 9.30 p.m. by your time and the temperature is 70° F in the shade.

Dearest David, I think that we should make a midsummer vow to write more often to each other. You enjoy my letters, I enjoy yours. We are like those Etruscan couples who sit conversing on their tomb. We belong to an earlier and more conversational world, and tend to finish our sentences and tie up our shoelaces.

I like to think of you among oak trees. Have you ever tasted Oak Honey? It is made by bees who lick the slight gumminess on oak leaves in spring. It is dark green, and has a delicious arboreal taste. The gumminess is only there for a short season, so I suppose you would have to take the honey early, before it is contaminated with clover and what not. You have bees. You have small oaks. Think of this next year. It is a product of France. If it is made in your locality, you would not need to disturb your bees – which is, God wot, a dangerous thing to do.

I see, from your Proustian indication, that you have more than bees. 'Even Puss feels the heat' you say. One does not refer to a cat as Puss unless it is domesticated, and comes home for the night. I am so glad.

A friend of mine who is familiar with pythons says that if you gave your python a guinea-pig and went away for a month it would look flaccid by the time you came back. She used to frequent a Snake Temple in Malaysia, where the pythons drooped from rafters, and fed on hens – in their feathers. I once came on a snake (black) swallowing another snake. The swallower was firmly coiled, to get a good stance, and the top third of it was erect. The swallowed was about halfway down, and protesting with wavings and wrigglings. I hoped to watch this to the end, but the swallower saw me, and flounced away, still with raised head.

This was in North Carolina, halfway up a mountain. There was a sawdust pile near our cabin, and there were rattlesnake tracks on it. Valentine, who was convalescing from influenza, sat for hours hoping for a rattlesnake, but she never saw one. . . .

You swim in pools, you play chess in the shade. Coq de luxe! My river is so diminished with drought that the moorhens wade across it. My kitchen floor is encumbered with watering-cans, to hold wash-water from the sink. The garden is like a brickfield, the earth is so warm that everything sown in it grows immediately, reaches the height of six inches, and then wilts for thirst. I have the promise of a vast crop of white currants, but unless it rains soon, they will drop off.

But I have a kingfisher.

And I have a great deal more to say, but I will keep it for next time – except to say that Fanny must be a heroine and the Parent's Reward.

Love   Sylvia

Dearest Sylvia, I wish you could have been here last week – not that I had a spare room. William was here with Linda and two children and an old schoolfellow of Linda's to look after them. The horn and his wife in a tent on the lawn, and a neighbour kindly put up the flute and lent a caravan to the bassoon and her lover.

They gave three very successful concerts, and their playing was very good indeed. I enclose a programme of the first concert. . . .

They stayed eight days and then dashed back to the youngest child. William is said to look like me, but he is really very like Ray's brother Tom, who is an excellent viola player.

But the marvel is William's wife Linda. She has a questioning intimate merry eye and is always bursting with laughter. So we were happy. . . . There were a few dramatic moments when we were invaded by hornets (they have a nest in a hollow elm a few yards away, and I am going to climb up a ladder and exterminate them with a poison gas fusee when I feel brave enough).

Unlike bees and wasps, which go to bed at night, hornets are attracted by bright lights, and there are always one or two glaring at one through the window-pane like miniature tigers with red eyes in the kitchen which has no curtains.

Since they left I have washed and ironed nine pillow-slips, various towels and two sheets (single – double I send to the laundry) indelibly marked with greasy crayon, for Merlin thought they would serve as canvases for his compositions.

At the bottom of the Dervilles' orchard is a tall hedge containing wild plum trees the fruit of which is vastly superior to the large prunes they grow. So Linda made several pots of jam, and as there is one tree loaded with unripe fruit I shall make more jam next week.

I have a hive of bees but no honey extractor (they cost about forty pounds in France) so the Dervilles, who have seven hives, have not one either.

After I had taken the honey an old man who had an impediment in his speech and only spoke patois arrived with an extractor which must have been one of the first ever made. It was a long battered filthy tin tube, impossible to clean and with no tap at the bottom. It worked erratically; however, I now have ten kilos besides what is left of the one we ate in comb. And the honey is almost the best I ever tasted. I am asking Richard to find my old extractor at Hilton Hall and send it out if it exists.

However, what wasn't extracted went back to the bees in heavily dripping combs. The season seemed at an end: they killed the drones, but yesterday honey was coming in fast, and there was an excited contented hum. It may be a field of sunflowers about a mile away.

Well, then I went to an enormous party given by my dear friends the Elstobs. They are poor as mice but bought a ruined farmhouse and spent two years and their last pennies rebuilding it themselves, and to my joy and amazement have sold it for about 200,000 francs.

So they invited about a hundred people, and there were tables all round the courtyard groaning with food and every delicacy. But no knives or forks. So soon one saw ladies who had spent hours in putting on their maquillage dipping their fingers in mayonnaise and smearing it all over their faces like gypsy children. There were three twenty-litre containers – one small barrel of wine.

Next day I went back to lunch and helped with the left-overs, and there were still about ten of the original guests left.

Well, all this has left me a bit exhausted, and I lie down at frequent intervals – to regain my strength before the arrival of Frau Doktor Liselotte Glage, who is writing a book about my revered aunt Clementina Black. What? You have never heard of my aunt! Tut! Tut!

All my love   David

13: viii: 1976   *Lower Frome Vauchurch*

Dearest David, One has only to keep an Aunt long enough for her to become a Collector's Piece. You will have no trouble with Frau Doktor Liselotte Glage. She will know everything about your aunt Clementina. All you will have to do will be listen and say at intervals, Wirklich!

I wish I could feel as easy about your hornets. Can't you suborn some young person to climb the ladder and do the brave deed? I have long left off doing brave deeds myself. One must have some of the advantages of old age. Sit in the shade, dear, and eat honey.

I was attacked by what I called wild bees and the local inhabitants hornets in North Carolina. We had been lent a cabin halfway up a mountain, so far up that we needed a fire at night. There was a bare patch nearby which we tidily used as a rubbish-pitch, and I was tweaking sticks out of it when the wild bees attacked me. The cabin had been lent us by some good kind Quakers. Quakers do not hold with funeral rites, the bare patch we used as our rubbish-pitch was the grave of one of their children, *obit* halfway up the mountain. It was all rather unfortunate. . . .

Except for one half-baked thunderstorm I have seen no rain here since mid-June. The meadows look as if they were covered with brass filings. I sink to the ankles in dust if I walk on garden-ground. No strawberries, no raspberries: a vast brief crop of white currants. No green peas. The roses fell off the bush as soon as they opened.

And owing to Fortune's malice, *no figs*. The fig tree was deluded by the mild winter and put out nothing but leaves. (However, a neighbour's fig tree is fruiting as never was.)

I shall put out a book [*Kingdoms of Elfin*] in the New Year, and you will get a copy. I am working on the proof now. If I could rewrite it from start to finish, it would be rather good. If I could breathe anything but dry air, I might think it better. I plan for a perpetual bronchitis kettle. Nothing else will save me.

You will die by hornets. I, parched by dry air. What a pity!

Are your wild plums called quetsches? They make a delicious jam, and you can put them up in syrup. They are cheap and low; and a standby in Paris bistros.

I wish I had heard the Wildboar Wind Quintet. I remember William's oboe long ago, at Hilton, musing and mewing in a distant room. When I saw him there he was so like Ray it stopped my heart. He had her wild-deer glance.

Much *much* love, my dear David.   Sylvia

13: ix: 76   *Lower Frome Vauchurch*

Dearest David, Yesterday I had Pat . . . here, with her Brian. I have never seen her look so well, so young, so happy. . . .

They were off to Greece by car; and spoke of visiting you on their way back. I shall wait to hear your opinion. . . .

How are your hornets? How is your gamin cat? How are you, my dear? I am to send you Bea Lubbock's love. She was here last week, and told me this story about (Mayerling) Rudolf. She had it from her operatic brother-in-law,* who has a grace and favour apartment in the Imperial Palace. It was inhabited by Rudolf as a young man. One evening the Hapsburg White Lady appeared to him. He shouted at her to get out. He followed her, saw her going upstairs, then vanishing into a wall. He shot at her with his pistol. The bullet-marks on the wall excited so many enthusiastic souvenir-hunters, chipping bits off, that a glass panel was fixed over them. Thereupon, and to this day, fresh flowers were laid below it by the sweeping women. A cushion was placed on the step, everyone who went by knelt there, signed themselves with the cross. In fact, a *cultus* for Rudolf, who by now must be on his way to becoming a saint. So am I.

I have Tim on my plate again. A letter from the University of Texas . . . told me they are printing that *Book of Merlyn* you thought

---

* Paul Schöffler, bass singer with the Vienna State Opera, married to Mark Lubbock's sister Mary.

so poorly of: and would I write an epilogue to their edition? I felt that Tim should be attended by someone who could write in the English language, so I agreed. $500: very mingy considering that they charge $5 a peep to anyone who wants to consult one of the manuscripts they have collected.

Last week there was an equinoctial gale, and an owl began hallooing to the Hunter's Moon; and now it rains quite naturally, and is cool in the evenings, and grass is growing, and I am making sloe gin.

Love from   Sylvia

18 September 1976   *Le Verger de Charry*

Dearest Sylvia, Thank you for your delightful letter, to which I reply at once – not that it needs one. I suppose Pat will let me know when she is coming, and I shall be glad to see them – except between 3 October and 9th, when my sister-in-law Frances and probably also my daughter Henrietta will be here. . . .

Well, yesterday I went for a medical test to renew my French Permis de Conduire. The brutes have only renewed it for a year, and then I shall have my urine, blood pressure, heart and eyesight tested again. When they eventually decide that my urine makes me unfit to drive, I shall have to risk my life on a *mobilette*, for that doesn't need a licence, though it is more dangerous.

I waited till William and Linda had gone away after their concerts (a hornet sting on the lip or finger would make it impossible to play the oboe) and then one morning decided that I would no longer be craven. So I put on a bee-veil and gloves and gumboots and climbed up the ladder at 6 a.m., lit a fusee, which gives off poison fumes, popped it into the hollow elm and stuffed it up with an old shirt – all without seeing a hornet. I was lucky, as a few minutes later a couple of early foragers came back and were puzzled. However, it was the end of all the others.

My other bit of news is almost too painful to tell. Just over a week ago I went for a long walk, and Agrippa followed – first lagging behind – then dashing past me like an explosion of black fur. He followed about a mile to the fir wood where I was collecting cèpes (*Boletus granulatus*). This bored him, and he wandered off and has not been seen since. I think he has been shot, as the shooting season opened then, and the French shoot cats.

I shall not have another. The same thing is bound to recur, and anyhow at present I don't want one. He might conceivably come back.

I have been living largely on cèpes and am trying my hand at preserving them. The peasants nowadays sterilise them like bottled fruit – in water with a pinch of salt – but the old way was to pack them in lard and bring it to the boil and then stopper it up with a waxed cork. I have tried the first and am going to try the second. One can use the lard again. I have made a bottle of sloe gin and another of sloe marc de pays, which is cheaper. I got 5 litres of it at 14 francs a litre. Gin is 32 francs a bottle. As there was the largest crop of sloes ever known I picked 2 kilos of them, boiled with 2 kilos of windfall apples, and rubbed it through a sieve for hours on end. Then boiled it and then added 1¾ kilos of sugar, and it has turned out a delicious sloe cheese.

Well, then I made a lot of delicious jam, but full of stones, from wild plums – and some wretched plum and apple from windfalls from the Dervilles' orchard. I am rather crazy about wild food at present and am going to make rose-hip jelly and/or syrup.

The other thing I am eating at almost every evening meal is sorrel. I saw some in the market at Cahors, and the man insisted on giving me almost an armful for one franc, when I only wanted enough for one soup and one omelette. . . .

How mingy the Texans are getting! Really they have oil bubbling up in the campus and ought to be richer than ever. I can't remember a thing about *The Book of Merlyn*. Well, what a boring letter I have written – but I suppose I had better post it, and anyway it will enable me to send you my love – real enduring love, dearest Sylvia   David

26: ix: 1976   *Lower Frome Vauchurch*

Dearest David, I grieve about Agrippa – more, I grieve about you. It is so painful pretending to be sensible about a knot of feelings, all of which are irrational: irrational to hope, irrational to pine, and, after so much emotion, irrational to get over it.

You are feeding on cèpes. Tonight, I shall dine on grey mullet. This is the story of its catching. Yesterday was very dusky and sultry, and my friend Colin – who is a skin-diver – decided to go fishing in Portland Bay. He knows it well, and there is a particular wreck on the bottom where he is always sure of finding a mullet or a bass. He swam underwater to the wreck, sure enough there was a fine grey mullet. He aimed, shot it; at the same instant the wreck was brilliantly lit; as though he had pressed a button with the trigger and set off a dozen arc-lights. It was still glittering plain as he rose to the surface. And was whacked on the head by a roar of thunder, and such a pelt of rain that the sea spouted up all round.

The sea floor of the Bay is a city of wrecks, all with their habitués. There is one where conger eels dwell like quiet gentlemen in their club.

I hear a leisurely splashing from the river. It is the aquatic cow, who morning and evening goes for a walk in it. The river runs full and fast. . . . By now you may have read how our drought has been followed by torrential rains. According to Londoners this was caused by powerful Ugandan Asians performing a rain ceremony in Hyde Park. In Devonshire, on the other hand, it is attributed to Local Government. Local Government put stand-pipes in every town street, and since then it has rained every day. Whitehall ought to make more use of these mystic powers.

A great many odd things happened during the drought. Ladybirds came into the house for shade, and my sorrel became uneatably sour – pure oxalic acid. The young leaves are better; but still need a great deal of garlic to soothe them.

It was a relief to see your writing on an envelope and to know that you had not been stung to death by hornets. But do be careful of the survivors. They have probably sworn a vendetta. As you have made their family tree uninhabitable, they will probably have settled in a new home under a woodpile or a rubbish heap.

Is *Up She Rises* the ancestral book you told me about? I shall make a point of living through the winter so as to read it. *Kingdoms of Elfin* should be out early next year. What a pair we are!

> Madam, how does my gay goshawk?
> Madam, how does my doo?

If you hadn't intervened, dear David, I should have gone on writing poems and hiding them in hatboxes, and being an ornament to the Plainsong and Medieval Music Society, and publishing such learned treatises on the Hoquet in the Fourteenth Century at long intervals. How glad I am you intervened. And how grateful.

With loving love   Sylvia

7: xii: 1976   *Lower Frome Vauchurch*
Dearest David, Ignoring Christmas, I will wish you a happy Shortest Day, and a prosperous Enlargement. The shortest day is Bea's birthday, and the Chilean midwife had no sooner shaken a yell out of her than she bore her off and pierced her ears. It would save a lot of trouble if the other rites, baptism, confirmation and so forth (vaccination, for instance) could be done at the same time. I suppose they all passed over your head. I have noticed a remarkable

absence of the Holy Ghost about you. I don't think your ears are pierced, either. . . .

I am waiting for the next thunderstorm. They have been coming and going all day, with hailstones knocking on the windows like skeleton knuckles. The Siamese cats ignore them, but my indigenous British blue hurls himself into the spareroom bed and writhes the blankets over him. . . .

With a *great* deal of love   Sylvia

1977

4: ii: 1977   *Lower Frome Vauchurch*

Dearest David, Here I am, knocking on your door. But where are you? in your woods, in Spain, in the Caucasus? And how are you? The last I saw of you, you were getting the better of hornets. Hornets seem a long time ago – distant as wood strawberries and chanterelles.

I am in a morass. I have not had a dry foot for months. I am also in a doldrum. This book has had good reviews, and as a result, I can't write. Like a stormcock, I can only sing in a blighting wind; praise has inhibited me – even though I know it is a tribute to my old age; or perhaps because I do know. A letter from you, my dear David, would do me a great deal of good.

Some time this autumn you will get a parcel from the University of Texas, with their reprint of White's *Book of Merlyn*. They asked me to write an epilogue, and that is one reason why I asked them to send you a copy. They are a rum lot. Their first letter began 'I must indulge your patience', and later they sent me a cable beginning *Dear Miss Townsend Warner*. I felt rather piqued since they didn't include F.R.S.L.

Since they err, I suppose they are human.
Love   Sylvia

11 February 1977   *Le Verger de Charry*

Dearest Stormcock, I am sure that perched high above the rushing Frome, you are singing madly. However, since you say you are in the doldrums and would like a letter, I sit down at once to thank you very much for Robin's copy of the *Kingdoms of Elphin* [deleted] *Elfin*. (Your quotation from Peacock must be responsible for my misspelling* – also that, like the erring Texans, I am human.)

Well, you ought to get my book *Up She Rises* soon. Indeed it may have crossed *Elfins* in the post. It cannot be wetter in Dorset than here. But I have crocuses in flower, daffodils in bud, and the avenue of almonds leading to the château is in full bloom, and on one of

---

* A quotation from *Gryll Grange* by Thomas Love Peacock, author of *The Misfortunes of Elphin*, faces the contents page of *Kingdoms of Elfin*.

[these] hot sunny days my bees were coming home with their knickerbockers heavy with pollen.

I lead a double life when I am alone, for the characters [and] incidents in my new book are more real than the few neighbours I see. I live almost entirely with them – have very little control over them – and often wonder whether it is worth while putting on paper the absurd tragedies of their lives. However, there they are, and I am their scribe. When I have visitors they retreat into the background, and I was lucky to have a Tasmanian young woman (twenty-four years old) who flew out from Toronto to spend Christmas – three weeks – with me. A biologist studying methods to avoid the pollution of rivers. . . .

I am coming to England for the whole of the month of July. The University of Birmingham is making me a Dr of Litt. I mean to drive to England and all round it – up to Yorkshire and Northumberland with William, to Wales with one cousin, to Somerset with another, and to you if invited to lunch. Also I shall stay at Hilton Hall, now inhabited by Richard and Jane, and their sons at week-ends. Richard commutes to London and Macmillan as required. Well, what else? Most of the taps leak, and hot water runs away. Everything is frantically expensive – but one person doesn't eat much – and luckily wine is cheap: 2.55 a litre, and I bought a barrelful at 1.40 a litre. I hope it doesn't turn into vinegar. But there are the usual rumours of someone buying an option on *Aspects of Love*.

I am eighty-five in March and keep going fairly well.

I have no cat. My last two were both most certainly shot. But I put out all suitable scraps for a short-tailed marmalade animal.

Love from   David

23: ii: 1977   *Lower Frome Vauchurch*

Darling David, Your letter – thank you for writing it so soon – did a great deal to lever me out of my doldrums. They were post-influenzal depression, bloated by the incessant rain. The post-influenzal depression is better now, the weather isn't.

I shall be delighted to see you, with attendant cousin, in July. By then you will be a Dr of Litt. Do they need any special kind of food to go with their dignity? I shall be very happy to supply it – in reason: the turtle soup will be tinned. One of the results of being included in Europe is that it has become impossible to get any of the former European foodstuffs that one used to find at the grocers: a few dried mushrooms penetrate the iron curtain. If one is very lucky one can sometimes find wine vinegar from Belgium. I count the grains of Italian rice, polenta has vanished. If you would like to shed a ray of sunlight on my declining days you will bring me some chestnut *flour*: it is impossible to make soup or sauce with the purée, and my chestnut soup was a speciality of the house. Though it were as expensive as coffee, I would pay for it with rapture.

Up She Rises hasn't come yet. I think it was the one you told me about. I am sure I shall enjoy it. You are one of the few people I re-read. I have just been reading Peter Quennell's *Marble Foot*. I was pleased to learn that Tommy horned him. His account has an air of magnanimity, and in the next chapter he is being moral about it. I am also reading Golo Mann's *Wallenstein*. It would be easier to read if Mann did not give heavy nudges in every other paragraph: Wagnerian nudges, on the lines of 'What did I tell you in bar 740?' It is a Tower of Babel story. Negotiations (incessant) were conducted in Italian, German, Bohemian, French, Spanish, Dutch, English, Latin. No wonder that Wallenstein turned to the simple language of the sword. Winter fed the wolves. Horseflies swarmed over the battlefields in summer.

Love   Sylvia

5: iii: 1977   *Lower Frome Vauchurch*

Dearest David, *Up She Rises* came two days ago. I am no further than Portsmouth, but I must now and at once write to you that I love Clementina with as much reality as if she had come to life in a story by Defoe, and that I followed her every mile of the journey. It is a triumph of narrative: *you tell it as she would remember it*: the mutton cutlet and mashed turnip, the very small teapot, the hot bath before the fire, the carnation in the conservatory, and her mind always ahead of her feet, even the places where she rested, or slept dry, things she would put behind her. Oh! that villainous Yorkshire laundress: the cheese on the other hand was better than Scotch cheese. Borrow would have hugged you.

You set me thinking. The journey is the artery of fiction from the *Æneid* on. Stationary stories are as special as orchids. Jane Austen, H. James, are an order of enclosed contemplatives. Stendhal – I never cease to bless you for telling me to read Stendhal, as you did at the end of that long walk in the Essex flats – is always on the move, if only dodging the police. And the fun they miss, these lenten orchids. What fun you must have had, travelling with Clementina.

Thank you, my darling David   Sylvia

Dearest Sylvia, At eighty-five I find I forget what I have done, and I missed the four books by or about Tim White – not in their places. I racked my brains wondering to whom I had lent them and then found them yesterday tucked away on a top shelf – hidden while I was away in England. So I have spent an hour reading parts of your biography. It is, of course, brilliant, but that's not the point – nor its wit. What is so moving is the sweetness of your character, the gentleness with which you handle that 'feral' creature.

I went for ten days to England, because my darling Henrietta fell thirty feet on to concrete and smashed most of the bones on the right side of her body. She was very lucky that neither head, spine or internal organs were damaged. She is in the new Charing Cross Hospital in Fulham Palace Road and rapidly recovering but has suffered and is suffering a great deal of pain – agony. Owing to the smashed ribs they did not dare to give her a general anaesthetic when they drove steel pins into her thigh bones. And the leg is on a windlass so it shall not shorten. So, in spite of drugs, it is like medieval torture. However the pins may have been removed by this time and the windlass relaxed.

She is the most beautiful of my daughters and very close to me – a curious mixture of Grant and Garnett – without Stephen. She has written me two letters with her right hand – the broken arm is healing, and she ended the first with 'life is so precious'. I stayed with Angelica in her house in Islington and travelled to Hammersmith every day. London seemed to me horrible, very dirty and very exhausting and full of horribly ugly buildings. It was wet and cold.

Soon after I got back here I woke up one morning to find two inches of snow! They say the grapes are done for and almost all the fruit.

I am trying to finish a novel about French and English and have scrapped a romantic ending with two lovers trapped in a dugout dying from asphyxiation and made them not lovers because of being trapped. When rescued the book peters out.

I am wildly excited because an Australian scientist has discovered how to store solar energy and make it transportable. It makes nuclear energy unnecessary. In the Voyage to Laputa Swift kept imagining things which have come true. He had a sort of second-sight without knowing it.*

* David wrote to *The Times* (12 May 1977) emphasising the importance of this discovery, which proved a false dawn. In the Voyage to Laputa Swift described one who 'had been Eight Years upon a project for extracting Sun-Beams out of Cucumbers', anticipating the discovery of the action of sunlight on chlorophyll and the production of Vitamin C.

I shall come and visit you in July and bring sweet chestnut flour.
Very much love   David

10: v: 1977   *Lower Frome Vauchurch*

Dearest David, Thank you for praising my gentleness towards the feral Tim White. When I began that book I disliked him – a braggart, a self-admirer, a Mr Facing-Everyway. It was Ray who taught me better. She must have seen some good in him, and there must have been some good in him to admire her as he did, and be influenced by her. Looking at him that way, I began to take him seriously. . . .

Poor daughter, poor father! I hope Henrietta is released from the windlass by now. She must have great courage to write with her broken arm that life is precious. *Her right arm* – I think she is an artist. Doctors are very bornés. It never occurs to them to try if hypnosis might replace a total anaesthetic.

Hailstones have rattled on my windows, the morning garden has been stiff with frost: my nose has been as red and raw as Marian's; but the garden seems to be none the worse for it, and my garlic is like a lying illustration on a seed-packet. I think there must be a tincture of last summer's heat in the soil

I sent you a copy of *Kingdoms of Elfin* (it is selling well in U.S.A.). Didn't it reach you? Or are you silent because you don't approve? I think you would approve of the last story, it brings that note of sadness in, is a coda in the relative minor.

As for Swift's second-sight without knowing it, it is my belief that inventors are prodded into inventing what the common mind has long wished for; and that Astolfo was the first promoter of flying machines; unless it was Icarus. Did you read that they have found a prehistoric *spoked* wheel in Switzerland?

True love   Sylvia

20 May 1977   *Le Verger de Charry*

Dearest Sylvia, Tonight my memory seems to have gone, and I don't know when I wrote last or what I said in my letter.

But I have a strong memory of being sent all the stories in the *Kingdoms of Elfin* by the editor of the *New Yorker* and writing you a letter about them.

But as you ask: Did I get a copy of the book? Did I read it? What do I think? I have this evening discovered two stories in it, not sent by the *New Yorker*, 'The Climate of Exile' and 'The Late Sir Glamie'. They are magnificent. Your wit, your knowledge, your impudence, is there in every line. I love them both and shall now go back to re-reading the *New Yorker* ones.

In your letter you speak of being waterlogged. But here things are far far worse. Out of habit, wet peasants have put rows of melon seed into the earth, and they have all rotted. The soaking hay has begun to rot near the roots. Rain comes every day and sometimes all night as well. It has never been known before. And I have what the French terrifyingly call *angina*, which is what we call quinsy, and all my doctor does is to tell me to spit. And the chemist wants me to push suppositories up my anus!

Only the *sun* will cure me. And every day is dull and heavy and wet.

The Times did eventually publish my letter – on the 11th or 12th – but I haven't seen it and only know that it appeared because of a letter from a lunatic, claiming intellectual kinship with me.

Well, we did have one fine day and an old rustic arrived to say there was a swarm of bees. So I went up a ladder and brushed them into a wastepaper basket and put them into a small ancient hivelet that I possess.

But bees hate being brushed. One should shake a swarm, but I could not shake the gigantic oak on the bark of which they had clustered.

However, I took them, being stung round the wrists, and gave them to an enthusiastic friend, who set to work and made himself a magnificent beehive. But the next few days it rained, and I lay awake thinking of the bees starving. So I made syrup and went to transfer them into their new home. It was raining, my friend's wife held a garden umbrella over the bees, while I pulled up one frame after another and put them in their lovely new hive. And then put a feeder with a quart of syrup on top. I hope they are all right. I was glad of the glass of wine, when I had pulled off my soaking mackintosh and veil.

The queer thing is that my own hive (which did not produce that swarm) is *full of honey*, and I am going to take some of it when the sun shines again and I have borrowed an extractor. The honey last year (not finished yet) was dark, glutinous and delicious. I hope to buy you some farine de chataigne tomorrow when I go to Cahors. It is too luxurious for our shops in Montcuq. And then I will send it by the next friend's car.

I have in recent months written a book – happily going on from bit to bit, and now, looking at it, I see that it is *pointless*. So I am rather in a quandary. I shan't put it on the fire, because some later inspiration may come to me. But I am a bit sick of the thing. The people are real people to me. But are they worth writing about?

Lots of books aren't worth being written. I think the best thing is to put it [on] one side and think about something else.

Henrietta still suffers a lot of pain and makes progress, but she won't eat enough. How does one cure that disease?

All my love, dearest Sylvia   David

Thank you so much for the copy of *Elfin*.

27 May 1977   *Le Verger de Charry*

Dearest Sylvia, I have now read all the stories in *Kingdoms of Elfin*. They have made a very different impression from the pages of the *New Yorker*.

I think they are magnificent. Unequal perhaps, but quite unlike anything written before. It is rather as though a child who was quite certain of the facts of its imagination had dictated them to – Voltaire perhaps – and imposed her vision on that sceptical creature, who had a full knowledge of the boring ceremonial and etiquette of courts. Except for your three refugees taking shelter with Mustafa, you do not mention homosexuality – and the little boys are chosen to grow up with green ribbons round their wrists. But the Irish fairies were paederasts and indeed gave the name Fairy to many of our acquaintance. And Oberon's revenge on Titania was because of such a quarrel. But I think your view is the best, for some charm of innocence or inexperience is preserved. I think also your Elfin ladies were foolish and rather blind to throw out their lovers when their hair turned grey.

I hold a brief for the white-haired experienced lover who is more interested in the sensuality and pleasure of his partner than the boy who makes her throw up her heels among the raspberry canes. But perhaps, at eighty-five, I am prejudiced.

'Fox Castle', which depends on the fact of expulsion, is one of the best.

I chanced to re-read one or two of my grandfather's stories in *The Twilight of the Gods* and wish I could see how you would have handled, let us say, his story 'The Purple Head'. You would have enriched it so much.

I was interested in one of them, 'The Poet of Panopolis', because it dealt with Nonnus, a poet quoted by Peacock, who wrote an immensely long poem about the exploits of Dionysus and then, in old age, a versification of the Gospel of St John. But was he an apostate? Or perhaps a true poet, who felt that his work was more important than its subject? We shall never know.

I am planning to come to England in July and drive all round it. If this succeeds, may I come to lunch with you about the 22nd? But I may overestimate my physical powers, as I do get tired more easily now. But I will write about this again.

Very much love and admiration.   David

Darling David, I hope your mysterious malady, for which you are to spit and use suppositories, is being mended by *the sun*. If it is quinsy, keeping your feet warm and *dry* should help. I have only once been ill in a French province, and then I was so much elated by my Racinean eloquence describing my symptoms (j'ai vomi une matière visqueuse) that I recovered in a flash. But you are too acclimatised to talking French, so that won't get you the same tonic effect.

But, my dear, take care of yourself a little. The only person I know who had quinsy said that hanging by the neck would have been a flea-bite in comparison. Besides warm dry feet you should eat plenty of garlic. Try snails, well fortified with garlic butter. . . .

I hope that the bees you moved so tenderly to their new hive were grateful – and settled. Bees are as opinionated as cats. A beekeeping parson assured me that nothing could persuade his bees to swarm on any day of the week except a Sunday: at Mattins: and that his congregation, already swarming in pews, took it much amiss. His tone was boastful, as with everybody who keeps a dangerous animal. But when cats are opinionated it is usually because they Know Better. No cat will look at food if it has been injured or badly scared. They say they can't digest food while they are still digesting shock. I expect your Henrietta is a cat. Besides, one would need to be as strong as a crocodile to eat hospital food. Those menus, so promising to the eye; and it all comes out of a freezer, its paper bag removed and a little warm gravy poured over it. I learned this from a young man who had worked in a hospital kitchen. He said he had never seen originally good honest meat so injured and maltreated.

Do you remember Horace Walpole writing early in May to say that spring, as usual, had come over from France to spend the winter in England? It has been like that: a falsely beaming sun and a shrewish north-east wind. We need rain – but we shall get it, no doubt. A Jubilee and a Bank Holiday should haul down rain upon us. Loyal townspeople will be as cross as wet wasps, rustics will say these new Bank Holidays aren't as good as the old ones, but could be worse.

Your letter was in *The Times* very much as you wrote it to me, but nobler, and more Godlike. . . .

Take care of yourself, very dear David.

Love from   Sylvia

Dearest David, From the start I have hung on your approval, waited for your verdict – even when I flouted it. You can imagine how pleased I am with your praise of *Elfin*, and with your analogy of the child 'quite certain of the facts of its imagination'. As for speculating how I might have handled 'The Purple Head', I would never lay an impious hand on your grandfather. My father's copy of *The Twilight of the Gods* (bought in 1888) I read and re-read when I was a child – old enough to know it wasn't quite true, but knowing it was veracious. Even then I was enchanted to see how demurely he twitched the carpet from under the feet of Authority – Bishops, Lucifer, Brahmins, Distributors of Elephants. He corrupted my youth, and I am eternally grateful to him: I believe the current phrase is formative. I was born under a Garnett star. And 'Virtue and the Tiger', in my *Cats' Cradle-Book*, shows how your grand-father 'formed' me.

No, I don't mention homosexuality. Even if I had known that Irish fairies are paederasts, I doubt if I would have gone to the Kingdom of Nephin to explore for it – though in the first version of 'The Blameless Triangle' Mustafa buggered the lot, with no ill-feeling on any one's part. But elfins, as I saw them, seldom love, unless they are very young, like the girl at Blokula, or love a mortal, like Tiphaine. Perhaps their longevity keeps them cool-blooded, or their extreme self-consciousness. Un amour de convenance is more their line. I am still finding out more about them. If I am spared I may do another volume. There are three stories already – and a heavenly amount of research involved. Oberon, for instance, was hermeticist, and had a Lullian Wheel, and a bowl of prophetic goldfish.

I shall be here all July, please come to lunch – to stay, if that would be most restful for you, at any rate, to stay long enough for an after lunch siesta. I am deplorably the worse for this last year's wear and tear, and a prey to vain regrets – that I shall never see the Aurora Borealis again, or listen to larks – too deaf; or walk up hills – too lame; or re-read *Clarissa* in small type – too lazy to get her in a later edition than my sharp-eyed great-grandfather's.

But you enjoyed my book, and you are coming to lunch.

True love   Sylvia

Sylvia sent David, with her next letter, a duplicated typescript of *Twelve Poems* (posthumously published in 1980).

Dearest David, Long ago you liked my poems. Here are the latest – probably the last. They were read at the S.T.W. morning at the Aldeburgh Festival, and so well read by Peter Pears (who being a singer has breath control and does not gasp for breath at every comma) that I forgot my manners and thought rather well of them.

And the next day I was driven home by way of Ely. I had forgotten how lovely its plain statement nave is, and the sumptuous austerity of those leagues of flat rich country around, growing tall corn and beans, as though for some godlike Mr Jenks of the Horse Marines – and growing very fine oak trees. I wondered what had become of the acorns you set in the Essex Marshes. By now, if they grew, they should be tall enough to rustle over – over what? Much the same satisfied uninhabitedness, I suppose. There is an atomic station at Bradwell Juxta Mare, but it cannot have sprawled so far.

Love   Sylvia

Dearest David, Will the 29th July suit you? It is a good date for me, though I could manage the 30th, if that would be better for you. I hope you will trust my cooking enough to come to lunch. And who will come with you, for I hope you won't be driving yourself: Dorset is a thick soup of caravans and traffic blocks percolating to the beautiful sea. Hot Cross Soup.

I shall think of you on Friday, being made a Doc. of Litt. I hope there will be a great deal of ceremony, that you will be robed and hooded, and given a bouquet and an illuminated scroll, and that Birmingham will be at its brightest. And that Richard won't mislay you in those environs. I would like to picture [you] arriving by canal in a state barge; but that is too much for my wilder hopes.

And I shall address this letter to Hilton Hall behind its grand gates. I hope it doesn't look too sleek. I recall it in its apples on the floor, coffee-pot on the hob days – gaunt and hospitable. . . .

Much love   Sylvia

From David's pocket diary for 29 July 1977:

Go down to lunch with Sylvia. Tried to find a taxi and got het up. Arrived in time. Perfectly delightful visit. Picked white currants. Nice girl [Antonia von Trauttmansdorff], neighbour, devoted to Sylvia, came.

Dearest David, When do you go to that orchard of sinless heathen apples in Cashmere? Or perhaps you are there already? In that case I must hope that this will be forwarded by whichever of your publishers I decide to be the most punctilious. I have some more or less recent poems I want to send you. Opportunities to be read in Cashmere are rare, not to be neglected. . . .

I have been reading a book about Catherine the Great. It was her aunt-in-law who I found more interesting: the Tsarina Elizabeth Petrovna. She was the daughter of Peter the Great; sumptuously beautiful, her beauty overcomes the bad artists who painted her; vehemently pleasure-loving and vehemently pious. At intervals she would leave balls, theatres, dresses, diamonds, and go on pilgrimages, travelling for weeks, dragging her court with her, putting up in a château if one came in handy, but also in wayside inns, and at the end of it *hurl* herself into some monastery, with confessions, penitential exercises, fastings, devotions, as at other times she would hurl herself into bed with a lover. A very honest woman. And merciful. She refused ever to sign a death-warrant.

Antonia, whom you met here, has been reading your three autobiographies (this sounds as though you were the Trinity). The leap from Elizabeth Petrovna is not so wide, for it was your childhood visit to Russia that she particularly admired. We plan to spend the winter improving our minds (the Royal Society and the Cambridge Platonists – do you remember taking me to Little Gidding, and the passing fox-hunt?), experimenting in cookery, and exploring our native land. She has just come back from Bury St Edmunds, where she was subpoena'd as a witness to character for a bungling burglar, and spent two nights in a Christian home. Unused to Christian homes, she found this a peculiar example of splendeurs et misères, sleeping in fully-floral nylon sheets, prevailingly purple, and leaving them to breakfast on a choice of cereals. I had urged her to stay at The Angel, but the Christians were imposed on her. The burglar's judge was as merciful as Elizabeth Petrovna. Numbering all the man's previous sentences, he remarked that they seemed to have done him no good, and gave him a very short one.

It has been a very prolific summer. Everyone with a garden is pressing other people (also with gardens) to accept potatoes and runner beans. I keep my garlic to myself.

Please write and tell me about far Cashmere.

Very much love
                                                              Sylvia

It seems to me that I have already sent you, given you, those *Twelve*

Poems. When you were here, perhaps. It was a great pleasure to see you, a great compliment that you came so extravagantly by train.

22 October 1977   *Le Verger de Charry*

Dearest Sylvia, You sent me *Twelve Poems*, one of which is constantly in mind when dear Rachel Devas brings her infant Claire Noëlle to visit me.* But of the twelve I like best 'Earl Cassilis's Lady', because I think you are very like her, and when I read it I think of you. But I like them all. . . .

As you see I am not in Cashmere, or even Kashmir, and I am rather worried because my dear Shusheila, who sent me the warmest of invitations in June, has not replied to two letters suggesting that I accept it. Of course the thought of the invitation being accepted may well appal her. . . . anything may have happened. I don't expect to go, which will save me enough to live here for another two years. But what did Kingsley make Athene say to Telemachus (if it was that couple) about living like a stalled ox (in *The Heroes*)?

I have just indulged in an orgy of squid or calamari. In Italy they serve these delicious denizens of the sea – I can't call them fish – as little rings of wash-leather. The way to cook them is to fry them gently and then stew them in wine (chopped up) with tomatoes and aubergines for three hours in a gentle oven – garlic and herbs, of course. I had been expecting a hungry South African to share the dish, but he didn't come.

Angelica is coming to see me on a short visit – arriving at Cahors Station twenty-six kilometres away at 5.30 a.m. That means waking up and leaving here at 4.30 in order to meet her. I only hope I shall.

I have been feeling older lately. My hands tremble, and I have a fear of going blind in another few years. But what the hell.

My contact in Macmillans is not only Richard but his colleague Alan Maclean. . . . He is anxious to make me write brief lives of the famous people I have known. It won't be lives but impressions. He says it will make me rich, but actually I don't very much want to be rich if I am not going to India or China. I have all I need and enough tomato chutney for two years. Very good it is too. I should buy a silk suit in India.

My Henrietta has made an astounding recovery and has passed an examption [?examination/exemption] in face of severe competition to go to London University to study English Literature. She had to

---

* See above, p. 185.

write an essay on *Huckleberry Finn*, which she hadn't read, after mugging up Pope and the Lake poets. Why she wants to learn all about Saxo Grammaticus instead of reading *Hamlet* by herself is a mystery. But it will force her to keep regular hours. She is desperate to find a room in central London. You haven't a friend who has one to let, I suppose?

Here it has begun to be autumn with high winds. In the market there are the last little melons going for fifty centimes each and sacks of gleaming chestnuts and proud geese going to their deaths with Roman fortitude. Figs too.

I had a bad patch unable to put two words together. Everything I wrote was like yesterday's toast. But I think I have recovered. My novel is exactly where it was when I came to see you. Finished but needing something.

But I have just written a very indiscreet account of Vanessa Bell.★ People won't mind the usual indiscretions, but I think I shall have to bowdlerise characteristics like possessiveness and the capacity to come to believe what is useful about one's own motives, etc. But the real difficulty is to convey the strength, the hidden amusement and the physical beauty.

If I write about Tim I shall use your life as a crib shamelessly. You mustn't mind. Then I should like to do Edward Thomas and Arthur Waley and my mother. If I do this book it will be largely cooking up and blending what I have already written – e.g. an obituary of Virginia Woolf with a long article about her in the *American Scholar*. Angelica sent me the last volume of Virginia's letters – the love-letters to Vita Sackville-West are a considerable improvement on those about the eternal servant problem. The chief change for the better in English life today is not having servants living in. Forgive this long diatribe.

I send you all my love   David

I have just read Virginia's description of Tommy's wedding to Julia Strachey which took place in St Pancras Church. You will be glad to know that the service was held up at the end because Lord Tomlin could not let himself out of his pew – persisting in thinking that the hinge was the latch, so the signing of the register was delayed until he was liberated.

12: xi: 1977   *Lower Frome Vauchurch*

Dearest David, . . . I am sorry about not going to Cashmere, and the sorrier since you are anxious about the fate of your hostess. Piety seems to be back in the saddle again – cf the young woman

★ Not included in *Great Friends*.

233

who quoted Lucretius in the first chapter of *No Love*.* I heard a booming voice praising Hinduism only this morning on the wireless: those orthodox Russian bassos, Tibetans roaring from the pits of their stomachs – there seems to be something about piety that sends voices below the bottom line of the bass clef. The voice of reason, for me, is an explicit tenor.

Do you remember (I don't) who it was who plucked out a white hair, looked at it, and said, Fie! Virgil seems to have been of the same mind, writing of the turpitude of old age. You didn't seem old to me this summer, I hope your resignation to it is premature. My own is belated. My legs are so swollen I can't think of them as my own. I fondly believed it was British genius, and gout. But I am assured it is only what I may expect at my age. Well, here we are, my dear; and let us rejoice that we still have our minds our own and have not turned to God.

As I wrote those words, *the light went out*. The electricians are discontented with their lot (reasonably, I think, they are not paid travelling expenses) and plunge us into darkness from time to time. Like Theodore saying, 'I heard a noise in the ditch, and thought it was a rat. But then I thought, Who made that rat?', I suspect God is turning on and off the electricians.

I am in the depth of pleasure reading Goethe's *Roman Elegies*. They have been translated by a man called [Zeydel] with the translations on the page facing the originals, and sometimes I leap the gap and find Goethe the kind of man I would have bedded with myself: he is so honest in his voluptés, the lady's back and the creaking bedstead.

There is a terrific south-west wind, a wet gale, that has lasted two days. Does it bellow in your woods? I woke up last night thinking of the Lord Protector dying in just such another. Is it true that when he was a baby a monkey plucked him from his cradle and ran over the roof with him? You'd know, he belonged to your part of the world.

You have made tomato chutney. I have been busy with sloe gin. . . . It is a seasonal pleasure squirrelling away the fruits of summer. They seem to feel it themselves. I have noticed that the last roses live much longer in water than their ancestors from the same bush did.

A voice has been raised in the wilderness in the main review of the

* 'It was her view, constantly expressed, that it was religion alone that had always prevented the advancement and enlightenment of mankind, that all wars and pestilences could be traced to religious causes, and that but for the mistaken belief in God, mankind would already be living in a condition of almost unimaginable bliss and moral elevation.'

234

New Yorker, saying that there has been more than enough of Virginia Woolf. It will be a pleasant change to have Vanessa. Remember to put in how she drove under the rainbow. In a train, if I remember rightly. I have seen a rainbow *between* me and the sun; and I expect everyone to believe it.

Take as much as you please about Tim if you do him. I came into the world to be useful to others, as Stockmar remarked. Why has no one written a life of that cryselephantine humbug? I had a snatch at him, long ago in *Vogue* – those bright days when we both wrote for *Vogue* – usefully pandering for King Leopold of the Belgians. But he merits a full-length frontal exposure.

Goodnight, darling David. My love, my long true love.

Sylvia

Verb sap. My sloe gin will be ready for drinking by April.

1978

Dearest Sylvia, How are you bearing up against the torrents of rain
and the hurricanoes of this winter?

I imagine you on an island, living on red currant jelly and potato
skins, and hope the postman has waders and this letter will reach
you.

I think of you often, partly because a neighbour called Rachel
Devas has a prodigious infant who sums one up in a clear steady
gaze, is learning to walk and make noises, while my hands tremble
and I mislay balance.

I am very well, much better than two years ago. However, I have
cataract, but as no one knows how long it will be before I go blind
and they operate, I don't think about it. Otherwise Fortune smiles
on me and my daughters. Fanny, who came with me, I think, to
visit you, is extremely happy with work. She is stage manager of a
peripatetic opera company and has just been playing the part of Ida
in Strauss's *Fledermaus* and being a great success.

One kindly person said he couldn't look at anyone else on the
stage. Whether that was because Fanny is so big I don't know.

No, it was Nerissa who came with me, I feel sure. She has started
painting and is happy.

Angelica has sold her beastly house in Islington and bought a
warehouse at Rotherhithe. The river runs against the wall.

The most extraordinary piece of good fortune has happened. A
lovely young woman of twenty-three concealing her age and
inexperience bought an option on film rights of *Lady into Fox* – paid up
– and now has raised the money necessary and has nine fox-cubs in
training. Two she is bringing up herself, and seven are being trained
by professionals. They start 'shooting' the film in October, and she
has asked me to fly out and spend the winter with her in Australia!

I have accepted. I don't mind a bit whether the picture is good or
bad, as the cinema is a different world, but the script was good. She
sent me a photograph of herself with the cubs in her arms. She is
called Mrs Joanne Lane. With all that, I shall be paid some
thousands of pounds! I don't know how many, as my agent has the
contract, but my guess is ten.

A picture of *The Sailor's Return* has been made, but I sold the rights for nothing a long time ago. But just imagine basking in the winter sunshine, summer there near Melbourne, with kangaroos getting suddenly into the picture by mistake. Well, dearest Sylvia, I ask you, don't miracles occur?* I am coming to England in July. May I come and see you then – or, if I have gone blind, sit and hold your hand in mine?

Very much love   David

3: ii: 1978   *Lower Frome Vauchurch*

Dearest David, How heavenly to get a letter from you full of confidence and good fortune. I am so glad you have all these things to look forward to. I wish (moderately) that fifty per cent of them will come to the boil.

There seems to be something charming about old age. I too, in my quiet way, spend a great deal of time writing to feminist presses (Virago and so forth) that I shall be delighted. About one thing I . . . really am delighted. *After the Death of Don Juan* is to be re-issued. It is a good book, and was swamped by 1938–39 events. It may well be swamped this time too, but at any rate it has got its head up.

I am pleased with your doctor's good opinion on you, though they give with one hand and take away with the other. You are very much better than you were two years ago – and have cataract. I was yesterday assured by my doctor that there was nothing wrong about me, and that my heart might sweep me off at any moment. Let us disregard these crows, and look forward to meeting in July. By then you will have discovered the charm of kangaroos and wattle. A call to Gräfin Antonia von Trauttmansdorff (she saw you last summer, and envied me) . . . will tell you if I am here to have my hand held or among the glorious dead.

I learn from yesterday's *Times* that you wrote a book about telling taradiddles for your country's good.† I *long* to read it. Can I?

I hope we may meet in July. You were so handsome and well-beseem that it was a glory to know you. I, alas, am shockingly decayed. But not in love.

Always   Sylvia

Sylvia died on 1 May 1978, before they could meet. David survived till 17 February 1981.

* David did not go to Australia, and the film eventually foundered.
† David had concluded his wartime work with the Political Warfare Executive by writing its official, and secret, history.

Index

Aberdeen, 154

Ackland, Valentine, viii, ix, 48, 53–5, 109, 140–1, 144–5, 154–6, 193, 212; *Whether a Dove or a Seagull*, 55

Albert Hall, 35, 39

Aldeburgh Festival, 160, 230

Alderney, 72–3, 104, 116

Aldington, Richard, 17n

America, United States of: publication in, 25, 27, 102; visits to 41–4, 50–1, 78–9, 89–90, 92, 100–2, 106, 109, 114–15, 157; ex-Miss, 203

American Association for the Advancement of Literature, 166

Ancienne Auberge, *see* Saint Martin-de-Vers

Andrews, Julie, 114, 116n

Annenberg, Walter, 166

Aquitania, S.S., 41

Arles: Musée Arlaten, 177

Ashburnham, Mrs, 35

Ashcroft, Peggy, 196

asparagus beetles, 152, 154

Aston, James, *see* White, Terence Hanbury

Aubeterre, 200

Austen, Jane, 55, 223

Austin, Texas, 112

Australia, 236, 237n

autumn, 69, 147

Avila, 188–9, 191

Bagenal, Tim, 108

Barcelona, 188–90

Barry, Mrs Elizabeth, 22

bassoonists, 166, 168

Beardsley, Aubrey, 178

Beckford, William, 113

bees, 31, 86, 107–9, 117, 122–4, 132, 143, 151, 163, 226, 228; *see also* honey

Behn, Aphra, 22

Békássy, Ferenc, 203

Bell, Angelica, *see* Garnett, Angelica

Bell, Anne Olivier, 86, 132, 200

Bell, Clive, 65

Bell, Quentin, 86, 132, 154, 200

Bell, Vanessa, 1, 55, 203, 233, 235

Bernardette of Lourdes, 192

berserk student, 208

Bétharram, 192

Betjeman, John, 162

Bigots (club), 93

Bingham, Henrietta, 18

biography, writing of, 73–4, 84

Birmingham, University, 222, 230

Birrell, Francis, 2, 173

Birrell and Garnett (bookshop), 2–3, 30

Black, Clementina (DG's great-grandmother), 194n, 223

Black, Clementina (DG's aunt), 215

books, weeding and rearranging, 116, 164

Border country, fierce history of, 86–8

Borrow, George, 223

Borzoi 1925, 3, 21

Boston, Rev. Thomas, 160

Boughrood Castle, 167–8, 172, 183–4, 196–8, 200

Bracegirdle, Anne, 22

Brenan, Gamel, 51–2, 136–7, 179

Brenan, Gerald, 51n, 52, 137, 191, 198, 200; *St John of the Cross*, 191

Brett, Hon. Dorothy, 110

Brewer (publisher), 50, 52

British Museum, 1, 22, 78

Britten, Benjamin, 160

Brooke, Rupert, 203

Bryanston School, 67

Buck, Percy, 1

Burnett, Frances Hodgson: *Little Lord Fauntleroy*, 212

Burnett, Ivy Compton, 212

Burt, Fred, 152n

Bury St Edmunds, 231

Butler, Fanny, 125n

Butler, Samuel, 125n: *The Way of All Flesh*, 125n

Butler, Thomas, 125n

Butler, Victor, 31

Butt's Intake, *see* Duke Mary's

Cahors, 89, 92, 155

Caithness, 125

California, 91, 112

Callow, William, 139

Camelot, 114n

Campeche, 113

Canary Islands, 188–9, 191–2

238

244

My feel on the day ?... I 3
211 pleasure at her skill — still

TV Ballet Tango By Legless Man
& one now in wheelchair

Old lady getting Photo'd
at the Library

Repetition words (3) fund
everybody does it

92 Sylvia believed Farewell was a vb.

Who remember No Love
By D G

Concert aspects of Love became
a show
U OK

161 unheard of   151 Tell MB this
story

To prepare a young
person for the modern
world strikes me as a
very wicked thing
E Waugh.

Mrs Beeton was a trained
musician

151 mistake
Timon 149